The Uses
of Adversity

The Uses
of Adversity

*Failure and Accommodation
in Reader Response*

Edited by
Ellen Spolsky

Lewisburg
Bucknell University Press
London and Toronto: Associated University Presses

Associated University Presses
440 Forsgate Drive
Cranbury, NJ 08512

Associated University Presses
25 Sicilian Avenue
London WC1A 2QH, England

Associated University Presses
P.O. Box 488, Port Credit
Mississauga, Ontario
Canada L5G 4M2

The paper used in this publication meets the requirements
of the American National Standard for Permanence of Paper
for Printed Library Materials Z39.48-1984.

Library of Congress Cataloging-in-Publication Data

The Uses of adversity : failure and accommodation in reader response /
edited by Ellen Spolsky.
   p.   cm.
  ISBN 0-8387-5112-1 (alk. paper)
  1. Reader-response criticism. I. Spolsky, Ellen, 1943–
PN98.R38U8   1990
801'.95—dc20   88-43297
                                        CIP

PRINTED IN THE UNITED STATES OF AMERICA

Contents

Note on the Lechter Institute

The Institute for Literary Research at Bar-Ilan, until 1985 under the directorship of Harold Fisch, has now been renamed the Lechter Institute in gratitude for support from the Lechter family of Montreal, Canada. The Lechter Institute is pleased to pay a debt of thanks to its secretary, Shulamit Zohar, for her substantial help in bringing this volume to press.

Introduction

Ellen Spolsky

In May of 1985 the Institute for Literary Research at Bar-Ilan University in Israel held a conference on "The Literary Text and Its Audience." The topic was not entirely new, and reader-response criticism had, five years since, arrived at the mature stage of having been anthologized.[1] As I reflected on the papers presented at the conference and the discussions that followed, it became clear to me that because the subject of reader response was no longer new and its general claims were now common currency in literary studies, some rather subtle re-vision had shown itself. The assumption of earlier work—that communication depends on shared grammars and communities of readers with the same ideas of how to interpret[2]—was questioned in several ways and shown to be a misleading oversimplification. This collection of essays, deriving from the conference, suggests that attempts to explain the communication of meaning will at the same time reveal the varieties of at least partial failure that accompany it and will also demonstrate how that failure can itself be functional.

It must be emphasized that the papers were not all written with this adversity in mind; as editor, I exaggerate this aspect by their groupings, which indicate what I see as their common assumptions or conclusions. These are, in some cases, at least a swerve away from the authors' intentions. I have, further, placed my own essay about failure first in the collection, in the hopes of prejudicing your reading of the other essays.

The first four essays are theoretical considerations of the relationships between audiences and texts. E. D. Hirsch suggests that toleration of error, the intention to expect and to grant some leeway in speaking, is the basis for the ability of audiences to "accommodate" already familiar written words to their current contexts. He then emphasizes the limits of such accommodation. If his belief that such accommodation has limits is correct, then time and cultural differences are bound, eventually, to make some texts unreadable. Meir Sternberg spins gold from straw by considering

9

Aristotle as a reader of his own text, investigating his failure to draw the available inferences from his own insights about plot and action. He ends by making an argument about a necessary condition of a literary theory on the basis of what Aristotle and Lessing (among others) didn't understand about the progress in time of reading experience.

Claude Gandelman's essay is itself an example of Hirsch's principle of accommodation: Hegel's dialectic was conceived as working in history but in this essay is extended to an aesthetic dimension. The argument suggests that if the dialectic between master and slave is understood as a dynamic between an author or authoritarian text and an audience, meaning is produced through aggression and conflict, through the failure of the master to retain mastery.

The insights derived from analysis of specific texts, even more than the theoretical papers, indicate the need for a new stage of thinking about the theory of audiences and their responses. In some of the essays (chapters 5–7), texts are found to be premised on the incompetence of their intended audiences. They are seen to instruct these audiences in the proper way to read them, on the necessary presupposition that whatever codes or procedures readers would otherwise bring to the task of reading would be somehow inadequate or inappropriate. Thus, Betty Rojtman has the biblical narrative itself modeling the appropriate hermeneutic for its interpretation. Harold Fisch explores several facets of prophetic communication by using Ezekiel as the example of the speaker who fails to communicate through the medium of a preexistent grammar. He shows the relationship between the prophet and his audience to be antithetical and uneasy. The prophetic text insists on its hearers being witnesses; however, this role is a burden that they are not quick to accept. In Tova Cohen's essay we find other examples of teacherly texts—Hebrew poems of the Enlightenment, whose poets require their audiences, though "liberated" from the bonds of the traditional orthodox hermeneutic situation, to reinvoke those very procedures in order to measure the distance the poems witness between the tradition and their own skepticism.

A second group of essays (chapters 8–12) is bound by the diversity of ways in which each investigates a specific instance of resistance. Kathryn Hellerstein finds resistance to inherited codes in the language of the Yiddish poet Molodowsky, made possible by the double semantic basis (Germanic and Hebraic) of the Yiddish language. The poet uses a set of Yiddish words with Hebrew roots as an etymological metaphor for the old code—the repressive tradition rejected by the speaker of the poem. Sharon Baris discusses the failure of interpretation aboard the ship *Bellipotent* in Melville's *Billy Budd*. The one who could act the role of Daniel and interpret for the literal (innocent) Billy remains silent while Billy dies for not having been read aright. Kinereth Meyer sees Yeats also involved in a struggle with traditional codes or myths, questioning, in "Leda and the Swan," whether a poet can resist being raped by tradition and create something new under the great wings.

Jane Tompkins, in a discussion of the academic rejection of Margaret Mitchell's *Gone with the Wind* despite the book's great popular success, raises the issue of whether a text can actually force certain readers to misread it. The misreaders here, Tompkins claims, were the male critics of the academic establishment whose misreading was a way of rejecting Mitchell's assertion of female power. In their joint linguistic and literary study of Flaubert's *Bouvard and Pécuchet*, Roselyne Koren and Judith Kauffmann conclude that Flaubert concluded that concluding is impossible. Their essay is set at the conclusion of this collection to raise this inquiry.

If I have misread some of the essays I've edited—retuned them to harmonize with my minor key—I hope thereby to have provided some new examples of the ways to fail and material for the study of the ways in which readers accommodate. The first step in understanding accommodation is the recognition that truly common grammars probably do not exist. The second is the continuing exploration of the ways in which texts are nevertheless understood.

Notes

1. Susan Suleiman and Inge Crosman, eds., *The Reader in the Text: Essays on Audience and Interpretation* (Princeton: Princeton University Press, 1980) and Jane P. Tompkins, *Reader-Response Criticism: From Formalism to Post-Structuralism* (Baltimore: Johns Hopkins University Press, 1980).

2. See Jonathan Culler, *Structuralist Poetics* (Ithaca: Cornell University Press, 1975) and Stanley Fish, *Is There a Text in This Class?* (Cambridge: Harvard University Press, 1980).

The Uses
of Adversity

Part I
Theoretical Positions

1

The Uses of Adversity: The Literary Text and the Audience That Doesn't Understand

Ellen Spolsky

What is the Problem?

In retrospect it might be said that Saussure's *Cours de linguistique générale* (1915) was like the proverbial bottle that seems half full to the optimist and half empty to the pessimist. Responding to his claim that in the language system "there are only differences," American structuralism in general, and linguistic structuralism in particular, set itself the task of identifying those differences in the structures that make language work. In France, however, the next phrase of Saussure's sentence weighed more heavily: "with no positive terms." The negativity seems to have fascinated the continental structuralists; with some marked exceptions (Claude Lévi-Strauss, for example), they were more distressed by the gap opened by the lack of "positive terms" than they were intrigued by the possibilities of significant structure. The absences and the spaces, the free-floating relativism of a Saussurean system of distinctions rather than of meanings preoccupy the work of Barthes, Blanchot, Beckett, Foucault, and Derrida.[1]

American structuralist theories, on the other hand, with pride of place going to generative grammar, are positive theories in the sense that they are theories of how things work. Indebted indirectly to Saussure's notion of a grammar as a description of *langue* as opposed to *parole,* the study of literature in America has in recent years borrowed from generative grammar the constructed notion of a competent or ideal speaker or reader who has internalized the grammar. Throughout the 1970s, articles, books, and collections testifying to a new awareness of audience participation in the reading process proposed as the object of study not a text, not a verbal icon, but a relationship.[2] In these studies, neither text nor reader has an independent existence. Both the theoretical studies of read-ing and the readings of specific texts focus on the multiple corre-spondences between readers, texts, readers' interpretive abilities, and the model of that ability. Because these very correspondences (according to the details of one's theory) either allow understand-ing, or actually constitute it, most reader-oriented criticism in America reveals its optimistic interpretation of Saussure by deny-ing, implicitly if not explicitly, the possibility of "wrong" interpreta-tions. They should not occur. That they do, however, means that a theory which doesn't account for misinterpretation is an over-idealization.

The theory that could explain all language—or all human symbol-making and symbol-using capacity, including error—would be too powerful: that is, it would be too general to be either explanatory or predictive. If a system predicts where and how error will occur, no misstep or failure exists; the system would have accounted for (i.e., would have predicted and explained) the failure. The error would be "right."

Does this mean that error can never be accounted for the-oretically? Indeed this question about the relationship between a positive theory (i.e, a theory of reading and understanding), and a theory about the failure of understanding is one of the most puz-zling questions in all the language-related disciplines. What is gained by exclusion or inclusion? What is the relationship between the excluded and the included?

There is, of course, a logical sense, in which a "positive" theory (e.g., a competence theory) entails its opposite: if a theory states the rules to generate meaning, it also implicitly tells what con-stitutes failure to generate meaning—namely, the nonfunctioning of those same rules. In practice, however, the inverse of a competence theory is not an incompetence theory. A good example is Wayne Booth's 1961 discussion of narration. Booth tells us that the reader counts on a narrator (a reliable narrator) to perform certain func-tions: for example, a reliable narrator provides information the reader could not otherwise know and also can mold the beliefs of the reader—that is, "define for us the precise ordering of values on which our judgment should depend."[3] An unreliable narrator, how-ever, does not fulfill the inverse of those functions, nor does an unreliable narrator necessarily fail to fulfill those functions. He or she may yet provide information to the reader, and, furthermore, he or she may contribute to a definition of values, although not by means of a simple inversion. An inferential procedure, more complex than the inferences needed when the narrator is reliable, could both deliver information and help define the ordering of values. Incompetence and failure, it would seem, are more variegated than competence. Perhaps like marriage, all competence grammars resemble one another, but each misunderstanding is unhappy in its own way.

The crucial theoretical question is whether or to what extent the failure, the misses, the negatives, the factors that have so far escaped systematization within the positive theories are not random exceptions, but are themselves systematic. If so, are they systematic in the same way? Does their systematicity undermine a theory of meaning, or does it simply escape that theory?

The example of the development of the theory of generative grammar in America is instructive. It has always excluded the explicit study of noncompetence from its purview, and we can see in the history of that exclusion both advantages and disadvantages. Early on, Chomsky separated out the realm of what he called performance as not amenable to the same kind of systematic study as was the grammar itself. This position was strongly attacked by other theorists (e.g., Dell Hymes and William Labov) who recognized that many of the factors that had been excluded as random performance factors were not only systematic ones but themselves dependent on competence. In response to this criticism, the terms of the Chomskian distinction have changed somewhat. Performance is now understood to be a smaller category than it originally was including factors like stuttering or slurring due to exhaustion, but not all kinds of phonological variation; the more interesting theoretical distinction is now between the grammar and the use of that grammar (pragmatics).

The argument, however, continues about whether or not the kinds of competence studied under the rubric of language use are systematic in a way that is similar enough to the autonomous grammatical system to have implications for the way the grammatical system itself is described, or whether they are entirely outside the system. Many scholars in England and America who study pragmatic subsystems such as speech acts and conversational rules tend to see the systems they describe as nonthreatening additions to an autonomous grammar (e.g., J. L. Austin, John Searle, J. Sadock, H. P. Grice, G. Lakoff, E. Schegloff, K. Bach and R. M. Harnish, and S. Levinson). Work by William Labov, however, on variable rules in phonology and by R. Jackendoff, and Schauber and Spolsky on preference rules in semantics raises questions about the nature of the rules in which a theory of language should be written. These rules suggest that the kinds of systemization they have described outside that autonomous grammar actually entail revisions in the autonomous grammar itself. Two fields of linguistic study are explicitly devoted to the description of versions of incompetence: the first is the study of language learning in both children and adults, and the second is the study of the language of brain-damaged adults such as aphasiacs and schizophrenics. Most of these studies claim to have implications for the construction of the autonomous grammar.

In the broader field of human sciences, the same debate is enacted. Michel Foucault's exploration of the systematic marginalization of lepers and then of madmen in Europe is an example of the recognition of a system at work in the domain of the excluded. His work, he claims, invalidates the claim of Saussure and the semioticians that "meaning" or semiotic exchange is the model for the understanding of human civilization. He argues instead for "a refusal of analyses couched in terms of the symbolic field or the domain of signifying structures, and a recourse to analyses in terms of the genealogy of relations of force, strategic developments, and tactics. . . . One's point of reference should not be to the great model of language *(langue)* and signs, but to that of war and battle."[4] Derrida, though he stays within the realm of language, also focuses on the relentless and systematic spoiling power of the excluded, such as the marks of genre, or traces of negative or ironic meaning. He also sees the inversion of an established hierarchy as systematic in the sense of predictable and inevitable, rather than random, but does not share Foucault's belief that analyses can produce knowledge. He concludes instead that the existence of excluded traces undermines rigorous theory construction.[5]

Theorists of failure, then, must resist the temptation to search for what seems to be ephemeral anyway—the total system, the unified science, the epistemological theory of theories that will explain competence and misunderstanding at once, because such a theory would be too powerful, that is, like Tolstoy's happy family, too general to be of any interest. It would be a tautology with the phenomena studied—that is, with the world. This is true whether the overgeneralization is optimistic or pessimistic. Thus, they must also resist the kind of positive idealization that ignores failure as a kind of "performance error" that will go away when the speaker/ hearer has either had a good sleep, grown up, or learned what the community expects. They must also resist the kind of negative idealization that swallows all symbolic activity into indeterminacy.

Interpretation Overcomes Difficulty

Saint Augustine approved of riddles.[6] Recognizing that the active seeking of answers is useful, he thought riddles were a good way to teach: train minds by making difficulties for them to solve. The more recent critical literature on difficulty is not as clear about the uses of adversity. Some reader-critics have admitted to difficulties in understanding some texts; they have understood the job of criticism as helping themselves and others to recognize puzzlement itself as meaningful. Among these critics misunderstanding is marginalized with regard to an assumed "normal," understandable language, although misunderstanding itself is neither accidental nor meaningless. Rather than undermining human language and communication, it is seen as providing enriching possibilities. A second group of readers views misunderstanding not as an epiphenomenon but as a necessary feature of human language, inevitably, systematically, and usually surreptitiously sabotaging the possibility of determinate meaning. The job of the critic, then, is to expose this hidden disruption and corruption inherent in language. William Empson's 1930 *Seven Types of Ambiguity* is a good example of the first group of theories. In the preface to the second edition of his book (1946), he responds to critics who demanded a more rigorous definition of "ambiguity."

> We call it ambiguous, I think when we recognise that there could be a puzzle as to what the author meant. . . . The criterion for the ordinary use of the word is that somebody might be puzzled, even if not yourself. Now I was frequently puzzled in considering my examples. . . . It seemed to me that I was able in some cases partly to explain my feelings to myself by teasing out the meanings of the text. Yet these meanings when teased out . . . were too complicated to be remembered together as if in one glance of the eye; they had to be followed each in turn, as possible alternative reactions to the passage; and indeed there is no doubt that some readers sometimes do only get part of the full intention. In this way such a passage has to be treated as if it were ambiguous, even though it may be said that for a good reader it is only ambiguous . . . while he is going through an unnecessary critical exercise.[7]

Note that the text is ambiguous to begin with, and the solution the meaning "teased out" does not simplify the ambiguities; criticism does not make the puzzle go away. All good poetry is supposed to be ambiguous, he says later, and part of the reason for that

ambiguity (and why it will not go away) is the way the reader relates
to the artistic creation:

> Whenever a receiver of poetry is seriously moved by an apparently
> simple line, what are moving in him are the traces of a great part of his
> past experience and of the structure of his past judgments. Considering
> what it feels like to take real pleasure in verse, I should think it
> surprising, and on the whole rather disagreeable, if even the most
> searching criticism of such lines of verse could find nothing whatever in
> their implications to be the cause of so straddling a commotion and so
> broad a calm.[8]

Cleanth Brooks, in "The Language of Paradox," also insisted
that the difficulties or ambiguities of poetry were not something
that one wanted to make disappear. The language of paradox, he
said, is "appropriate to poetry," though poets themselves may be
more or less unaware of their use of it. "The tendency of science is
necessarily to stabilize terms, to freeze them into strict denota-
tions; the poet's tendency is by contrast disruptive. The terms are
continually modifying each other, and thus violating their dictionary meanings."[9]

Michael Hancher, in an attempt to describe the speech act of
interpretation, describes two important features of it that may but
need not both be present in any one interpretation. He notes first
that Austin categorized interpretation as a "verdicative"; it is the
speech act that gives a judgment and "presupposes a definite *difficulty* of judgement," something it is "hard to be certain about."
Because interpretation is associated with difficulty, and because it
may even, according to Hancher, arise out of difficulty (i.e., be
called on to settle a difficulty), it is often associated with failure,
though failure is not entailed. According to Hancher, Austin
thought that verdicatives were "a difficult business but not an
impossible one."[10] This "non-easiness condition," as Hancher calls
it, implies the second feature of interpretation, i.e., that expertise is
involved. Hancher notes that expertise implies either relative difficulty, or just being in a position to know. Hancher cites the example
of a textbook editor interpreting "for college undergraduates
Milton's reference, in 'Lycidas,' to 'the pilot of the Galilean lake.'
What distinguishes the speech act of interpretation [in this case]
from description is not any lack of certainty but the presumption of
the need for expertise."[11] As Empson suggested, some poems are
harder for some folks than for others.

Both the condition of "non-easiness" and the connection of
expertise to the practice of interpretation suggest that some of the

newer kinds of specialist criticism belong in the category I am building of theories that consciously acknowledge difficulty and the possibility of failure. Feminist criticism, for example, is founded on the difficulties that women experienced in reading a literary canon written almost entirely by men. Feminist critics in the early 1970s accepted without debate the marginalization of failure, identifying the difficulties women have reading literature and criticism written by men with the exclusion of women from the center of cultural consciousness in a patriarchal society. Judith Fetterley describes the difficulties she encountered as a woman reading American literature:

> Our literature neither leaves women alone nor allows them to participate. . . . The female reader is co-opted into participation in an experience from which she is explicitly excluded; she is asked to identify with a selfhood that defines itself in opposition to her; she is required to identify against herself.[12]

I suggest that this nonease is actually not so far from Austin's or from Empson's puzzling ambiguity. Fetterley reports not being able to do what seems to be expected of her. Indeed, as Hancher's analysis would predict, her perception of this unease immediately evokes a call for further interpretation:

> The first act of the feminist critic must be to become a resisting rather than an assenting reader and, by this refusal to assent, to begin the process of exorcising the male mind that has been implanted in us. . . . And the consequence, in turn, of this re-vision is that books will no longer be read as they have been read and thus will lose their power to bind us unknowingly to their designs. While women obviously cannot rewrite literary works so that they become ours by virtue of reflecting our reality, *we can accurately name the reality they do reflect* and so change literary criticism from a closed conversation to an active dialogue.[13]

Sandra M. Gilbert tells a parable about the literary education of a bright young student named Henrietta Adams:

> Why . . . did Hen experience an odd sensation of uneasiness every time she opened a book? She had, after all, learned to "submit" herself to the "established truths" so clearly stated by the texts she read. As Oedipus, she had interrogated, and yet acquiesced in, the fatality that causes a man to kill his father and marry his mother; as Pip, she had learned never to trust a fatal *femme* like Estella Havisham but rather to lower her expectations and make her own way in the world; as Huck Finn, she

had lit out for the territories, escaping both the false gentility and the constricting domesticity of a slave-owning society ruled by fussy ladies like Aunt Polly; as J. Alfred Prufrock, she had worried about "the overwhelming question" toward which flighty women who "come and go / Talking of Michelangelo" might paradoxically lead her. . . . Why, then, did Hen feel anxious about literary study?[14]

Gilbert's story of Hen continues into her summer vacation, during which, we are told, she feels so much more comfortable reading novels by women.

The next step in the development of feminist criticism, then, was inevitably to notice, as Nina Baym did, that male critics had to be resisted as strongly as male authors did. Their readings, she claims, are "uncongenial, if not basically incomprehensible, to a woman."[15] As an example of an incomprehensible or an unprocessable critical text she quotes Leslie Fiedler on *The Scarlet Letter:*

> It is certainly true, in terms of the plot, that Chillingworth drives the minister toward confession and penance, while Hester would have lured him to evasion and flight. But this means, for all of Hawthorne's equivocations, that the eternal feminine does not draw us on toward grace, rather that the woman promises only madness and damnation.[16]

Our attention is drawn to Fiedler's use of the "us", by which, Baym argues, he makes the novel "inaccessible to women and limits its reference to men."[17] We may recall again Hancher's features of interpretation: a condition of unease, a connotation of failure, and the assumption of the need for expertise. According to Baym, the implication of Fiedler's "we" is that only he and other male readers have the required ease and expertise to prevent failure.

Stanley Fish's 1967 reading of Milton's *Paradise Lost* shares several crucial features with difficult, failure-prone, resisting readings. It seems as well to offer some new insights into our exploration of acknowledged misunderstanding. Like Empson, but unlike the feminist critics, Fish proposes that his author is a conscious manipulator of the reader. Unlike Empson, but like the feminist critics, Fish expects the reader to be able to get out of trouble, not only to recognize but to resolve the difficulties the text makes. The "fit reader" makes mistakes in reading (in interpretation), and then recognizes those mistakes and interprets them as analogous to his moral state. The reading becomes a dialectical experience: the reader is forced to acknowledge his error, correct it, and thus move toward truth. Remember that Fetterley also understood "progress" (in the sense of movement toward better interpretation) to depend on changing literary criticism from a closed conversation to an active dialogue. Both the feminists and Fish are aware of the risk of failure. In *Paradise Lost,* according to Fish, we are asked to respond to the text and yet be prepared to resist it. Our stance toward it is of one armed with an understanding of the traps reading such a text involves. Readers might well misunderstand, be misled, fail to emerge from the confusion. Although the following passage is a quotation from *Surprised by Sin,* note how easy it is to read it as a feminist critical description of reading literature or criticism written by men:

> [As we read, we must] be prepared to discount [the effects of the text] in the light of better knowledge. We must commit ourselves and not commit ourselves at the same time. . . . The poem is a profoundly disturbing experience which produces something akin to a neurosis; the natural inclination to read on vies with a fear of repeating old errors and encountering new frustrations. In this, the poem is a microcosm of the world and the difficulties of reading are to be equated with [its] difficulties.[18]

Dissembling Texts Overwhelm Interpretation

A second set of attitudes toward the misunderstanding of texts is described by theories in which the reader (according to the theorist who in these cases is often separated from the reader) is not aware of misunderstanding. Here it is the nature of language to skew, slant, distort, confound, or frustrate the emergence and understanding of meaning, and most often while dissembling cogency. Misprision in these theories is blinding, all embracing, and inevitable; perspicacity is an illusion.

Among the early theorists to draw this pessimistic picture was the Russian, Sergej Karcevskij. The work of this Prague school structuralist is described by Peter Steiner:

> In contrast to his teacher Saussure, Karcevskij's semiotics of language emphasizes the essential rupture in the structure of the linguistic sign, the complex inadequacy of its constitutive elements. "Sign and meaning do not completely overlap; their limits do not coincide at all points; the same sign can have several functions, the same meaning can be expressed by several signs." . . . For him there is a deep juncture between the subjectivity of our consciousness and the inter-subjectivity of language. On the one hand, "no matter how 'socialized' the forms of

our psychic life are, the individual cannot be reduced to the social," and on the other hand, "every word from its first appearance designates a genus and not an individual." Karcevskij bases this claim on the fact that language must always fulfill a double function: to "furnish a means of communication among all the members of a linguistic community" and to "serve equally for the self-expression of each individual in this collective."[19]

The good news from Prague, however, was that

"The exact semantic value of a word" Karcevskij argues, "is not sufficiently established except as a function of the concrete situation." But since the reality to which the words are applied is infinitely change-able, every application of a linguistic sign extends it homonymically and synonymically. It is this incessant interaction of language with extra-linguistic reality that fuels the engine of linguistic development. At every moment language is not a fixed atemporal system but a fluid equilibrium which contains both elements of the past and those pointing toward the future. As Karcevskij puts it "the signifier (sound) and the signified (function) slide continually on the 'slope of reality.' Each one 'overflows' the member assigned to it by its partner: the signifier seeks to have other functions than its proper function; the signified seeks to express itself by other means than by its sign. . . . It is thanks to the asymmetric dualism of the structure of its signs that a linguistic system can evolve: the 'adequate' position of the sign is continuously displaced through its adaptation to the exigencies of the concrete situation."[20]

Taking a less benign view of the ability of the sign to "adequately adapt" within the concrete situation, are the deconstructionists who, as Stanley Cavell says, have "noticed the capacity of ordinary language to repudiate itself."[21] In their view, the issue is not the occasional failures of the system or the uncontrollability of a non-systematizable context, but the irreparable absence of a center of reference, a "transcendental signifier" that could anchor the sys-tem, prevent slippage. We must understand, according to Derrida, that signs cannot be "deciphered."[22] Interpretation cannot simply "tease out" meanings that had been embedded in a text, as Empson thought it would. The multiplicity of a text's meaning will result not from the poet's having intended ambiguity, or the language of para-dox, but from the nature of the sign. Paul de Man developed a theory of "blindness and insight" that seems to belong to our category of theories of misunderstanding in which the reader/critic is not aware of his or her own reading failures. In the critics he examines, de Man tells us in a foreword that a paradoxical discrepancy appears between the general statements they make about the nature of literature (statements on which they base their critical methods) and the actual results of their interpretations. Their findings about the structure of texts contradict the general conception that they use as their model. Not only do they remain unaware of this discrepancy, but they seem to thrive on it and owe their best insights to the assumptions these insights disprove.[23]

De Man thus espouses a view combining elements of Derridean belief in the disruptive nature of language, with the earlier view of Empson and Brooks that misreading should be corrected or at least accounted for, and that a critic, i.e., an expert reader, could set things right by telling the laity the truth about a text. Frank Lentricchia has taken de Man to task for his presumption of an "Olympian" stance:

Ought he not to be chastened by his acknowledgment that his own judgments must in some sense be blinded? Though he conveniently claims for himself the status of a reader "in the privileged position of being able to observe the blindness as a phenomenon in its own right," his announced position ("there are no longer any standpoints that can *a priori* be considered privileged. . . . All structures are, in a sense, equally fallacious") denies him the right to know anything "in its own right."[24] De Man's discourse alone, apparently, escapes duplicity and mediation because de Man alone occupies a perspective in which it is possible to separate fiction and reality, to judge fiction fallacious for not meeting the real in a relationship of adequacy, and to know the real unfallaciously—for itself.[25]

Despite his irritation with him, Lentricchia nevertheless praises de Man's perception that misreading, when it occurs in an "expert" that is, a well-trained reader is not a random, marginal occurrence but a phenomenon that reveals something important about language. When Derrida, for example, "misreads,"

it is most likely attributable not to the critic's professional limitations but to his having been deceived by a rhetorical feature of the text that is not recognized as such. The good reader . . . is the one who is sensitive to the ways, the cunning, unblinded modes of narration found in the highest literature, in which the text puts its own rhetoricity in question.[26]

In de Man's view, expertise is still on the side of demystification, as it was in Empson, Brooks, and Hancher; however, what needs to be clarified has changed. The text's ostensible ambiguities will be declared to be valued not when taken at face value as richness, "polarities," or paradoxes within the text, but only when, in the reading experience of a powerful and well-trained reader, they are shown to expose the indeterminacy of literary language or rhetoric.

For Harold Bloom the expert is the misreader, and the value of misreading lies in its being nothing less than the very source of creativity: it keeps the poetry coming. Misprision or willful misreading, by aggressively rejecting earlier vision, clears a space for re-vision. The poet is a son, an ephebe, in Bloom's terminology, who must revolt against father poets, those who came before, in order to write. Critics too, as in de Man, can be creative misreaders. "Reading is . . . a miswriting just as writing is a misreading. . . . all poetry necessarily becomes verse criticism, just as all criticism becomes prose-poetry."[27]

In Bloom, we find the same theory accounting for both reading and misreading because the distinction has disappeared. Only one way of "right reading" (interesting reading, strong reading, competent reading) is possible—and that is misprision. Interesting as the theory undoubtedly is, and even explanatory as an account of the continued production of poetry, it is less revolutionary than it may seem. The word "misreading" has simply been entered into a theory that is manifestly not interested in readers below the level of poet or prophet. Since these readers are, by definition competent, it means no more than what the word "interpretation" has always meant. Still needed, however, is a way to explain what it is about difficult poetry that sometimes stumps good readers. The level of idealization of Bloom's theoretical argument has risen too high to be useful in explaining perceivable differences between readers with different experience and between interpretations at different levels of insight. This is the same position in which we find Stanley Fish after the publication of his collected essays, with his own retrospective annotations, in *Is There a Text in This Class?* The level of generalization is so high as to reduce the power of the theory to explain what it seems to have started out to explain.

It is now time to admit that three or four of the distinctions that have been organizing the discussion in this essay are in fact too weak to fill that job. I began by separating optimists from pessimists and even tried to align them on opposite sides of the Atlantic ocean. That distinction breaks down, however, when so-called pessimists like Harold Bloom turn out to have produced a theory about the generation of poetry—surely a theory of "how things work," if an angry one. The distinction between theories in which misunder-

standing is recognized and corrected and theories in which insidious language failure passes undetected is muddled by the
admission of a reader like Empson that he has no intention of
"solving" ambiguities, and again by the claim of de Man to be able
to penetrate the blind spots of other critics. As for the distinction
between systematic and random failure, the testimony of the various theorists seems to testify to the existence of the former, and
personal experience, not always recorded in print, surely testifies to
the existence of the latter. All this means is that the border of the
untheorizable has been relocated. We have seen what looks like
systematic failure in several theories postulated at such an idealized
level as to be useless as an explanation of the misunderstanding that
called for explanation in the first place.

Although the unargued distinction between literary texts and the
world, science, or nonliterary texts was assumed by more than one
of the critics whose work I have quoted,[28] I find the opposite
assumption, also made, in passing, by a few of the critics, more
suggestive. Empson, for example, talking about dealing with ambiguity, compares his reading of difficult texts with "ordinary experience"[29] like playing catch; however, explaining the process is much
more difficult. Fish also allowed that the challenge presented to the
reader of *Paradise Lost* "is a microcosm of the world."[30] I am
inclined to follow this direction to see what can be gained by
assimilating the difficulties of reading and interpretation to other
kinds of misses or failures that are not necessarily linguistic, and to
hope that such a move will be a valuable idealization and not an
overgeneralization. Instead of asking what a misreading would be,
that is, instead of addressing the categorization issue of how readings and interpretations can be labeled deviant, we might turn our
attention instead to observing the functional power of the challenge
of the new. More than one of the theorists I have quoted notice in
the misreading they discuss something like a challenge and a response. It is not only de Man who sees blindness as a precondition
for insight. Bloom, in his "revisionary ratios," tries to detail the
ways in which something new comes out of something willfully
misread. Fetterley calls for a dialogue as if it would help, and Fish
goes even further, showing how salvation of the soul can result from
mistakes that are then corrected. Karcevskij claims that the possibilities of language change and creative language use in poetry
result from the inevitable slippage between the language system
and an individual's use of language.

Looking for the uses of adversity, assimilating the problem of
misunderstanding literary texts to the larger epistemological con-

text of interpretation and learning reveals several areas of research outside literary theory in which dissonance has been studied. We can take some comfort, for example, from E. H. Gombrich who talked about "the sacred discontent" that arises as the result of the perception that the expected and the actual do not match i.e., when the schema already in memory is inadequate to match the present experience. Visual perception, as Gombrich understands it, is a matter of discriminating. In order to process incoming sensory data, we rely on schemata already in place, i.e., innate or already acquired structures or conventions that can be adjusted as needed. Gombrich cites the difference between formulaic medieval art and Renaissance representational art:

> To the Middle Ages, the schema is the image; to the postmedieval artist, it is the starting point for corrections, adjustments, adaptations, the means to probe reality and to wrestle with the particular. The hallmark . . . of the postmedieval artist is not facility, which he avoids, but constant alertness. Its symptom is the . . . many sketches which precede the finished work and, for all the skill of hand and eye that marks the master, a constant readiness to learn, to make and match and remake till the portrayal ceases to be a secondhand formula and reflects the unique and unrepeatable experience the artist wishes to seize and hold.
>
> It is this constant search, this sacred discontent, which constitutes the leaven of the Western mind since the Renaissance and pervades our art no less than our science.[31]

The essence of Gombrich's 1956 Mellon Lectures in the Fine Arts, the idea that understanding and learning are accomplished by hypothesis testing, rejecting, and remaking, is by now widely accepted. Karl Popper, the historian of science and an important influence on Gombrich, has recently restated the case as follows in his dialogue with the neurophysiologist John Eccles in the conclusion to the jointly authored *The Self and Its Brain:*

> The epistemology fits together well with our present knowledge of brain physiology, so that both things mutually support each other. . . . I would suggest that a good conjecture and working hypothesis—a sweeping hypothesis—would be that all the integration processes or decoding processes [involved in sense perception] are of the critical or trial-and-error type. That is to say, that each of them, so to speak, comes with its hypothesis and sees whether it works. The nerve cell which reacts to an inclined line is actually ready to fire or tries to fire; or it actually fires, and, if the matching is successful, it fires more, or better, or whatever it is. There is a difference if the action matches, or if it finds

out that the action does not match. How this works in detail of course I, who am not a physiologist, would not dare to say. But I would say that it is a good working hypothesis that each of these integrative stages is essentially a stage of action, of actually doing something.

I might add that I think that the integration of the different senses and their mutual cooperation is very largely a matter of the mutual checking and mutual criticism, as it were, of one set of interpretations by another.[32]

Popper's major work on mistakes is his 1963 *Conjectures and Refutations,* the hypothesis of which has been summarized by Keith Oatley:

We only really learn by our mistakes (refutations). As we apply our schemata to the world by living, they fail in various ways and we can learn, change and develop by modifying our schemata or theories accordingly. Popper quotes J. A. Wheeler at the beginning of his book as saying "The whole problem is to make the mistakes as fast as possible."[33]

In both these theories, and in the work of the cognitive psychologist Jean Piaget as well, the experience of coming up against barriers, making wrong interpretive guesses, and failing to find satisfying and coherent matches between past experience ("schemata") and present needs are not marginal, not mistakes that can be ignored by an epistemological theory but are central ingredients to learning. According to Eccles, "All of life is learning."[34] Children and laboratory rats are not the only ones who learn.

The purpose of these excursions beyond the bounds of literary theory was to enforce the claim advanced earlier that misreadings are not marginal or random phenomena; they are not limited to literary texts but are a way of relating to the world and managing the "worldly pilgrimage," as Stanley Fish noted. I wanted to suggest that by assimilating the problems of misreading difficult literary texts to the larger cognitive issue of misunderstanding, we might find some answers to our literary questions.

The other half of the claim is that overgeneralization itself is a danger, which more than one theorist has fallen into, having noticed the generality and the systematicity of error. An attack on the optimism of the assumption that systems work, and the co-occurrent marginalization of error that afflicts many theories of language and reading, will be more useful if it is not itself an idealization. More attention to detail is now needed: after the paradigm change, some "normal science" has to describe not a single category, error, but, instead, the various categories of error in the margins of our vision.

This approach is nicely exemplified by Mary Louise Pratt's attack on Grice's cooperative principle and on reader-response criticism for not considering the *plurality* of readers or the various motives of the same reader, author, or text. Speaking of Grice's overarching cooperative principle, Pratt claims that assuming "rational cooperation toward shared objectives" is an assumption so oversimplified as to be a distortion. "One must be able to talk about reader/text/author relations that are coercive, subversive, conflictive, submissive, as well as cooperative, and about relations that are some or all of these simultaneously or at different points in a text.[35] We need to collect examples of how these relations do not work as people thought they might, and see if, by not fitting current theories, they provoke us to a new level of understanding.

If response theory can only account for correct or predictable responses, if it remains only a theory of successful reading, then it loses the possibility of dealing with those aspects of a text that are most likely to separate a literary text from a nonliterary one: its mysteries. "The study of literature," Geoffrey Hartman reminds us, "has to accomplish two things at once: it must acknowledge the otherness of a text, and it must accommodate that otherness." Reading literature is "a double process of familiarization and defamiliarization."[36] If the text has no strangeness, no difficulties, then it will probably be judged to have no literary value. A language theory is a response theory, but a literary theory probably has to be more.

Notes

1. The suggestion that optimism and pessimism are divided among theorists depending on what side of the Atlantic they inhabit was made to me by Betty Rojtman of the Hebrew University. It is a resonant overgeneralization.

2. Stanley Fish and Jonathan Culler were together responsible for the spread of the idea of an ideal or competent reader specifically paralleling the idea of a competent speaker in generative grammar.

3. Wayne Booth, *The Rhetoric of Fiction* (Chicago: Chicago University Press, 1961), 178.

4. Michel Foucault, "Truth and Power," in *The Foucault Reader,* ed. Paul Rabinow (New York: Pantheon, 1984), 56.

5. See *Of Grammatology* (Baltimore: Johns Hopkins University Press, 1976) and Richard Rorty, "Philosophy as a Kind of Writing: An Essay on Derrida," *New Literary History,* 10, no. 1 (1978): 141–60.

6. Augustine, *On Christian Doctrine* (trans. D. W. Robertson, Jr.) 2. 37.

7. William Empson, *Seven Types of Ambiguity,* 3rd ed. (London: Peregrine, 1961), 10–11.

8. Empson, *Ambiguity,* xv.

9. Cleanth Brooks, "The Language of Paradox," in *The Well Wrought Urn* (New York: Harcourt, Brace, 1947), 6.

10. Michael Hancher, "What Kind of a Speech Act is Interpretation?" *Poetics* 10 (1981): 269.

11. Hancher, "Speech Act," 268.

12. Judith Fetterley, *The Resisting Reader: A Feminist Approach to American Fiction* (Bloomington, Ind.: Indiana University Press, 1978), xii.

13. Ibid., xxii–iii. Emphasis is mine.

14. Sandra M. Gilbert, "The Education of Henrietta Adams," *Profession* 84 (1984): 5–6.

15. Nina Baym, "Melodramas of Beset Manhood: How Theories of American Fiction Exclude Women Authors," in *The New Feminist Criticism: Essays on Women, Literature, and Theory,* ed. Elaine Showalter (New York: Pantheon, 1985), 73.

16. Leslie Fiedler, *Love and Death in the American Novel* (New York: Criterion Books, 1960), p. 236.

17. Baym, "Melodramas," 74.

18. Stanley Fish, *Surprised by Sin: The Reader in Paradise Lost* (Berkeley: University of California Press, 1971), 207.

19. Peter Steiner, "In Defense of Semiotics: The Dual Asymmetry of Cultural Signs," *New Literary History* 12, no. 3 (1981): 419, 421–22. Steiner takes his citations of Karcevskij from "Du dualisme asymétrique du signe linguistique," in *Travaux du Cercle linguistique de Prague I* (Prague: 1929), 88.

20. Steiner, "Semiotics," 423.

21. From a lecture given at the Center for Advanced Studies, Hebrew University, Jerusalem, 1986.

22. Derrida, "Structure, Sign, and Play in the Discourse of the Human Sciences," in *The Structuralist Controversy,* ed. Richard Macksey and Eugenio Donato (Baltimore: Johns Hopkins University Press, 1970), 264.

23. Paul de Man, *Blindness and Insight: Essays in the Rhetoric of Contemporary Criticism* (New York: Oxford University Press, 1971), ix.

24. de Man, *Blindness and Insight,* 106, 10.

25. Frank Lentricchia, *After the New Criticism* (London: Methuen, 1983), 301–2.

26. Ibid., 307.

27. Harold Bloom, *A Map of Misreading* (New York: Oxford University Press, 1975), 3.

28. Cleanth Brooks, it will be remembered, opposed "science," in which he presumed words must be exact to literature in which paradox is valued. In fact it is by now widely recognized that advances in sciences require the use of metaphoric language in the early stages of exploration. Cf., Richard Boyd, "Metaphor and Theory Change: What is 'Metaphor' a Metaphor for?" in *Metaphor and Thought,* ed. Andrew Ortony (Cambridge: Cambridge University Press, 1979), 356–408. De Man also separates out literary discourse as special by virtue of its "rhetoricity."

29. Empson, *Ambiguity,* x.

30. Fish, *Sin,* 207.

31. E. H. Gombrich, *Art and Illusion: A Study in the Psychology of Pictorial Representation* (Princeton: Princeton University Press, 1969), 173.

32. Karl R. Popper and John C. Eccles, *The Self and Its Brain* (London: Routledge & Kegan Paul, 1977), 433, 435.

33. Keith Oatley, *Perceptions and Representations: The Theoretical Basis of Brain Research and Psychology* (London: Methuen, 1978), 241–42.

34. Popper and Eccles, *Self,* 425.

35. Mary Louise Pratt, "Ideology and Speech-Act Theory," *Poetics Today* 7, no. 1 (1986): 70.

36. Geoffrey Hartman, "The Culture of Criticism," *PMLA* 99, no. 3 (1984): 379.

References

Augustine. *On Christian Doctrine.* Translated by D. W. Robertson, Jr. Indianapolis, Ind.: Bobbs Merrill, 1958.

Austin, J. L. *How to Do Things with Words.* Oxford: Clarendon Press, 1962.

Bach, K. and R. M. Harnish. *Linguistic Communication and Speech Acts.* Cambridge: The MIT Press, 1979.

Baym, Nina. "Melodramas of Beset Manhood: How Theories of American Fiction Exclude Women Authors." In *The New Feminist Criticism: Essays on Women, Literature, and Theory,* edited by Elaine Showalter, 63–80. New York: Pantheon, 1985.

Bloom, Harold. *A Map of Misreading.* New York: Oxford University Press, 1975.

Booth, Wayne. *The Rhetoric of Fiction.* Chicago: Chicago University Press, 1961.

Boyd, Richard. "Metaphor and Theory Change: What is 'Metaphor' a Metaphor for?" In *Metaphor and Thought,* edited by Andrew Ortony, 356–408. Cambridge: Cambridge University Press, 1979.

Brooks, Cleanth. "The Language of Paradox." In *The Well Wrought Urn.* New York: Harcourt Brace, 1947.

Chomsky, Noam. *Aspects of the Theory of Syntax.* Cambridge: MIT Press, 1965.

Derrida, Jacques. "The Law of Genre," *Critical Inquiry,* 7, no. 1 (1980): 55–81.

———. *Of Grammatology.* Baltimore, Md.: Johns Hopkins University Press, 1976.

———. "Structure Sign, and Play in the Discourse of the Human Sciences." In *The Structuralist Controversy,* edited by Richard Macsey and Eugenio Donato, 247–65. Baltimore, Md., Johns Hopkins University Press, 1970.

Empson, William. *Seven Types of Ambiguity.* 3rd ed. London: Peregrine, 1961.

Fetterley, Judith. *The Resisting Reader: A Feminist Approach to American Fiction.* Bloomington, Ind.: Indiana University Press, 1978.

Fiedler, Leslie. *Love and Death in the American Novel.* New York: Criterion Books, 1960.

Fish, Stanley E. *Is There a Text in This Class?* Cambridge: Harvard University Press, 1980.

———. *Surprised by Sin: The Reader in Paradise Lost.* Berkeley, Calif.: University of California Press, 1971.

Foucault, Michel. *Madness and Civilization.* Translated by Richard Howard. New York: Random House, 1965.

———. "Truth and Power." In *The Foucault Reader,* edited by Paul Rabinow, 51–75. New York: Pantheon, 1984.

Gilbert, Sandra M. "The Education of Henrietta Adams." *Profession 84* (1984): 5–9.

Gombrich, E. H. *Art and Illusion: A Study in the Psychology of Pictorial Representation.* Princeton: Princeton University Press, 1969.

Grice, H. P. "Logic and Conversation." In *Syntax and Semantics 3: Speech Acts,* edited by P. Cole and J. Morgan. New York: The Academic Press, 1975.

Hancher, Michael. "What Kind of Speech Act is Interpretation?" *Poetics* 10 (1981): 263–81.

Hartman, Geoffrey. "The Culture of Criticism," *PMLA* 99, no. 3 (1984): 371–97.

Hymes, Dell. "Toward Linguistic Competence." In *Working Papers in Sociolinguistics.* Austin, Tex.: University of Texas Press, 1973.

Jackendoff, Ray. *Semantics and Cognition.* Cambridge: MIT Press. 1983.

Karcevskij, Sergej. "Du dualisme asymetrique du signe linguistique." *Travaux du Cercle linguistique de Prague, I.* Prague, 1929.

Labov, William. *Sociolinguistic Patterns.* Philadelphia: University of Pennsylvania Press, 1972.

Lentriccia, Frank. *After the New Criticism.* London: Methuen, 1983.

Levinson, Stephen C. *Pragmatics.* Cambridge: Cambridge University Press, 1983.

Man, Paul de. *Blindness and Insight: Essays in the Rhetoric of Contemporary Criticism.* New York: Oxford University Press, 1971.

Oatley, Keith. *Perceptions and Representations: The Theoretical Basis of Brain Research and Psychology.* London: Methuen, 1978.

Popper, Karl R. *Conjectures and Refutations.* London: Routledge & Kegan Paul, 1963.

Popper, Karl R. and John C. Eccles. *The Self and Its Brain: An Argument for Interactionism.* London: Routledge & Kegan Paul, 1977.

Pratt, Mary Louise. "Ideology and Speech-Act Theory." *Poetics Today* 7, no. 1 (1986): 59–72.

Rorty, Richard. "Philosophy as a Kind of Writing: An Essay on Derrida." *New Literary History* 10, no. 1 (1978): 141–60.

Sadock, Jerrold M. *Toward a Linguistic Theory of Speech Acts.* New York: Academic Press, 1974.

Saussure, Ferdinand de. *Cours de linguistique générale.* Paris: Payot, [1915] 1972.

Schauber, Ellen, and Ellen Spolsky. *The Bounds of Interpretation: Linguistic Theory and Literary Text.* Stanford, Calif.: Stanford University Press, 1986.

Searle, John R. *Speech Acts: An Essay in the Philosophy of Language.* Cambridge: Cambridge University Press, 1969.

Schegloff, Emanuel A. "Sequencing in Conversational Openings." *American Anthropologist* 70, no. 6 (1968): 1075–95.

Steiner, Peter. "In Defense of Semiotics: The Dual Asymmetry of Cultural Signs." *New Literary History* 12, no. 3 (1981): 415–35.

2

Author as Reader and Reader as Author: Reflections on the Limits of Accommodation

E. D. Hirsch, Jr.

Because I have often stressed the importance of authors' intent, I could not blame you for supposing that I value authors above readers. But on the contrary, I believe that living readers should take precedence over dead authors, and I am sympathetic to what is called "the readers' liberation front." Thomas Jefferson, the founder of my home institution, the University of Virginia, firmly held the principle that we the living must resist binding ourselves to the conceptions of the dead. He recommended revising the U.S. Constitution every twenty years, and he framed legislation to abolish property entail. Entail was the practice of narrowly prescribing in one's last will and testament exactly how one's property should be passed down through all future generations. Modern criticism, applying Jefferson's spirit to the literary sphere, has abolished intellectual entail. Dead authors may not restrict their meanings forever to some original historical moment nor narrowly control how their texts shall be passed down in perpetuity among future readers.

But simply to assert the rights of living readers over dead authors is not to say anything specifically useful for literary culture or academic learning. Having abolished the principle of literary entail, shall we also abolish the principle of inheritance itself? Shall we place no limits on our liberation from the dead hand of the past? That is a significant question for those interested in literary culture and writing in general.

Writing was invented to overcome the restriction of speech to one time and place. As Plato ruefully observed in *The Phaedrus*, however, writing abandons living conversation and suffers from the artificial yoking of two historical worlds. Obsoleteness is thus inherent in the very nature of writing. That disadvantage is, of course, trivial compared to the advantages that writing brings. The fixing of speech in written form makes its meaning permanently available and makes human experience cumulative to a degree that oral societies could not hope to match. By enabling the present to build on the knowledge of the past, writing has been the chief agent of intellectual progress. (You will notice that this general observation conceives of literature as a form of writing, not as a separate substance with its own special laws.)

This momentous, cumulative function of writing has required the concept of a *communication* between the past and present. Humankind advances in knowledge because what writing "says" is communicated to future time. But the model of communication is, as Plato observed, problematic. In normal oral communication speaker and audience inhabit the same moment, whereas in writing they occupy different moments, making the model of communication an analogy or metaphor rather than a reality. Communication through writing has always required imaginative adjustments.

In what follows, I shall be considering a technique that audiences in literate cultures have developed for overcoming the datedness of past writing—the technique of "accommodation." Since accommodation is to be my main focus, I shall not try to list all the multifarious causes of datedness such as changes of taste, or changes of technology and political power. I shall simply ask whether, after the abolition of entail, there are nonetheless appropriate limits on the reader's accommodation of dated texts to present circumstances.

In oral societies, as Jack Goody and I. P. Watt have explained, the accommodation of past traditions to present circumstances was accomplished by subtly changing the words that carried the traditions.[1] This means of accommodation, however, is not available to literate culture. *Scripta manent.* Writing stays. Because we cannot adjust the words, we must adjust the interpretation of the words. Thus, in literate cultures, writing gradually disclosed a dissonance between the beliefs of past authors and those of present readers. Writing thereby introduced a spirit of skepticism toward traditional views of the world. Nonetheless in those institutions where a great deal is at stake in preserving tradition and the authority of the text—for example, in religion and law—interpretive techniques have been developed to *accommodate* past texts to present readers.

In religion, the foundation of such accommodation is the distinction between the literal and the spiritual senses. That distinction is grounded as follows. When God revealed His truth to historical persons He accommodated His meaning to their historical understandings. Later, in the course of history, humankind will need to comprehend that already accommodated truth in different ways. Thus, when we interpret a holy text we must grasp the trans-historical principle behind it, not just its original historical sense. We must reaccommodate its eternal meaning to our own under-standings in our own time and place. According to this principle, the holy text has underneath its historical clothing (i.e., under its literal sense) an essential core meaning (i.e., its spiritual sense) that is true in all times and places. The interpreter's task is to present this core meaning in the idiom of the present day. On this con-ception of divine texts, the problem of datedness does not and cannot arise in a fatal form, as Augustine argued at length. When we adjust the divine text to historical change we simply follow the suprahistorical intention of the suprahuman author.

But what of nonreligious texts? Such an interpretive model seems appropriate for sacred scripture, since with an omniscient author we may perform indefinitely many acts of accommodation without fear of anachronism. With merely human texts (human authors being time-bound and finite), datedness could be a fatal danger. So we must ask whether the *communicative* model of interpretation used in religion is appropriate for accommodating the literary and legal texts of our tradition. Is it reasonable to make authorial intent part of our interpretive norm in the secular as well as the sacred sphere? Indeed, is a secular accommodation really possible if readers pay any attention at all to historical meaning and authorial intent?

Legal theorists draw a distinction between interpretation that submits itself to the historical intent of a law and interpretation that operates on the principle enunciated by Justice William O. Douglas when he was on the nine-man Supreme Court: "With five votes we can do anything." In the former case, interpretation is governed by a past intent; in the latter, it is governed by the present intent of the judges. In one case the meaning of a statute is determined by historical evidence, in the other by the will of an oligarchy. Which mode is preferable? Perhaps no single answer can be given for all circumstances. My argument will be that neither account in an extreme form is acceptable as a solution to the conflicting claims of the present and the past.

I want to argue first that the principles of accommodation are basically the same in religious and secular interpretation. The key distinction between the two spheres is this: the author's intention behind the holy text is omniscient and infinite, whereas the author's intention behind the secular text is finite and human. Nonetheless, when we try to accommodate the finite human text to the present, we are obliged to assume that it too has a spirit as well as a letter, a core meaning that can be transported from one historical era to another. This notion of a transhistorical meaning in literary texts is of course a radical doctrine in our historicist era. Nonetheless, the very *idea* of accommodation logically implies a transhistorical core meaning that can be applied to the present as well as to the past.

The distinction between letter and spirit is fundamental to all interpretive accommodation. If the letter of a past meaning could be directly applied to the present, no accommodation would be needed, for the spirit and the letter would be congruent. The distinction between the two arises only because the literal sense becomes outdated. Similarly, past *interpretations* of the spiritual sense also become passé and must likewise be discarded in favor of new interpretations of the spiritual sense. But how can we justify finding such a spiritual sense in the human-authored texts of literature and law.

Let us look at some examples of literary datedness, starting with a medieval text. The only story in Chaucer's *Canterbury Tales* that most of us would call dated is probably the "The Tale of Melibee." The spiritual sense of this tale is confined to a very explicitly articulated moral and theological system—one that is not widely accepted today. This point suggests a preliminary hypothesis about literary datedness that we can test against further examples. My hypothesis is that one reason a story becomes irretrievably outdated is that its *spiritual* (i.e., allegorical) sense cannot be accepted as literally valid. The spiritual sense of a text must seem acceptable to present readers, for when the spiritual sense is itself obsolete, all is lost.

This generalization would seem to hold for such works as the novels of Thomas Love Peacock and for that slowly dying masterpiece, Spenser's *Fairie Queene*. In both cases, the reader is compelled to supply allegorical meanings that are themselves passé. As with "the Tale of Melibee" we are not inclined to allegorize the allegory itself in order to accommodate the work to our own time.

To take such a further allegorizing step goes against the way we read literature. All stories that are interesting to us are made so through our application of ad hoc allegories, whereby we constantly find analogues with our own experience. If those ad hoc allegorical echoes are lacking, we find the story uninteresting. If an animal story pertained only to the animal point of view, it would be entirely uninteresting to us and would suffer a fate analogous to datedness. George Orwell's *Animal Farm* and Bernard de Mandeville's *Fable of the Bees* are read because they are allegorical of human experience. Even stories like *Black Beauty* are about *human* relations with animals. Readers of literature automatically make ad hoc allegorical connections with their experiences. But when the explicit allegory itself doesn't ring true, we do not make connections between the allegory and our own lives. Passé allegory removes the immediacy and impact of a story and condemns it to the lost land of Melibee.

This hypothesis also explains why much of our older literature is remarkably resistant to datedness. Most of the *Canterbury Tales* are unlike "The Tale of Melibee." They, like most good literature, refrain from expressing explicit general concepts through explicit systems of allegory and philosophy. That is what Sir Philip Sidney meant when he said (somewhat playfully) that the poet never affirms. The poet comes to us with a tale and lets *us* supply the conceptual systems under which the tale is applied to human life. When literature itself contains an insistently specific allegory, or is insistently rooted in a particular historical situation, those elements become quickly dated. They are, as Sidney so genially suggested, the elements that most easily tell lies. Both the historian and the scientist tell lies, Sidney says, because they earnestly try to tell narrow and particular truths with great exactitude. When their literal sense proves to be wrong, their story is superseded by other stories that try to tell those truths with ever more precision and detail.[2]

Hence, stories in literature, no matter how detailed they are in their concrete description of life, tend to support many different conceptual systems and apply to many different human experiences in different periods. I do not suggest that literature is innocent of conceptual systems. Quite the contrary, the conceptual element alone gives literature breadth and duration. Unless an example implies a concept, the example cannot embrace further examples beyond the one in the story. Rather, it is because the conceptual systems of literature are typically painted *inexplicitly* that they remain true of human life. Reading such conceptually inexplicit texts in subsequent periods, we can accommodate their broad concepts to current systems like Freudianism, or Marxism, which some currently believe to be valid. The characteristic lack of specificity in the concepts of literature helps it resist conceptual datedness. Broad, stone-age physics is still true, as has been observed; it is last year's very specific physics that has become outmoded.

Also through inexplicitness the law resists datedness. The laws that become outmoded are just those that have been painted with narrow rather than broad strokes. Justice John Marshall famously observed that the framers of the U.S. Constitution deliberately wrote it broadly and inexplicitly to enable readers to supply future accommodations. The statutes that are narrowest and most explicit are the first to become obsolete. So far then, it does seem to hold true that to be accommodated, a text's spiritual meaning must continue to seem valid to present readers.

We can test this hypothesis further with a more complex and therefore more typical example. W. K. Wimsatt has written a comment on Blake's poem, *London* that brings out very clearly the problem of the limits of accommodation. Because it is a short poem, I shall quote it in full:

I wander thro' each charter'd street,
Near where the charter'd Thames does flow,
And mark in every face I meet
Marks of weakness, marks of woe.

In every cry of every Man,
In every Infant's cry of fear,
In every voice, in every ban,
The mind-forg'd manacles I hear.

How the Chimney-sweeper's cry
Every black'ning Church appalls;
And the hapless Soldier's sigh
Runs in blood down Palace walls.

But most thro' midnight streets I hear
How the youthful Harlot's curse
Blasts the new born Infant's tear,
And blights with plagues the Marriage hearse.[3]

This universally admired poem is firmly established in the canon of English literature. Wimsatt, however, considered it an example of why we should *not* allow our interpretation of literary meaning to be accommodated in any degree to authorial intent. He says:

We are now seeking a maximum or crucial instance where a poet's private or personal and habitual meaning (as inferred from external documents) clearly clashed with what he managed to realize in . . . his poem. . . . The following [instance] may serve to define the issue. The materials are well known, but not the interpretive problem as I shall urge it. William Blake wrote in a sketchbook:

An ancient Proverb

Remove away that blackening church
Remove away that marriage hearse
Remove away that man of blood
You'll quite remove the ancient curse.

These lines remained in the sketchbook, where they deserved to remain. They are a raw expression of certain soreheaded antinomian
attitudes which are beyond doubt a part of Blake's biography at the
period when he was writing *London*.[4]

Wimsatt then goes on to focus on the phrase "marriage hearse."

Mr. E. D. Hirsch, as I have said, is well informed about Blake and
reliable, and I believe he gives us an accurate reading of a sort of
intention [for the phrase "marriage hearse"] which Blake probably did
entertain. . . . If there were no marriage, there would be no ungratified
desires, and therefore no harlots." One thing, however, which perhaps
he does not notice, or perhaps does not worry about is that these ideas
are silly. (Why wouldn't there be *many* ungratified desires, as many at
least as there were losers in stag combats, or wooers rejected, or
pursuers eluded, or matings frustrated? and *many* harlots? and *many*
whoremasters?) An admirer of Blake the poet might well be content to
leave these ideas, if he could, on a back shelf in the doctrinaire part of
Blake's mind. What if we actually do find them or manage to put them in
the poem? Won't this make the poem silly? And, since evaluation and
interpretation are at the very least closely related, won't we be in danger
of reading the poem as a pretty bad poem? And isn't this poem, in fact,
supposed to be a masterpiece, "one of the best city poems ever written"? Isn't it in fact a masterpiece?"[5]

Wimsatt has clearly laid out the puzzlements that arise when we
are interpreting a canonical text whose original implications do not
completely fit values and truths that current readers believe in. The
Blake poem is a particularly useful example of the problem, because the discussants have agreed on the premises of the problem.
Wimsatt accepts my view about what Blake originally meant, and I
accept his view that Blake's ideas about marriage (which Blake
shared with Godwin and other radicals of the early nineteenth
century) are silly and obsolete. We agree both about what Blake
intended by "marriage hearse" and about the datedness of his
ideas. How shall those agreed-on facts affect our accommodation of
the poem to the present day?

Wimsatt's answer is that we should not allow intention to place *any* limits on accommodation. He reads the poem as being *in favor* of marriage. He says:

> Blake's struggle with *London* was in part a struggle to make the last line of the last stanza viable. The tough fact was that the word "marriage" in the history of English usage and culture was not the name of an evil. . . . It was the name of a sacred institution and a first principle of stability for nearly every important value in a whole religiously and ethically oriented civilization and culture. . . . Let us imagine that some inquisitor of school curricula, reading Mr. Hirsch's gloss on *London,* were to file a protest against corrupting the minds of school-children by the required study of this depraved poem. . . . [An] answer that surely would not be long delayed would be to the effect that Blake's *London* in fact says no such thing.[6]

Indeed, Wimsatt sees to it that the poem says no such thing. He quotes with approval the comment of Joseph Wicksteed to the effect that the poem implies the "beauty of marriage." This direct inversion of Blake's intended meaning protects the poem from silliness and justifies it as a "masterpiece" that deserves to be taught in the schools.

But should one make a poem say, the opposite of what the author intended? My own preference in this case would be to leave the warts of datedness on the poem where they cannot be plausibly removed. Even if the price of this approach were that the poem should be excluded from early grades, I would be content for that price to be paid. *Amicus Blake, sed magis amica veritas.* Isn't that the best lesson for school children and everyone else?

What then are the limits of accommodation? Some flexibility in interpreting the letter of an older text is needed in order to apply its spirit to the present day. But what shall be the limit of this flexibility? Is there a rational demarcation principle between an accommodation that is justifiable and one that is not? Whatever this principle might be, we must clearly have transgressed it when we understand Blake's *London* as being in *favor* of marriage.

Let me briefly apply this observation to legal interpretation, which I conceive to be governed by some of the same intellectual and cultural issues as literary interpretation. Although the legal theorist Guido Calabresi cites many cases of accommodative distortion in statutory interpretation,[7] Wimsatt probably goes further than most judges, including Justice William O. Douglas, would be prepared to go. For example, it happened that Justice Douglas was a member of the Warren Court that upset an earlier Supreme Court ruling, the Plessy-Fergusson decision, in which the court had *ac-*

cepted the principle of separate but equal educational facilities. But in 1954, the court directly overturned this earlier interpretation as passé, banished it from the legal canon, and purged it from the legal curriculum. All of this overturning and banishing would have been unnecessary on the Wimsatt or pure readerly principle of accommodation. The court could have simply announced that the spirit of Plessy-Fergusson itself was against segregation, despite what the text said literally and the original authors intended.

Courts in a democracy are reluctant to make quite such radical "accommodations," though one hears of "Alice-in-Wonderland" interpretations occurring under totalitarian legal systems. In the United States, however, judges are reluctant to go as far as some literary critics, because judges want to preserve respect for the law's objectivity, and its governance by evidence and rational argument. (I would want to make the same point about literary scholarship.) But is there in fact a rational demarcation principle between justified and unjustified interpretive accommodations? Here I arrive at the positive proposals that I shall offer for solving this technical problem.

If a rational demarcation principle between justified and unjustified accommodation exists, we can predict that the principle will conform to common sense and existing traditions of responsible interpretation. What we need is a principle that illuminates rather than dictates the accumulated wisdom of our interpretive traditions. I believe that such a principle *is* available, and that, like everything else that is sound in theory of interpretation, it is based on ordinary linguistic practices.

In a recent issue of *Critical Inquiry,* I invented for another purpose the following example of a common speech practice.[8] Someone says that Jack had taken a trip in his new Toyota. The speaker is then told that he had mistaken the make of car. It was not a Toyota but a Datsun. To this the speaker replies, "I *meant* Datsun."

In this example I stressed that the speaker had said he *meant* Datsun, not that he meant to *say* "Datsun." I deliberately contrived an example in which the speaker meant to *say* exactly what he did say, namely "Toyota," but where he also quite properly insisted that Datsun was nonetheless what he *meant,* whether he said it or not. A literary analogue of this example was T. S. Eliot's observation that Edgar Allan Poe meant his most *memorable* year in *The Raven,* although he wrote (and meant to write) his "most *immemorial* year."

These discrepancies between what we mean and what we mean to say are instances of the *provisionality* of speech. Such provisionality is a feature of both conversation and writing. Although we may intend to speak truth, and to refer accurately to reality, we know that our human limitations may cause us to say things that are not strictly and literally true. Aware of our limitations, we speak provisionally and under correction. At a later time, we may have to amend the letter of our saying in order to preserve its spirit. That is why the speaker in my example was justified in saying he *meant* Datsun. I suggest that these accommodations of ordinary speech are analogous to our accommodations of older written texts.

I also suggest that this account of the provisionality of speech bears deep analogies with Gotlob Frege's important logical distinction between sense and reference. "Jack's Datsun" is the reference of the remark whose sense was "Jack's Toyota." I can not pursue this analogy with Frege's distinction further but mention it in passing in order to show how very far reaching and fundamental are the principles of provisionality and accommodation in our ordinary speaking and thinking. The pervasiveness and breadth of these similarities indicate that we are dealing with fundamental and non-arbitrary features of speech.

That is why we ought to have confidence in the wisdom of ordinary usage in providing us with the demarcation principle we are seeking. In ordinary speech we place limits on the distance we will accept between the letter and the spirit of words. We are willing to let the sense "Toyota" stand for the reference "Datsun," because we feel that the literal senses of the two are close enough to each other to be subsumed under a reasonably narrow generic grouping. This appropriately narrow class is taken to embrace the various true references of our words. In the Datsun example, the implicit generic grouping would be something like "the class of small imported Japanese cars, any member of which can be allowed to refer to or represent any other member."

By contrast, we would not usually accept "Dodge truck" or "Ferrari" as referring to a Datsun. The generic grouping would be too broad. The letter and spirit would be too distant, and we would insist that the statement itself should be changed, not just its interpretation. On analogy with statutory interpretation, we would revoke or repeal "Dodge truck" as being unreferential (unconstitutional), and we would legislate a revised text, "Datsun." If we believe that the original legislators (authors) in using the words "Dodge truck" meant to refer *narrowly* to a vehicle that turns out to be a Datsun, we should need to revise the statute. This illustrates the well-known advantage of broad over narrow language in law making. The proper limit of accommodation lies somewhere between being specifically wrong yet generically right (Toyota for Datsun) and being wrong in broader generic terms (truck for sedan).

The demarcation principle just described holds in typical communicative situations. We may be broadly tolerant in our uses of language, but there's a point at which we put our linguistic foot down. Typically, we will accommodate slight misstatements to a more accurate later reference. For instance, we would usually accept "cottage" as referring to cabin. But we would put our foot down at "mansion" referring to cabin. We would let "article" stand for "monograph" but not for "book," and "marriage hearse" for a repressive institution" but not for "sanctity of marriage." Thus, in the case of the Blake poem, if we wanted to carry out an acceptable accommodative interpretation, we would be tolerant of Blake's mistaken views of the relations between marriage and prostitution but not tolerant enough to say he meant that marriage is a good thing. At the same time we would accept repression. He was right about oppression, wrong about marriage. To have a poem in favor of marriage, we'd have to reauthor Blake's poem, or better, find a different poem.

Don't broad and narrow genres of meaning all lie on a single continuum? Isn't one man's Toyota another's Dodge truck? Isn't the demarcation principle after all just a matter of arbitrary convention? Of course conventions do play a decisive role in interpretive decisions, but "arbitrary conventions" is no description of the case. We need a basis for choosing appropriate conventions. Which shall we choose? The convention that we use in ordinary speech is that of not departing very far from a speaker's *intentions*. That is to say, convention alone does not adequately define the demarcation principle, because the conventions we adopt in interpretation are generally the conventions we believe the author to have intended. In law, we characteristically assume that legislators know and act under the same conventions as judges. That is our chief warrant for applying such conventions. The two principles are codependent. Conventions are bound by listeners' inferences about speakers intentions, and intentions are bound by speakers' inferences about listeners' conventions.

In the examples just mentioned (cottage/mansion, sedan/truck), the implicit demarcation principle that determined whether a text should sustain a particular accommodation was our conception of the breadth and character of the original intention. In literature, for instance, a very specific word may often stand for a very general range of applications. A Dodge truck in a poem could represent not only all wheeled vehicles including Datsun but, depending on the generic intention, ships at sea and rickshaws as well. On the other hand, when the textual intention-convention is more specific, as is usual in the law, our tolerance of legitimate accommodation will be less broad, and the distance we allow between original sense and later reference will be proportionally smaller. Ultimately, then, the limits of valid accommodation are determined by the breadth of the historical intention-convention that we infer.

Our consideration of the problem of past authors and present readers, a problem native to writing, has thus disclosed an interesting feature of verbal meaning in general. Meaning is best conceived not as a static object but as the continual unfolding by readers and listeners of a historical act of intention. In this process the author projects himself or herself as a future reader, submitting to future correction, and the reader continues the role of author. Both are governed by the unfolding of a historically defined principle that extends beyond the limitations of both into a continuous future. The logic of that unfolding is the logic of an ongoing decision procedure that is governed by a demarcation principle. Our meaning inferences continue to be governed (or should be) by the breadth and character of a principle that is defined by a past intention.

On this view, the limits of accommodation in textual interpretation are the same as the limits of accommodation in ordinary speech. As ordinary speakers we intend our meanings provisionally, and as listeners we tolerate a degree of error that is dependent on the nature of the speaker's intention. We are aware that human knowledge is finite, so we *intend* to give ourselves some leeway in speaking. We speak as listeners and we listen as speakers. We speak under correction, and we listen with an accommodating ear. We stretch or narrow our accommodative practices according to conventions that are ultimately determined by the breadth and character of a speaker's intentions. That is the appropriate accommodative principle for all merely human texts, including the texts of literature and law.

Notes

1. J. Goody and I. P. Watt, "The Consequences of Literacy," *Comparative Studies in Society and History* 5 (1963): 304–45.

2. Sir Philip Sidney, "The Defence of Poetry," *Sir Philip Sidney: Selected Prose and Poetry,* ed. Robert Kimbrough (Madison, Wis.: University of Wisconsin Press, 1983).

3. W. K. Wimsatt, *Day of the Leopards: Essays in Defense of Poems* (New Haven: Yale University Press, 1976) p. 31.

4. Ibid., p. 31.
5. Ibid., p. 32.
6. Ibid., p. 33.
7. Guido Calabresi, *A Common Law for the Age of Statutes*, (Cambridge: Harvard University Press, 1982).
8. E. D. Hirsh, Jr., "Meaning and Significance Reinterpreted," *Critical Inquiry* vol. 11, no. 2 (1984): 202–25.

References

Calebresi, Guido. *A Common Law For the Age of Statutes*. Cambridge: Harvard University Press, 1982.

Goody, Jack and I. P. Watt. "The Consequences of Literacy." *Comparative Studies in Society and History* 5 (1963): 304–45.

Hirsch, E. D., Jr. "Meaning and Significance Reinterpreted." *Critical Inquiry* 11, no. 2 (1984): 202–25.

Sidney, Sir Philip. "The Defence of Poetry." In *Sir Philip Sidney: Selected Prose and Poetry,* edited by Robert Kimbrough. Madison, Wisc.: University of Wisconsin, 1983.

Wimsatt, W. K. *Day of the Leopards: Essays in Defense of Poems.* New Haven: Yale University Press, 1976.

3

Time and Reader

Meir Sternberg

Time is the medium of narration, as it is the medium of life.
—Thomas Mann, *The Magic Mountain*

What's a "medium"? He's a means,
Good, bad, indifferent, still the only means
Spirits can speak by.
—Robert Browning, "Mr. Sludge, 'the Medium' "

My dramatis personae are Time and Reader in literary communication. My theme lies in the nature of this pairing, its constants along with some problematic variables, and their implications for how writers write and readers operate under the rules of the game. And my excuse for revisiting a scene I have often visited in the last twenty years[1] is the need for explaining the different views taken of it by other visitors past and present. I want to look at the temporal conditions of reading in close reference to some doctrines and trends in literary theory where they appear or disappear, or surprisingly fail to appear. Whether ancient or modern, all these approaches are well established and most of them insidious, because they mix genuine insights with persuasive dogmas or neatly erect local and contingent truths into general laws. This is what gives the challenge of sorting them out its relevance to any inquiry into the problem, as well as its historical and metacritical interest. What follows, then, is nothing so ominous as a consideration of the state of the art regarding either of my topics by itself, however appropriate such a stock-taking might be these days. Rather, it develops an argument meant to bring out what happens to the reader in temporal art by tracing what has happened to the reader in temporal theory, or its absence.

A Problem

To do justice to the relations between Time and Reader would provide matter for a small library, but to appreciate their omnipresence it is enough to think of what the literary text does to us in transmission and what we do in response. As a temporal medium, literature must unfold whatever it wants to present—an action, a character, a society, a theme, a figurative cluster or sound pattern—along a continuum of time, where elements emerge in an ordered and irreversible sequence. Therefore, however modest the text's aspirations along this dimension of arrangement or however ambitious along others, like space and viewpoint, the time axis always proves crucial to the reader. What may be to the author anything from a presentational blessing to a convenience to a necessary evil is to the reader the route whereby he or she progressively discovers and makes sense of the text. Confronted by a string of linguistic signs, the reader must piece them together from moment to moment in order to reconstruct whatever the text has constructed: the action, the character, the society, the theme, the figurative cluster, or the sound pattern. As in all temporal communication, therefore, the communicative transaction in literature entails a basic dissymmetry between encoding and decoding, constructive and reconstructive activity: between the author, presumed to know what he or she wants to present, and the reader, who can find it out only by trial-and-error methods, in and through its gradual presentation in time.

Authors, however, do not just resign themselves to this built-in dissymmetry. They artfully exploit it to control the reading process throughout, with a variety of ends in view. Because readers know nothing for certain except what is disclosed from moment to moment, this ignorance is both partial and restless. It is partial because we come to the reading equipped with certain aids to prediction—such as generic conventions of sequence—and readers bring them to bear on the information released during the process. It is also a restless ignorance; we readers cannot remain passive recipients, satisfied with our lot because we know no better. We do know better, if only from hard-earned experience and fresh pressures and expectancies of coherence. For at each point, the reader must integrate the information that has emerged so far, or else the work will fall into pieces. But however hard we try to fit those pieces together in the light of relevant norms and models, our efforts will always be foiled by gaps, doubts, and tensions yet to be resolved. The hero's motives remain ambiguous, the thematic pattern disharmonious, the speaker's attitude indeterminate between irony and plain speaking, or the action simply open to more than one line of development. Only the textual future, in the form of what lies ahead in the sequence, can settle such questions and decide between our hypotheses. But that future not only unfolds piecemeal, so that each stage gives a new twist to old puzzles and expectations. The new information also creates new uncertainties; and it may also lull the reader into false certainties. The character finally looks intelligible, the theme worked out, the tone settled, the movement of the action plain—only to surprise us by relapsing into darkness and ambiguity with the next bend in the corridor of time. And so on to the end, when the dissymmetry of temporal communication straightens out at long last and leaves us, if not with all that we want to know, then with what we presumably need to know in order to form in retrospect a more or less coherent pattern of meaning and experience.

Our movement between partial ignorance and partial knowledge along a predetermined course thus enables the author to lead and mislead us, to control our hypothesis making and mold our perspective throughout according to his or her designs. How this dynamic operates, how it interacts with other compositional factors, spatiality included, how it maneuvers between order and disorder, how its strategies vary from genre to genre and from text to text: such issues are highly problematic. But that it does operate, and to the most crucial effect, is beyond doubt. Nor can there be much doubt that its operations involve a complex of features and values distinctively associated with art, if not peculiar to time-art: from semantic richness to the pleasures of retardation and inference and surprise to the foregrounding of the discourse as artifact. For better or worse, time and reader are indissolubly wedded in the communicative circuit of literature.

Curiously, however, though time has been a frequent subject in criticism since the Renaissance and the reader has lately come into the limelight, the relations between them have received nothing like proportionate attention, least of all systematic treatment. With the result that although the "reading process" is often enough invoked nowadays, its workings still remain almost a complete mystery and even its effects are not much in evidence. At best, the operations silently performed on the way from beginning to end are more assumed than explained by the performers in their voice as interpreters and theorists. What do we really know about the very fundamentals of reading in time, e.g., the dynamics of expectation, of ambiguity, of misunderstanding followed by retrospective enlightenment, of repetition and variation, of focus shifting, of attitude change? Here official interpretation lags far behind immediate experience or intuitive practice, and theory even behind interpretation.

Optimists will say, not without reason, that literary theory is still in its infancy and we must hope and work for better things. But whether they *would* be "better" is actually part of the problem. To judge by the ongoing record, progress here is not just a matter of repairing omissions and generalizing insights into principles. It first requires coming to grips with an array of doctrinal obstacles, which amount to a persistent tendency to obscure and downgrade, to loosen if not break, the link between time and reader. Unless we assume what experience has taught us to question, that in matters of art the child is always wiser than its father, the how's and especially the why's of this tendency have a serious claim to notice. They indeed turn out to be instructive and recurrent, often converging though far from uniform. To a partisan who looks back in haste on the history of critical thought, it may perhaps appear as if theorists of different persuasions have joined in a conspiracy to cut asunder what art has twined together. Actually, that is not so much their intention, still less their concerted intention, but the result of each one's efforts to define literary art in its proper terms, which to others or ourselves are often improper.

Fictive Time Promoted, Reading Time Demoted: The Aristotle-Lessing Tradition

Consider Artistotle's *Poetics.* Except for what lurks between its packed lines, it has little to say about the reader and even less about time. Yet the *Poetics* has launched what has since become a traditional (though not always conscious) line of dissociating those nominal absentees: the diversion of the locus or focus of artistic temporality away from the reader and the reading to the world read about.

That such a diversion should proceed from the first (and perhaps most affective) functional theory of art may seem strange. If art is what art does, and if what art does (e.g., catharsis in tragedy) necessarily involves and affects the receiver, then how can its analysis fail to highlight the axis along which reception takes place and effect? Specifically, indeed, how does one account for this omission regarding an effect like catharsis, which takes time to form and takes form in time, by a process always cumulative and ideally made tortuous through peripety and discovery? Considering the role actually fulfilled all along by this dynamics of presentation and response, in short, whence the apparent disregard for it?

The quest for an answer brings us to the heart of the Aristotelian doctrine, revealing a scale of priorities that does not always follow even from its own premises. It is not only that Aristotle rules out the possibility of defining literature in terms of its medium or "means"—the language that the reader directly encounters when approaching a text. Nor is it only that Aristotle defines art in terms of mimesis, so that its distinctive features adhere to representational (rather than presentational) structure, i.e., to the analogy between the created and the natural world. Apart from its hierarchical force, debatable but grantable, the line drawn between the means and the object of imitation comes to assume specific temporal significance. In the context of "means," where time is really inescapable it receives little notice. In the "object," where the presence of time is optional—arguably even within literature itself—it assumes necessary and dominant status.

From the first chapter of the *Poetics,* Aristotle's inquiry into the literary "means" focuses on its material and lexical components (language, possibly supported by rhythm and melody) to the exclusion of temporal properties. Words feature as sounds, symbols, styles, parts and figures of speech, but never as a sequence. Chapter 12 may appear an exception to this rule, switching for a change to the *text* of tragedy as it extends from Prologue to Episode to Exodos, with choral commentary interspersed among the episodes. This division of the text-continuum, however, remains completely unaligned with the all-important division of the event-continuum into "beginning, middle, and end" or any other functional parameter. It thus plays no role in the model of tragedy, and commentators have indeed long dismissed it as spurious and jejune.

Nor is it possible to explain this omission in such terms as lack of sophistication or even of interest. For a truly functional treatment of sequence in language we have to go no further than Aristotle's own *Rhetoric,* especially the section on "arrangement" (bk. 3, chaps. 13–19). Here, apart from observing the principle at work, we can figure out certain basic premises and links that might otherwise remain obscure, operationally speaking at least. Why does Aristotle apply the same term to "arrangement" in discourse, *taxis,* as he does elsewhere to "order" in time proper? What does he mean by analogizing or assimilating human discourse to natural time as sequences with members ordered from prior to posterior (*Categories* 14a25–14b9)? For contrast—and future reference—let me therefore generalize a few points and perspectives conspicuously absent not just from the division of the tragic text but from the *Poetics* as a whole.

A public speech, according to the *Rhetoric*, falls into four parts— namely, Introduction, Statement (or Narration), Argument, and Epilogue. Only the two middle parts are essential, because "you cannot either state your case and omit to prove it, or prove it without having first stated it" (1414a31–32).[2] The presence or absence of the two others hinges on whether the distinctive effect of the part serves or disturbs the purpose of the entire speech. To qualify for end point, either must prove itself a means to the given end.

The Introduction, for example, is not whatever happens to start the discourse but a start with a marked sequential role, "corresponding to the prologue in poetry and the prelude in flute-music; they are all beginnings, paving the way, as it were, for what is to follow" (1414b19–21). A *ceremonial* speech, in which virtuosity pays and monotony displeases, should thus aim for a striking prelude even at the expense of relevance, such as an appeal to the audience to excuse any infelicities in the sequel. *Forensic* oratory, again, employs openings to the same end as the invocation in epic: to announce the theme, so that the audience may grasp it in advance and follow its development. In contrast, the Introduction is not essential to a *political* address: its topic being known beforehand, the statement of facts can profitably dispense with preliminaries. Yet even in this type of speech an opening still has "remedial" uses, geared less to thematic than to perceptual and persuasive effect. In its remedial capacity, it may serve to seize or on the contrary distract the audience's attention, to excite their goodwill, predispose them in the speaker's favor, or at least to dispel their prejudice against him. "Bring yourself on the stage from the first in the right character, that people may regard you in that light, and the same with your adversary; but do not let them see what you are about" (1417b7–10).

Such consistent reference of forms to functions already exhibits an alertness to more than one property of the verbal medium as a system of communication. If those properties are roughly divided into selectional or durational versus combinatory or sequential, then we can see how Aristotle's Introduction appeals to both even in its "thematic" role. For his approach brings into play not only the discreteness of the units in discourse, whereby the exordium may be included or omitted at will and all parts stretched or minimized, but their linear organization as well. Further, the selectional variables are themselves often governed by the potentialities and requirements of sequential impact. *Because* a ceremonial speech takes time and must generate interest throughout, it demands an Introduction for variety; *because* a forensic speech deals with a long or intricate subject, it provides an Ariadne's thread at the start and finishes with a review; *because* a political speech naturally assumes foreknowledge of its theme, it can afford to plunge straight into the heart of the matter. The pressures of duration, the insurance of glancing forward and backward, the freedom to skip a part; each involves some basic feature(s) of communication in time. The "remedial" effect even suggests how all language use develops as a process of impression-formation, moral judgment, focusing—one that must by nature follow some direction, because it cannot but unfold in some order, yet remains variously directible by art. Hence, the possibility of swaying the audience through first impressions.

Nor do the rhetorical manipulations of the medium operate within the limits of a fixed sequence of discourse, extending from Introduction through Statement and Argument to Epilogue. Rather, that sequence is open to variation in its internal ordering as well as in its makeup and length. After all, even the priority of Statement to Argument derives from considerations of effectiveness alone—how can you prove a case without having first stated or "narrated" it? Like the extremes, indeed, those middle parts lend themselves, if not to reversal, then certainly to discontinuous arrangement.

Thus, narration in oratory must be intermittent rather than continuous, the line of events broken up into such stretches as the audience will find easy to keep in mind. Statement and Argument accordingly alternate: "Show, therefore, from one set of facts that your hero is, e.g. brave, and from other sets of facts that he is able, just, etc" (1416b22–24). Likewise, this time from the side of Argument, with those probabilistic syllogisms called enthymemes: "Do not use a continuous succession of Enthymemes: intersperse them with other matter, or they will spoil one another's effect" (1418a6–7).

As with distribution, moreover, so with transposition. Here it is even more evident that, though discourse must order its components from prior to posterior, it may still contrive and permute their ordering with a flexibility denied to the operations of time in nature. Why, for example, place calls for the audience's attention in the Exordium? They may come equally well at any other point along the speech. "In fact, the beginning of it is just where there is least slackness of interest; it is therefore ridiculous to put this kind of thing at the beginning, when every one is listening with most attention" (1415b9–11). Or, where should one concentrate the gist of one's case for the audience's benefit? "Some wrongly recommended doing [it] in the Introduction. . . . What you should do in your Introduction is to state your subject, in order that the point to be judged may be quite plain; in the Epilogue you should summarize the arguments by which your case has been proved" (1419b28–32). In condensed as well as distributed form, then, the same element may in principle range all the way from start to finish, and in practice it will find a more or less appropriate slot according to the speaker's theory or mastery of the art of arrangement.

Its placing may vary still further to meet the shifts and exigencies of communication as a *dramatic* process—a conflict enacted in and through language. The shift in role between defense and prosecution, for instance, determines whether the speaker will operate on the addressee's prejudices in the Introduction or in the Epilogue: "The defendant, when he is going to bring himself on the stage, must clear away any obstacles and therefore must begin by removing any prejudice felt against him. But if you are to *excite* prejudice, you must do so at the close, so that the judges may more easily remember what you have said" (1415a31–34). Most remarkable of all are the sequential permutations within the stage of Argument. Which comes first, building up one's own case or breaking down the opponent's?

> If you are the first speaker you should put your own arguments forward first, and then meet the arguments on the other side by refuting them and pulling them to pieces beforehand. . . . If you speak later, you must first, by means of refutation and counter-syllogism, attempt some answer to your opponent's speech, especially if his arguments have been well received. For just as our minds refuse a favorable reception to a *person* against whom they are prejudiced, so they refuse it to a speech when they have been favorably impressed by the speech on the other side. You should therefore make room in the minds of the audience for your coming speech; and this will be done by getting your opponent's speech out of the way. So attack that first. (1418b5–23)

With the encounter between opponents cast as a prolonged struggle over the audience's mind, rather than over objective truth or justice, the making and unmaking of impressions overrides everything else. For maximum impact, and on pain of failure to obtain a hearing, the order chosen by the speaker must take its reference from his position within the overall order of speaking. Given the drama and the mental arena, timing is all.

All these maneuvers rely for their full power on the verbal medium, then, and none could be dreamt of in a medium other than temporal. Within rhetoric, moreover, all imply a view of communication that is in harmony with a nonsemantic poetics such as Aristotle's, because they work less according to cognitive than to affective principles.[3] Communication here primarily affects (or infects) states of mind rather than transmits information, let alone knowledge; its sequence twists and turns to generate a desired play of response (e.g., feeling, attitude, impression, attention, memory) rather than a pattern of meaning. The rhetoric is a rhetoric of impact, in short, and so is the poetics.

The finer and more impact-centered the *Rhetoric*'s sense of the medium's temporality, however, the more striking its abeyance in the *Poetics*—doubly so considering that the rest of language's features and differentiae, from sound to style, are in evidence. It is to the *Rhetoric* that we owe even the note on the communicative rationale of "beginnings" in epic and drama, followed by other suggestive art-life analogies regarding the operations of sequence on the addressee. Throughout the *Poetics* itself, Aristotle just disregards the medium's ordering dimension as an irreversible line along which the units of language unfold, combine, refer backward and forward to produce sense and effect. Although his theory begins by collocating poetry or dance with painting under "mimesis," the difference remains a matter of "rhythm, language, harmony" as against "colour and form." He does not even glance at the possibility of distinguishing what we call temporal and spatial arts according to the presentational conditions of their media.

On the other hand, Aristotle imposes temporality on the object of literary imitation. "Tragedy" he declares in arguing the superiority of plot to character, "is an imitation, not of men, but of an action and of life, and life consists in action, and its end is a mode of action, not a quality. Now character determines men's qualities, but it is by their actions that they are happy or the reverse" (chap. 6, 1450a15–20).[4] Unlike Plato, therefore, to Aristotle literary mimesis is the representation of a dynamic process, the object represented consisting not in states or traits or existents but in actions.

Now actions, of course, extend in time.[5] So if Aristotle went on to relate the process of their unrolling (as a series of events) to the process of their reading (as a series of effects), he might still indirectly introduce the relationship between time and communication that he omits to address directly. The one sequence would then interact with the other, what happens to the characters in fictional time would link up with what happens to the reader while following and experiencing their fortunes in presentational time.

Yet Aristotle makes no such linkage, to the demotion of the axis

and drama of our reading vis-à-vis the characters' living. The im-
balance gains further interest from the point that the artistic effects
of imitation do not presuppose sequential development—the affective *or* the objective. Neither counts here as a condition for mimesis
or hence as a universal of art. If this sounds surprising, as it well
may in view of Aristotle's notorious claims for plot, it is only
because those claims have overshadowed an unobtrusive twist in
the passage from the opening to the body of the *Poetics*. Note that
the above quote, enjoining "an imitation, not of men, but of an
action," appears as late as the sixth chapter, just where the focus
has narrowed to literature and above all tragedy. The five opening
chapters, surveying the field from an interart perspective, are not
nearly so uncompromising. They maintain a much more flexible
(and, given the facts, reasonable) balance between "action" and
"men . . . character . . . qualities," between dynamic and static
existence, as imitable objects. In introducing those objects, typically, chapter 2 modifies at least the emphasis of "not men, but an
action" into "men in action"; then it goes on to subdivide the entire
range of artistic work ("in painting . . . dancing, flute-playing . . .
in language, whether prose or verse," all literary genres included)
according to the "men" rather than the "action." Earlier still,
dancing is even said to imitate "character, emotion, and action," in
this order (1447a26–28). Nowhere along the opening do we find
mimesis reserved for time and change in the world of literature, still
less in art at large, least of all (and the supreme test) functionally.

On the contrary, when chapter 4 comes to speak of the pleasures
yielded by imitation as such, it is the spatial domain—forms of
animals, corpses, portraits—that provides all the examples:

> Objects which in themselves we view with pain, we delight to con-
> template when reproduced with minute fidelity: such are the forms of
> the most ignoble animals and of dead bodies. The cause of this is, again,
> that to learn gives the liveliest pleasure, not only to philosophers but to
> men in general. . . . Thus the reason why men enjoy seeing a likeness
> is, that in contemplating it they find themselves learning or inferring,
> and saying perhaps, "Ah, that is he." For if you happen not to have seen
> the original, the pleasure will be due not to the imitation as such, but to
> the execution, the colouring, or some such other cause. (1448b10–20;
> cf. *Rhetoric,* 1371b4–10)

The very distinctive paradox of art—that what causes pain in life
gives pleasure in the rendering of life—thus operates independently
of represented as well as of presentational features. A portrait
satisfies the human love of inference and artistry no less than a plot;

and, judging at least from their relative frequency of citation here, in a more evident way. Space is the equal of time; the world at rest offers as worthy a field of mimesis as the world in motion. Only, portraiture and the like just happen to be outside the scope of the *Poetics*.

Given this equality, the medium logically rises superior to the object of imitation in all that regards distinctive value, for an art like literature *may* in principle choose (or move) between rendering temporal and spatial reality but *must* render either along a continuum of time. Actually, for reasons deriving from Aristotle's general philosophy and special interests, the very opposite happens by fiat: mimesis in language is confined to actions. The preliminaries once over, even "men in action" suddenly turns and hardens into "actions, not men." Hence, dispensable as it remains to the universal effects of art on the receiver, the actional sequence yet comes to play the key role in this poetics of literature. Poetically speaking, what makes literary art here is the temporality of its object, located in the causal movement of the plot—from happiness to unhappiness or the reverse—in mimetic relation to the sequences of nature. Object- or world-oriented, this approach leaves no room for temporality elsewhere: it reduces the defining factor of language to the position of a means, an inert material adapting itself to any form, a vehicle rather than a system of rendering, with constraints and latitudes of its own.

Where, then, has the *Rhetoric*'s fine sense of "arrangement" in language gone? The question has never been posed, as far as I know, but the context rules out any easy answer. Enough evidence exists to dismiss the condescending explanation in terms of Aristotle's blindness to language, in as well as out of sequence, while the orthodox appeal to its ranking low in his poetic hierarchy would be beside the point, because the question concerns the medium's properties (and the services it may thereby render to its alleged superiors) rather than its relative importance. For the same reason, it would hardly improve matters to invoke the opposition, exaggerated by some Aristotelians, between rhetoric and poetics, moving and making, communication and representation.[6] At this level of generality, the equivalences certainly cut across the boundaries. Over and above their common working in time, the two processes share a dominant orientation to the audience and to teleologies of impact at that. Not simply goal-directed but audience-directed and in this sense communicative, both teleologies are powerful enough to exercise control over matter and manner with a view to shaping our experience. When it comes to their respective powers, moreover, the rhetorical or oratorical end (persuasion) is itself second to the poetic (e.g., catharsis) because its achievement must still reckon with certain external pressures: from public opinion, from the opposition, from the need to develop an orderly argument, from truth to fact or life. So exactly in such a poetics, where the affair with the reader labors even less than social rhetoric under constraints outside itself, one wonders all the more why the temporalities of discourse have fallen into neglect. Where else can they operate so freely? Where else does communication likewise stand out as the affective face, goal, and, hence, determinant of representation?

This neglect of arrangement, I would suggest, has indeed something to do with a blind spot of Aristotle's, with his scale of literary components and with his opposition of rhetoric to poetics; but they come together in a more insidious manner. It is as if only because rhetorical discourse has no definite subject matter ("object"), as Aristotle constantly repeats, that its medium imposes itself on whatever matter the speaker may bring to it for effective linear arrangement. By contrast, the poetic work having not just a definite but a dynamic object to render, and the object already contains and prescribes the line of development—from happiness to unhappiness, say—and the medium must adapt itself as best it can. All that remains for it to contribute, as it were, is the material (e.g., words, meters, styles) in which to embody the form supplied and predetermined by the higher component.

What escapes notice is that it also contributes, as much as ever, not merely *to* arrangement but the very conditions and options *for* arrangement, down to artists' ability to actualize and linearize the object they have in mind into an artifact accessible to the audience. One need not quarrel with Aristotle's premises, surely, to recognize this oversight. For precisely where the rendered life appears in a dynamic guise—as a story not a description, a progress not a portrait—its rendering entails at least double linearity. Granted the need for literature to construct a plot, the very linearity of plot development requires a matching medium to enable and signify it to make it communicable at all. And granted the need to signify a plot line, the signifiers themselves must fall into a discourse line, into a movement where the author causes and the audience receives effects, into language in action as well as language of action. (A modest, yet typical example would be the *unfolding* of theme launched by, among other beginnings, Homeric Invocation and dramatic Prologue: "A foretaste of the theme is given, intended to inform the hearers of it in advance instead of keeping their minds in suspense" [*Rhetoric* 1415a8–24].) By a still closer analogy to rhetoric, if the signifiers must fall into linearity, then the line of discourse composed for them by the artist need not follow but may well impose itself (rationale and all) on the line of events, notably by twisting it out of chronological, "objective" order. Even by reference to Aristotle's own concerns—as I shall later specify—such imposition may fulfill distinctively poetic as well as "thematic" and "remedial" functions. Take a staple of tragic plotting: for a surprise or discovery to be sprung on the audience, the objective sequence of events must be deformed into the most affective—that is, what happened early in the world must emerge late in the discourse to heighten our understanding and experience of that world by shock tactics. Whatever the choice made by the artist between reflecting and twisting, the two sequences remain interdependent in the artwork and everything turns on their interplay. The privileged status assigned by Aristotle to the representation *of* time, however, unhappily obscures the working of presentation (or communication) *in* time.

Throughout the ensuing analysis, the object retains its centrality and criterial force at the expense of the medium that not only transmits but in fact often shapes it to poetic ends. Aristotle's emphasis steadily falls on the making and makings rather than the reading of plot, though his own argument affords ample opportunity to show how the mimesis of a developing action also develops our reactions. As regards the missing of opportunities, indeed, his approach bears a curious relation to much of what is nowadays known as reader-response criticism. Dismissing the notion of an objective text in favor of its interpretation, this criticism naturally orients itself to the reader; yet it all too often fails to give proper (or any) attention to the dynamics of reading in time, to interpretation as a process and a processing.[7] Never losing sight of process, conversely, Aristotle locates it not in the audience (let alone the interpretation) but in the object qualified to affect them. To him, considering the poem (i.e., the plot) "in itself" entails the determination and ensures against the subjectivity of reader response; yet the rage for the objectivity of plot structure minimizes, again, the temporalities of its impact even on the properly responsive mind. This clearly manifests itself in the *Poetics'* few overt references to time, whether in its durational or its sequential aspect.

The first reference to duration ("length" or "magnitude" in Aristotelian parlance) appears as a generic contrast, from which the Renaissance and Neoclassicism derived the so-called Unity of Time. "Tragedy endeavours, as far as possible, to confine itself to a single revolution of the sun, or but slightly to exceed that limit; whereas the Epic action has no limits of time" (chap. 5, 1449b12–15). Does the difference lie in the represented or the presentational time of the action? No wonder that so few interpreters have favored the latter alternative. To Else, that " 'one circuit of the sun' represents the maximum length of a single span of uninterrupted attention, and therefore of a single poetic experience"[8] is surely to postulate an audience with superhuman powers of endurance and concentration. Empirically, moreover, the notion of a daylong stage performance clashes (while a reduced chain of events accords) with Greek practice; and theoretically, it clashes with Aristotle's object-centered logic of analysis.

It is not only that Aristotle casts the variable of duration in terms of the time it takes the action to work itself out in the fictional world. He does not even imply the linkage to perceptual duration and effect whereby his followers were to motivate the unity of time—namely, that the closer the correspondence of the enacting to the enacted period, the greater the realism and credibility of plot. (Thus Boileau's *Art of Poetry* jeers at those dramas where the hero "begins a child and ends the play of age.") The original comment on time limits no more appeals to the psychology of verisimilitude than of attention or any other audience-directed criterion. It simply records the disparity between tragic restraint and epic license as a formal plot convention, with implications now restricted to the length of the two genres and later (chapters 24 and 26) extended to their economy and cohesiveness.

When the question of length comes up again in chapter 7, however, its handling first seems to mark a shift from fictive to perceptual duration. What, Aristotle asks, is the proper magnitude of the artwork? And his answer operates in terms of perspicuity, intelligibility, what a subject (reader, beholder) may apprehend in temporal experience. By reference to such criteria alone are the lower and upper limits of size determined: "An exceedingly small picture cannot be beautiful; for the view of it is confused, the object being seen in an almost imperceptible moment of time. Nor, again, can one of vast size be beautiful; for as the eye cannot take it all in at once, the unity and sense of the whole is lost for the spectator." In the following movement from the dilemma to the solution, the argument keeps up the perceptual frame of reference, and even notes a secondary dividing line: between spatial and temporal apprehension. Just as bodies and paintings require a size "which may be easily embraced in one view; so the plot, a certain length is necessary, and a length which can be easily embraced by the memory." The limits of physical extension are the limits of coherent retention.

The opposed demands of unity and complexity having thus been resolved in principle, it still remains to give the principle an operative application. What size is it that lends itself to easy coverage "in one view" or "by the memory"? At this juncture, however, Aristotle does not go on to specify the limits of length in the same perceptual terms, by reference either to some inclusive norm bearing on the mind's powers of coverage or (like present-day psychologists) to experimental testing. Instead, he falls back on his old reference point, translating the rule about perception time into the objective coordinates of world time:

> The proper magnitude is comprised within such limits, that the sequence of events, according to the law of probability or necessity, will admit of a change from bad fortune to good, or from good fortune to bad. (1451a11–14)

Though rather unexpected, this claim is not so gratuitous or discontinuous as it may look. For the end points mark extremes of the human condition, good versus bad fortune; as such they join forces with the movement leading from one to the other (by tight causal linkage) to compose an artifact of optimum memoribility, and hence of optimum extendibility.

The tie-up is certainly novel and brilliant. The fact yet remains that this last step involves a conceptual leap back to Aristotle's normative base of operations. The argument shifts from the human subject laboring under constraints that bear on the entire field of perception (i.e., on fitting parts together into unity) back to a privileged object that he may confront: the mimesis of an action, excluding all bodies and states, all their representations in the verbal as well as in the pictorial medium, certainly all medium components that do the presenting. This bias makes an enormous difference to the rule's applicability, even within literature itself. For in applying to mimetic rather than to physical extension in time— let alone to magnitude in general—this rule covers only one of the two dimensions of "length" entailed by literary mimesis.

Indeed, insofar as memory operates not on units of discourse (e.g., sounds, words, lines, sentences) but only on units of happening, then an action will necessarily surpass any object of description in both memorability and extendibility. Due to its causal unity, it outranks the loose, additive, "episodic" chronicle as well. It may be drawn out to a greater length than either without loss of coherence. All this is true, and far from trivial, but still one-dimensional. Even if we leave aside the problem of how the mind nevertheless embraces and stores a description (e.g., a portrait in color or in words), one need only think again of the *Rhetoric* to find certain queries about the medium for action itself clamoring for notice. There, when it comes to "arrangement" of and in language, the audience's memory figures as a constant point of reference. By analogy, then, how does the reader assimilate and remember a line of discourse, if only in relation to the line of events? How does the segmentation of the tragic text (e.g., into Prologue, Episode, Exodos, Chorus) affect the integration of the tragic process? Where do discoursal aids to followability and memory come in—such as introductory prospection, final retrospection, intermediate calls for attention—or for that matter obstacles, like temporal displacement? And does not discourse have its own logic and rules and variables of coherence, its own resources for memorability, along with its own extension in time? For a miniature but impressive case in point, observe how closely the opposition drawn by the *Rhetoric* between "free-running" and "periodic" style corresponds to the key opposition in the *Poetics* between episodic and causal plot:

> By "free-running" style I mean the kind that has no natural stopping-places, and comes to a stop only because there is no more to say of that subject. This style is unsatisfying just because it goes on indefinitely—one always likes to sight a stopping place in front of one. . . . By a period I mean a portion of speech that has in itself a beginning and an end, being at the same time not too big to be taken in at a glance. Language of this kind is satisfying and easy to follow. It is satisfying, because it is just the reverse of indefinite; and moreover, the hearer always feels that he is grasping something and has reached some definite conclusion. . . . It is easy to follow, because it can easily be remembered; and this because language in periodic form can be numbered [i.e., divided into perceptible parts], and number is the easiest of all things to remember. (1409a28–1409b5)

The language-plot homology in pattern and mental patterning along a sequence is inescapable: since its two members necessarily coexist and interact in the final literary product, one might expect to find it at least mentioned.

But the *Poetics* recognizes none of these points of contact, neither here nor anywhere else, including the long discussion (chapters 19–22) of the verbal medium. So the reference of the limits of duration to the limits of plot coherence in chapter 7—from happiness to unhappiness or the reverse—drastically narrows the focus. The whole field of observable experience shrinks into the dynamics of events, and the whole range of pattern making, further, into the storage of this dynamics in the memory. If before even the statics of painting enjoyed equality as a problem in assimilation, now in the context of literature it is either double (mimetic as well as physical) temporality or nothing—hence no mention of language—as though only what constitutes a process in the world deserves analysis in terms of its processing in the mind. The limit of magnitude ultimately derives, in short, not so much from the universal limitations of reading as from Aristotle's delimitation of what is fit to be read in temporal art—not from the temporal perception of an object but from the temporal object of perception.

As with duration, so with its internal ordering or sequence. In the *Poetics,* these two aspects of time form two conditions of beauty, "magnitude" and "wholeness" respectively, not for nothing treated in the same chapter.

> A whole is that which has a beginning, a middle, and an end. A beginning is that which does not itself follow anything by causal necessity, but after which something naturally is or comes to be. An end, on the contrary, is that which itself naturally follows some other thing, either by necessity or as a rule, but has nothing following it. A middle is that which follows something as some other thing follows it. (1450b26–32)

If magnitude concerns quantity, then wholeness is a matter of qualitative relations. It turns on the causal unity which delimits and runs through a sequence of events, so concatenating them that if any part "is displaced or removed, the whole will be disjointed and disturbed."

Where and how does that well-made sequence exist in time? Surely not in the finished literary product, for there the transposition or removal of a part always makes a difference to structure and response. (Recall how shrewdly the *Rhetoric* traces the play of form and impact in ordering.) Aristotle might expect episodic serialization from this rule—on the grounds that the presence or absence of a link makes itself felt only within a chain—but he would hardly deny that the best poetic arrangements do not simply meet the condition of wholeness, and for good reason. Thus, if a "beginning" has only consequents but no antecedents, then the plague that induces the Thebans' appeal to Oedipus does not mark the "beginning" of *Oedipus Rex*. The plague opens the drama as fashioned by Sophocles, not the chain of events that gives it its coherence, where the first cause goes as far back as Laius's oracle before the very

birth of Oedipus. It is, after all, to bring to light the first cause and
its successors up to the present crisis that Oedipus turns detective;
the plague rather serves as a middle, a mysterious effect to be
traced back to its origins, a point of departure for the journey into
the past. As in all detective stories, the two beginnings (like the
entire sequences that they launch) fail to coincide and the chrono-
logical-causal one emerges only toward the end. Far from being an
exception or a blemish, moreover, the *Oedipus* disarrangement
embodies the norm of the "complex" plot, with its unsettling
reversals and recognitions that no "simple" march of incidents can
make up for. Hence, wholeness applies to the order of happening,
not to the actual plot that may twist its chronology in artful imitation.[9]

What heightens the importance of this finding is the need to dig
for it below the surface of the *Poetics*. Aristotle presupposes two
distinct sequences of events, each with its own mode and frame of
existence in time. One is the "whole," straightforwardly proceeding
in the fictional world from earlier to later and from cause of result;
the other is the "plot," unfolded by the discourse in the order most
suitable to the work's purposes. In the Aristotelian scheme, further,
their divergence has implications for literary theory and practice
and even ranking, because the best type of plot contrives discrepancies between the orders of occurrence and presentation. By
chronological deformations, such as the Sophoclean or Homeric
plunge *in medias res,* it disturbs our sense of a whole and may not
restore it before the end, when the story line stands revealed from
start to finish. The *whole's* temporary ill-formedness is the *plot's*
optimum well-formedness. Much of literature's affective power accordingly arises from the interaction of the two sequences: the
(chrono)logical and the plotted, the concatenated and the
seemingly disjoined, the underlying and the overlying. Why then
does Aristotle omit to articulate this key distinction—as the Russian formalists opposed *fabula* to *sujet* more than two thousand
years later—and why does he reserve the "beginning to middle to
end" analysis for the "whole"?

Again, as with magnitude, the reasons largely go back to the
disregard for the organizing properties and potentialities of the
literary medium. Its temporal features, for one thing, enable not
only the unfolding of a chronology but its ordering (reordering,
disordering) into any number of plots. But Aristotle, holding the
mimetic sequence to be independent of verbal reference or representation, unthinkingly extends this freedom to the modes of presentation, as if materiality and linearity (or *lexis* and *taxis*) went

together in the medium. Actually, of course, even though an action can find its representation in a medium other than language, it cannot be represented at all, let alone flexibly re-presented, except in a medium that accords with its own temporality. So far from monopolizing time, the object of mimesis depends on discourse time for its very coming into existence and effect as an artifact, and even more as one favoring a divergence between whole and plot. Specifically, therefore, as long as the emphasis is on the common reference of whole and plot to the objective world-in-motion, rather than on their variance and interplay within the discourse arranged about that world, the pairing of them conceals as much as it reveals. In fact, it conceals exactly what it could be made (and what Aristotle himself might want it) to reveal: the workings of communication in mimesis, the poetic equivalent of the *Rhetoric*'s arts of arrangement, with all differences in object and end duly observed.

For another thing, the medium's temporal features impose what I called a dissymmetry on the structure of communication, which makes it necessary for the theorist to view ordering procedures (like everything else) from two sides. Thus, from the artist's side, the whole is given by aesthetic fiat (i.e., beginning, middle, end) and the plot remains to be constructed; from the reader's side, it is the plot that is given in the text, and the whole needs to be reconstructed from the text as it unrolls from one moment to another. With poetics defined as an art of making, however, the theory's emphasis naturally falls on the strategies of construction as opposed to reconstruction: on the well-formed pattern that the artist must start from rather than the manipulated end product that the reader will encounter and work back from, on how the artist makes sense *by* making plot rather than on how the reader makes sense *of* plot. The communicative dissymmetry left out of account, the very centrality of time's role in the fictional process of change and its rendering comes at the expense of the process of reading.

This line of approach has left its mark on literary study from the Renaissance to the present day, by various routes and sometimes in unexpected places and guises.[10] Its most notable development—and in turn an inspiration and a battleground for future theories—occurs in Lessing's *Laocoon* (1766):

> If it be true that painting employs wholly different signs or means of imitation from poetry—the one using forms and colors in space, the other articulate sounds in time—and if signs must unquestionably stand in convenient relation with the thing signified, then signs arranged side by side can represent only objects existing side by side, or whose parts

so exist, while consecutive signs can express only objects which succeed each other, or whose parts succeed each other, in time.

Objects which exist side by side, or whose parts so exist, are called
bodies. Consequently bodies with their visible properties are the peculiar subjects of painting. Objects which succeed one another, or whose
parts succeed one another in time, are actions. Consequently actions
are the peculiar subject of poetry.[11]

The rule is this, that succession in time is the province of the poet, coexistence in space that of the artist. (109)

This is more than a variation on the Aristotelian scheme, with some
breaches closed and emphases changed. As regards the "means of
imitation," Lessing's distinction goes beyond the material features
of the signs ("forms and colors" versus "articulate sounds") to their
modes of arrangement ("in space" versus "in time"). And as regard
the object of imitation, if not diverging outright from the *Poetics,* he
at least resolves any indeterminacy it may leave as to whether the
rendering of an action is integral to all mimesis. For Lessing opposes two kinds of equally legitimate object: body (whose parts
"exist side by side") and action ("whose parts succeed each
other"). In the end, he does arrive at the same conclusion as
Aristotle about literary mimesis, but by a wholly different reasoning. Literature must represent actions in order to maintain a harmo-
nious ("convenient," *bequem*) relation with its medium. To avoid
friction between signifiers and things signified, poetry must be all
"succession in time," just as painting must be all "co-existence in
space."

Despite the common terminal, then, the threefold difference in
route might seem to promise a far greater concern with reader and
reading process. Surely, if media contrast in their modes of arrang-
ing signs, then the contrast must affect the receiver's encounter
with each arrangement. (Speaking of the constraints on the perception of size, we recall, even Aristotle only analogizes but does not
quite equate the problems of apprehending a body "in one view"
and embracing a plot "by the memory.") Moreover, if objects
likewise contrast in their modes of extension, then the contrast
between time and space entails certain differences in the way we
perceive and reconstruct each of its members; and one would
therefore expect to find them specified, along with optional but still
distinctive resources like the unfolding of actions in *non-*
chronological order. Most promising of all is the last stage of the
argument, which combines the two sets of oppositions into two
opposed arts: literature versus painting. The ground offered for this
combination suggests nothing less than a reversal of Aristotle's

scale of priorities. In Aristotle, the object of literary mimesis must develop in time because it relates to life, and life is motion. For Lessing, the object must develop in time to suit with the medium. And once the medium assumes such importance as to determine the object itself, the question of presentational resources and effects comes to the fore.

Unfortunately, none of these expectations is realized, none of the implications pursued. Lessing's interest lies not so much in the reader's reconstruction as in the artist's construction of temporal art, and what is more, in construction limited to the rather negative or preventive aspect of temporal matching. This may well be the reason for his failure even to allude to displacements of actional order, which are liable to disturb the peaceful relations envisaged between signifier and signified (or for that matter between the arts, since painting shows no comparable scrambling device until the advent of Cubism). This is certainly the reason why Lessing rules descriptive writing out of literature. The consideration that such writing activates the reader by forcing him to retrieve a spatial object piecemeal from a temporal sequence would carry only negative weight. For the reading operations initiated and sustained by this cross-pairing are dismissed by Lessing as a sheer nuisance:

> The details which the eye takes in at a glance, he [the poet] enumerates slowly one by one, and it often happens that, by the time he has brought us to the last, we have forgotten the first. Yet from these details we are to form a picture. When we look at an object, the various parts are always present to the eye. It can run over them again and again. The ear, however, loses the details it has heard, unless memory retain them. And if they be so retained, what pains and effort it costs to recall their impressions in the proper order. (102)

Gratuitous "pains and effort" in reassembling parts into a whole: to this Lessing reduces the perceptual activities launched by verbal description—by the discontinuity between the flow of language and the coexistence of body elements.[12] To him such activities have neither attraction nor value. Worse, by making the signifiers perceptible at the expense of the signified, they destroy artistic "illusion," which requires a transparent (and hence matching) medium: the poet should "bring his subject so vividly before us that we are more conscious of the subject than of his words" (88).

Thus Lessing starts by upgrading the medium into a determinative force and ends by downgrading it into a self-effacing servant, indeed a "means" in the full sense of the word. He first arrives by one route (via harmony) at the Artistotelian imposition of a dynamic object of mimesis on literature; then he goes on or rather doubles back to arrive by another route (via illusion) at the hierarchical precedence of object over means, representation over presentation, world-time over discourse-time. Ironically enough, the reader is brought in only to justify the reestablishment of that precedence, designed to spare him "pains and effort": to minimize his own role and participation for his own good, as it were. Even more ironically, the reconstructive activity athwart-the-medium thus derogated and spared the reader comes to occupy a place of honor in plastic communication. A counterpart to descriptive writing in literature (temporal medium, static object) would be "the pregnant moment" in painting (spatial medium, kinetic object, pregnant with developments to come as well as intimations of the past). Far from banned as a mismatch, however, the painterly "pregnant moment" recommends itself to Lessing because it "allows free play to the imagination. The more we see the more we must be able to imagine; and the more we imagine, the more we must think we see. . . . When, for instance, Laocoon sighs, imagination can hear him cry" by projecting itself into the future (16–17).[13] The addressee's operations on and along time would seem to be in *inverse* proportion to the temporality of the art. All this in effect divorces medium-time (as a necessary vehicle of literary mimesis) from reading-time (as a flexible constant of literary perception and integration), so that the reader gets reduced to a passive assimilator of a sequence of events.[14]

This passive conception is thrown into yet stronger relief by the fact that it does not embrace the whole of the literary sphere itself. For Lessing's insight into media goes not only beyond Aristotle's concern with material variables but also beyond his own affair with the combinatory dimension of signs. Less famous yet semiotically no less important is his reference of the poetry versus painting antithesis to two further oppositions: auditory versus visual and arbitrary versus natural signs. And in terms of these oppositions, we find the reader adjusting, responding, and contributing to his medium as much as the beholder does to his. Thus, given literature's distinctive sign system, "in poetry a robe is no robe. It conceals nothing. Our imagination sees right through it"; hence, Virgil's Laocoon may wear his priestly regalia, whereas the sculptor's must be stripped of them or else our eye will wholly miss the expression of the body (39–41). More generally, where a painter's rendering would fail, a poet's may succeed, due to "the infinite range of our imagination, and the intelligibility of its images. These may stand side by side in the greatest number and variety without concealment or detriment to any" (43). All the stranger, then, that only when it comes to the medium's axis of extension do the reader's imaginative and gap-filling powers suddenly wane or vanish, to leave a mind passively following the line of least resistance devised for its benefit. Exactly here the timidity of the poetics grows discontinuous with the thrust of the semiotics. Like Aristotle's framework, Lessing's indeed assigns to both time and reader a place but not a common theater of operations.

That Lessing, like Aristotle before him, casts his theory of temporal art in reference to the writer rather than the reader is, therefore, neither an accident nor a mere terminological choice.[15] Nor is this common orientation unrelated to their hierarchical ranking of world and language. Both focus on the writer as one who composes a sequential object into literary art, rather than on the reader as he gropes his way along a sequential medium toward a reconstruction of that object and the designs underlying its mimesis. Neither sees the two as equal but dissymmetrical partners in a temporal transaction, where one progressively creates a world through language and the other progressively re-creates that world from the language. With that dissymmetry in role out of view, no wonder so little attention is paid to the main point: that from the reader's side, the presentational sequence is *always* of crucial importance as the axis of discovery and sense making, no matter whether the represented sequence outranks it in terms of aesthetic value.[16]

In this respect, Lessing's treatment of time finally emerges as even less reader oriented than Aristotle's. Neither deals with the moment-by-moment procedures of reading that would constitute interpretation in the modern sense. Communication, however, has temporal aspects other than the play of meaning—like feeling, apprehending, pattern making. And here Aristotle's functionalism has certainly given poetics a good start. He relates duration to memory, wholeness to a sequential coherence liable to undergo twists in the finished ordering, types of change and ending to the desires of the audience, and tragic plot (act of horror, recognition, peripety) to tragic effect (pity and fear), all in terms that are indeed general and slanted but at least constructive as well as preventive. Even if he does not give those relations a firm temporal anchorage, so as to link causal to affective or perceptual dynamics, his system occasionally enables one to repair the omission from within.

With his sharper sense of the temporality of the medium, Lessing only divorces it more sharply from the temporality of reading as distinct from writing. In a monograph on the subject, typically, he even neglects to touch, let alone to dwell or enlarge, on Aristotle's specific time rules and their functional consequences.[17] He is more concerned with the limits of literature as imitation than with what the reader fashions or experiences within those limits; more with the kind of text the reader should find than with the kind of operations he performs on what he does find. In short, he is more concerned with the preconditions than with the actual working conditions of aesthetic perception in time.

Time and Space Joining Forces against the Reader: Some Modern Themes

If the Aristotle-Lessing tradition plays down the reader's role and route in literary art by foregrounding the temporality of the represented object, a later one plays down the role of time itself by pushing into the background even the temporality of the representing medium. We again find the bond between reader and time loosened by some demotion of the axis along which the reading process extends and meets its adventures. Now, however, this is done in favor of an art or dimension other than temporal.

This tendency, often reflecting the battle waged by modernist art against the tyranny of time, assumes various forms in poetics and aesthetics. Some are even more amusing than self-defeating, because they so obviously fly in the face of the rules, whether in iconoclastic heat or with a view to shocking the bourgeoisie of the academe and the marketplace. What can one do except smile when urged to see the ideal novel as a loose sheaf of pages, freely arrangeable and reversible in the interests of an infinite play of meaning? More seriously, instead of denying temporal art its very temporalities, others wave away their distinctiveness by claiming them for all art.

This line originates in those pan-artistic Neoclassicists who applauded Poussin for creating pictures that aspired to the condition of narrative, and it is vigorously pursued by Etienne Souriau in "Time in the Plastic Arts."[18] Souriau denies the monopoly of temporal art on either fictional or perceptual time. In regard to fictional (what he calls "intrinsic") time, his argument does not go much beyond Lessing—whom he never mentions throughout—still less beyond the admirers of Poussin. The emphasis falls on the plastic artist's evocation of movement within the represented world, mainly through the "choice of a prerogative ['pregnant'] moment that is still capable of keeping its relation with a long unfolding of continuous action" (129). Again, in regard to time as an axis of perception, the claim that one cannot "appreciate the full beauty of a painting without a period of contemplation" (123) repeats with eloquence what oft was said and seldom disputed. Souriau, however, does venture into relatively new paths when he challenges the monopoly of the temporal arts on what we called prearranged sequence or direction as well as on duration. "In a musical, theatrical or choreographic work, the order of successive presentation is set, constant, precisely measured and determined"; but not uniquely so. "The lover of cathedrals is held to an extremely set order"; in the art of landscaping, the path drawn through the garden "conditions the successive and ordered appearance of the view"; even in painting and sculpture, the movement of the beholder's eye can be gently directed (125–26). Taken together, these parities are supposed to eliminate "the ill-founded contrast between the arts of space and the arts of time" (123).

Carried away by enthusiasm, however, Souriau overreaches himself and not without confusion. Speaking of temporal lines, he is apt to confuse duration and sequence, of which the latter subsumes and entails the former but not vice versa. He thus uses "succession" in both senses, usually to favor his plea for time-as-common property. Consider the shift from the stronger sense in the avowal that a poetic or cinematic work "is unfolded *in successive moments*" to the weaker sense in the rhetorical question, Can a painting be fully appreciated "without a period of contemplation wherein successive reactions take place?" (123). And when expressly setting out to prove that temporal as well as spatial arts find it difficult to impose their chosen sequence on their addressee, most of the examples he cites actually illustrate, if anything, lapses of durational control: "The reader of a poem is free to slow down or hurry his reading, to linger in meditation or to come back several times to a loved passage" (125). Of the four reading "freedoms" listed, the first three are certainly beside the point.

Even more serious is the failure to distinguish constraint from license in the two groups of arts. Roughly, by "constraint" I mean the set of rules, features, and conditions adhering to the medium itself; by "license" I mean the area left free for individual performance or variation. Thus, the already cited shift from the poem "unfolded in successive moments" to the painting contemplated with "successive reactions" also correlates with a shift from temporal constraint to spatial license. The poem's successive unfolding is a fact that, whether viewed from the author's or the reader's side, necessarily regulates both the duration and the sequence of communication. The successive reactions evoked by the painting, however, are subject to no such laws and control in either respect. They are actually not so much evoked as evocable, for Souriau is no less aware than Aristotle that with a painting "a single glance which catches a view of the whole is possible" and, aesthetically, "even of great importance" (123). And if full appreciation takes time—from thirty seconds to ten minutes (131–32)—its sequence yet remains undetermined and will vary even among beholders who form or carry away much the same overall impression. Nor do the spatial (or, as Souriau will have it, plastic) arts show a uniform interplay of constraint and license in their temporal aspect. Three-dimensional artworks like statues or cathedrals cannot indeed be embraced at a single glance. But to say that the spectator must trace their parts "one after the other and in a certain order" (124) is to cast duration as direction—to equivocate between the actual orders more or less freely followed by different perceivers of space and the predetermined order of reading under the arrow of time. Nowhere as in the comparative study of the arts is it so vital to differentiate the conditions that a medium presupposes from the conditions that it emulates in a valiant but often vain attempt to better, extend, or even transcend its own.

Finally, to the extent that Souriau does make this distinction, he gives it an evaluative turn, thus again reducing time in temporal art to its lowest common denominator. The very fact that time is more tractable in temporal art, he claims, only makes its patterns and effects less artistic than their hard-earned counterparts fashioned in the teeth of space. A revealing and typical yet none too obvious sophism, this, to which we shall return.

By the time Souriau's plea for equality appeared, however, it had already both lost and gained force due to a change in the conception of literary form. As if in anticipation of his argument, some literary movements and theorists had been making the opposite claim—not that spatial arts are endowed with temporality, but that temporal arts are endowed with spatiality. These two approaches seem diametrically opposed in focus and thrust and the view of art's center of gravity. Yet they meet and join forces to demote time and its workings in literature. Of the two members of this strange coalition, the literary side even goes furthest in this respect. Time is not important enough to quarrel about; it is space that matters. Hence the calls, from the most diverse quarters and nowadays as vocal as ever, for a shift in orientation. A literary text (or corpus) should be grasped as a simultaneous rather than unfolding whole; in terms of its thematic or figurative network rather than plot sequence, and of analogical versus chrono-logical relations.

A well-known case in point is Joseph Frank's "Spatial Form in Modern Literature,"[19] which now gains fresh salience as a counterpoint to Souriau. Applying Lessing's method to modern poetry and narrative, Frank finds them moving away from the temporal pole assigned to literature by Lessing in the direction of spatial form. Imagistic poetry, according to Ezra Pound's own definition, thus presents an intellectual and emotional complex in an instant of time, striking the reader's sensibility with an instantaneous impact. When Pound and Eliot have a number of images to present, as in the *Cantos* and *The Waste Land,* they aim at the same effect by "undermining the inherent consecutiveness of language, frustrating the reader's normal expectations of a sequence and forcing him to perceive the elements of the poem as juxtaposed in space rather than unrolling in time" (10). The word groups still follow one another in time, as they must, but their meaning comes to depend on our simultaneous apprehension in space of otherwise disconnected units. The modern novel, with its larger units of meaning, can preserve coherent sequence within each unit and yet achieve the same spatialization of form by disrupting the temporal relations between the units. Flaubert's fair scene in *Madame Bovary* halts the time flow of the narrative, cuts back and forth between the various levels of the action to bring out ironic similarities, and fixes attention on the interplay of relationships within the immobilized time area. On a much larger scale, Joyce's *Ulysses* makes "a vast number of references and cross references that relate to each other independently of the time sequence of the narrative" (16). To give the reader a picture of Dublin as a whole, Joyce strives for an impression of simultaneity, a sense of activities occurring in different places at the same time. To integrate the pieces, "the reader is forced to read *Ulysses* in exactly the same manner as he reads modern poetry, that is, by continually fitting fragments together and keeping allusions in mind until, by reflexive reference, he can link them to their complements" (18). Such works will leave us simply bewildered if we assume that, because language proceeds in time, a modern novel must be perceived as a narrative chain of events.

Like Souriau, then, Frank in effect denies Lessing's premise ("if signs must unquestionably stand in convenient relation with the thing signified, then . . .") and hence the conclusions drawn from it. Of these two conclusions, however, the literary theorist challenges the one left undisputed by the art critic. While Souriau takes issue with the dictate that "signs arranged side by side can represent only objects existing side by side," Frank shows the historical contingency of the rule that "consecutive signs can express only objects which succeed each other." However operative in previous ages, Lessing's ideal harmony gives place to "internal conflict between the time-logic of language and the space-logic implicit in the modern conception of the nature of poetry" (13). In short, modern literature aspires to the condition of painting, and its reader must accordingly adopt the techniques of the beholder. On the subject of readerly beholding, Frank's comments are sharp and various. But they center around the question of spatial organization: how we integrate fragments into a mood, a contrast, a society, a picture of life. The temporal axis of the reading comes in only to be blocked, frustrated, and thus forcibly transformed into the simultaneous perception desired by modernist writing. It is this that makes the theory's divorce of the reader from time more trenchant and disturbing, because more well defined, than in any other instance considered so far. The divorce no longer results from plain oversight, polemical heat, or doctrinal bias for or against. Rather, it appears to come in response to the directives issued by the literary structure itself as a premeditated art.

But it is to Roman Jakobson that we have to go for the most radical and influential theory along these lines. Jakobson claims in fact that the poetic function—"the set *(Einstellung)* toward the message as such, focus on the message for its own sake"[20]— attaches not at all to the fictive sequence and only to acts of violence perpetrated on the linguistic sequence. Unlike all the theories mentioned so far, his shows little interest in the temporal axis of the world—in plot, action, narrativity—because the rendering of a world ("the referential function") is deemed as nonpoetic within as without literary art. But nor does the poetic function derive from the temporal axis of the discourse as a sequence of linguistic signs. On the contrary, its distinctive feature consists in the imposition of spatial or suprasequential pattern on that temporality; in Jakobson's own terms, "Equivalence is promoted to the constitutive device of the sequence" (358). A literary text is accordingly a stretch of language so crisscrossed by a network of equivalences—prosodic, syntactic, semantic—as to make the poetic function predominant over all others.

This carries to an extreme a position independently reached and preached by many moderns. While such critics as Frank limit their claims about the triumph of supratemporality to particular authors, corpora, or movements, Jakobson extends his to the whole range of verbal art, arguing for their universal applicability to the poetic as poetic. To him, moreover, this is not one aspect or form of literary

organization but its very locus ("empirical linguistic criterion")—
something like a be-all and end-all.

A Meeting of Extremists and a Question of Empirical Adequacy

On the face of it, then, the approaches radicalized by Aristotle
and Jakobson could hardly be more opposed. Each defines poetic
art in terms of the very structural component—world and language,
respectively—that the other dismisses as least poetic, because least
distinguishable from its nonpoetic fellows. Within these components themselves, moreover, poeticity adheres to contrasting dimensions: sequence versus equivalence, movement versus
parallelism, fictive time versus compositional space. Finally, the
twofold opposition in the locus of the poetic goes with a sharp
divergence in the view of the literary paradigm: epic and drama
versus poetry. So the one's pride is the other's embarrassment.

As extremes often do, however, these actually meet at a number
of suggestive points. To start with, both models define poetic structure by reference to (1) a single necessary-and-sufficient condition
that (2) ignores or suspends the time axis of the language, but (3)
proves so exclusive in operation as to become empirically untenable. Naturally, since the conditions are mutually incompatible, to
enforce both at once would be more or less to depopulate the
republic of letters (which makes the prospect of a combined, "two-
dimensional" theory somewhat bleak). To enforce either, however,
would be to expel from that republic some of its most reputable
classes. Each would exclude the genres that form the other's poetic
paradigm. Much poetry and all weakly representational or even just
descriptive writing, governed by principles other than causal sequence, fall outside Aristotle's scheme; narrative and drama, resisting subjection to verbal equivalence, have no place in Jakobson's.[21]
So, unless one would have whole genres regulated by patterns and
along dimensions that go against their grain as well as their history,
both schemes must at least be denied general applicability. And
their symmetrical inadequacy points a larger moral. Although literature is a time art, it does not lend itself to (Aristotelian) definitions
in terms of the flow of its world; because literature is a time art, it
will not be reduced to the (Jakobsonian) freezing of its medium.

Hence, the temporality of the medium as a sequence of signs
comes to the fore; after all, in biblical parlance, the stone rejected
by the builders must become the cornerstone. Equally spurned by

the ancient champion of plot and the modern advocate of configuration, this Cinderella yet establishes its claim to primacy. To be sure, it no more forms a sufficient condition for literature than does either of its glamorous rivals—arguably, even less—since this feature of sequentiality is common to all linguistic discourse and to all media, from dance to film, that unfold along a continuum of time. But it is at least a necessary condition; a constant dimension of structure, an ever-present source and resource for effect, and therefore a natural starting point for giving the reader his due place as well.

Necessary or Operative Conditions? Time as the Line of Least Resistance

By itself, assigning time and reader their proper place need not amount to much beyond getting our logical priorities right. Necessary features do not always make operative or valuable features of communication, still less aesthetic dominants. And this holds as true for properties of the verbal medium as for any other component of discourse. Take the role played by the (ortho)graphic as opposed to the phonic system, especially in poetry. In Western culture, literary writing is made up of letters, with their own shape, system, and combinatory possibilities. Yet the attention of readers has traditionally focused on the patterns formed by the sounds that the letters stand for (meter and rhyme, above all) rather than by the letters themselves. Still, few would seriously quarrel with that orientation—not even those who, like myself, happen to be intrigued by literature's (ortho)graphic codes and devices. For whatever their material priorities within the medium, sound patterning has indeed gained aesthetic (i.e., functional, communicative) priority over the substance that realizes it for our eyes in verse. It is all, then, less a question of logical status than of contextual operation—of poetic force and relevance.

From this functional viewpoint, with its shift from literature to literariness, our theories display a new unity in variety. There is more than a hint that the neglect or demotion of medium-time springs from a belief that it is too much of a given: its organization of the text is too "necessary," too easily achieved, too similar to the workings of everyday discourse, too automatic to carry poetic weight. Hence the temptation to develop a model of literary structure where that weakness will be replaced (controlled, played down, shored up) by some other feature, sometimes introduced as more primary but always taken to be more potent, challenging, distinctive.

This lies behind much specious reasoning and empirical slanting in otherwise diverse approaches to temporal art. Souriau's last-ditch vindication of time in the spatial arts is an attack on its facility in all others:

> In so far as there is a difference, in regard to time, between the plastic arts and others, the advantage is on the side of the plastic arts. I do not hesitate, in fact, to say that time is more important aesthetically, and more worthy of study, in painting, sculpture, or architecture than in music, the dance or the cinema. . . . Why?
>
> Because, in the arts which are obviously temporal, time is the palpable stuff of which the works are fashioned. The symphony, the film, and the ballet are spread out, laid down on a bed of time; the time spent by the auditor or spectator is practically predetermined. His psychological experience must pass through a mill, as it were, where the work is measured out to him moment by moment according to the creator's will. The composer and the dramatist are the masters and the tyrants of a direct and obvious time. . . . But the painter, the architect, and the sculptor are masters, by a more subtle magic, of an immaterial time. . . . This time is never suggested except by means that are indirect, oblique, and subtle. . . . They are the key to the greatest success in these arts. Plastic time is an essential time. (140–41)

Note how the language of facility ("palpable stuff," "predetermined," "measured out," "direct," and "obvious") opposes the language of value ("indirect, oblique, and subtle"). Given such a line of argument, actual or implicit, one might expect literary scholars to counter by challenging the premise that (good) art must go against, rather than with, the presentational conditions of its medium. Instead, we often find the premise itself shared: only its unfavorable consequences are warded off from literature through a shift of literature's focus or essence from the temporal imperative to some duly distinctive liberty, preferably one difficult to take. No wonder, then, that modern literature turned to spatial organization in despite of time—or so its manifestos proclaimed—in order to rid itself of traditional artistic liabilities: plot, continuity, narrative interest, the *line* of least resistance. With time no longer judged against the norm of harmony (classic or neoclassic) but of difficult beauty, such a shift had to come sooner or later. Actually, according to an approach like Jakobson's it did come much earlier, at the very birth of poetic art; and not only with a view to differentiating more from less accomplished forms or periods. While all other verbal behavior follows a sequence, verbal art forces it into systematic equivalence.

Even the Aristotle-Lessing camp, with its insistence on the aesthetic primacy of time, is not quite an exception to this rule. For the temporality they promote belongs not to the medium, shared by all forms of communication through language, but to the world it evokes. Within their models of literature, the necessary (presentational) condition is more assumed or posited than activated, whereas the nonnecessary (representational) feature—not that they call it so—gets imposed by fiat as the poetic capital.

With Aristotle this may even help to explain the shift of emphasis from the opening to the body of the *Poetics* as well as the shift of focus from the *Rhetoric* to the *Poetics*. It would appear that Aristotle sees literariness where he sees interest and value and function. He restricts the field of literary mimesis to actions, those causally concatenated sequences with their exciting changes of fortune, crimes, discoveries, and peripeties; here poetic distinctiveness and impact lie. Nor is it an accident that he dwells on the highlights rather than the workhorses within the causal chain. And in effect, he goes on to distinguish good from indifferent plots by their artful twisting of the natural ("whole") flow of the action itself, not indeed into spatiality but out of chronology.

Lessing, with his different line of argument, goes in a sense even further. True, he explicitly derives the need for literature to represent a sequence of events from its mode of presentation as a sequence of signs. This concordance, however, is only designed to invert logical into poetic priorities—to ensure such harmony between the two sequences as will reduce the temporality of the medium to a transparent envelope and will leave our attention free to focus on the temporality of the action, where it properly belongs. In *Laocoon*, the effacement of the signifier continuum, vis-à-vis the object signified, is what distinguishes artistic from everyday discourse:

> It is true that since the signs of speech are arbitrary, the parts of a body can by their means be made to follow each other [in description] as readily as in nature they exist side by side. But this is a property of the signs of language in general, not of those peculiar to poetry. The prose writer is satisfied with being intelligible, and making his representations plain and clear. But this is not enough for the poet. He desires to present us with images so vivid, that we fancy we have the things themselves before us, and cease for the moment to be conscious of his words, the instruments with which he effects his purpose. (101–2)

Although intelligibility will do for the practical ends of "prose," poetry settles for nothing less than illusion. And the illusive rendering of the world demands an unobtrusive management of the word, so as to produce a concordant extension of *res* and *verba*. Even though the sign in language remains by itself arbitrary—artificial, insistent, opaque—the sign *sequence* in literature yet can and should assume a "natural" look by limiting itself to iconic arrangement. Once signification is reserved for action, the signifying sequence of language will merely reflect and make transparent the signified sequence of events. Hence, again, the veto on description as an incorrigible double offender, whose signifiers cannot but steal the show in combination as well as individually.

Lessing's equation of the poetic with the effaced sign clashes head-on with its modern equation with the perceptible sign (manifested, for instance, in Jakobson's claim that "This function, by promoting the palpability of signs, deepens the fundamental dichotomy of signs and objects"). As with other diametric oppositions we have encountered, however, the lines finally converge in divesting the presentational sequence of poetic effect. Whether poetic signs must be subdued or foregrounded is a moot point; that their serialization has no distinctive power unless properly restrained in favor of some other structure is common ground. Its very status as a necessary condition for literature gives medium-time only a negative or at best a neutral role to play in the generation of literariness. And in view of this startling consensus, the analogy with the relations between the orthographic and the phonic components of literary writing looms larger than ever.

Whence the Effect? Time in Control of Spatial Form and Actional Sequence

It is therefore important to realize that no such analogy holds: its functional basis only serves, in fact, to bring out the difference. Any sweeping demotion of presentation time, in the name of whatever theory, is doomed to failure; the demoted factor proves for once ever-operative as well as inescapable. It is not only that the models and ideals promoted at its expense are all poetic as well as logical variables, prized in certain genres, trends or eras and avoided if not disdained in others. (One thinks of all the writing marked by plotlessness, descriptiveness, or for that matter adherence to the speech patterns of everyday life.) Literary artists, notably including those who appear or pretend to strive against time, have always embraced the opportunity to lead the reader along a course predetermined from beginning to end—where effects can be timed, traps laid, curiosity and suspense and surprise manipulated, hypotheses and attitudes shaped throughout, in line with the overall strategy. It has yet to be shown that a single work of temporal art, outside the *jeu d'esprit* variety, has failed to exploit the resource for controlling impression-formation built into a medium where elements and patterns emerge in an ordered succession. Indeed, perhaps the most telling measure of its potence is the control it exerts on those very structures and dimensions invoked by theory to mold it into respectable poetic form.

Take the most common manifestation of "spatial" form in the represented world of narrative, dramatic, or cinematic art—the analogy between characters or events. All such analogues fall into patterns on the basis of similarity and contrast, equivalence and opposition: they cohere as foils, mirror images, counterparts, variations on a theme. And this type of linkage or relation, consisting in the simultaneous perception of the members analogized to each other, holds regardless of their order of appearance. Job's initial and final prosperity, or Cain murdering Abel in the first fraternal conflict of Genesis and the brothers' designs on Joseph in the last, are as analogical as states, incidents, or agents that immediately follow each other: Hannah's barrenness versus her rival's fertility at the beginning of Samuel; the series of plagues inflicted on Egypt, or Abraham, Isaac and Jacob as patriarchal figures. The very logic of analogy might therefore seem to operate in terms of devised coexistence, so transcending or suspending the flow of time in otherwise temporal arts as to reduce (normatively, to elevate) them to the eternal present of the spatial medium.

For all its plausibility, which has given it such wide appeal, this is a false conclusion.[22] Temporal art can indeed establish spatial patterns, but even such patterns cannot (and usually would not) evade the conditions of temporal perception, where everything must emerge in preordered sequence. The logic of composing such relations is the same in the temporal and the spatial arts; the logic of disclosing (or from the reader's viewpoint, discovering) them is poles apart. Since a literary text must be read sequentially, even the view and with it the shape of such a synchronic pattern as analogy is determined by the amount of information the reader possesses at any given moment in the reading process. And since this information may easily be distributed, the reader's view may undergo significant changes during the process, from modification to rever-

sal. For instance, two characters who initially strike us as psychological or spiritual twins may prove to be opposites as we "get" to
know them better; and vice versa. If we have to go outside time to
perform the spatial linkage, we must remain within time to find out
its true bearing after a series of shifts and twists. Hence, in a time-
art-like literature, there is no "spatial" but only spatiotemporal
form, no analogy immune against chronology, no synchrony independent of diachrony, no equivalence except in and along sequence.

This resource of *spatial dynamics* gives the artist such powers of
control over the reader's activity (pattern making, understanding, or
judgment) that no wonder we find it exploited through the whole
range of literature. One of the many examples I have analyzed to
demonstrate this key principle is the analogy between Odysseus
and Agamemnon in Homer's *Odyssey*. Throughout the opening
books, the references to the two characters abound in points of
similarity; for example, each is a king returning from Troy to a home
invaded by some suitor(s) of his wife. Therefore the reader grasps
them as straight analogues and begins to fear that Odysseus may
suffer the same fate as the murdered Agamemnon. But having
started by highlighting the similarity between these Returners, in
the interests of suspense, the epic then proceeds to reveal the
hitherto concealed dissimilarity, in the interests of characterization.
The initial correspondence modulates into a full-fledged contrast as
the text brings to light the whole set of Odyssean accomplishments
that have more than once enabled him to emerge victorious from
ordeals that no Agamemnon could survive. With the reversal of the
analogy, suspense turns into confidence; the misleadingly one-
sided character sketch into a complex portrait; and our schematic
view of Odysseus, as just another conventional soldier, into a
heightened appreciation of a unique hero. Due to the artful distribution of the points of contact along the reading sequence, the equivalence pattern that would remain static in spatial art springs here
into dynamic life, changing its form and its function alike at every
phase of its metamorphosis.

What is true of ancient epic holds equally true for modern literature, including the intertextual analogy drawn between Leopold
Bloom in Joyce's *Ulysses* and Homer's Odysseus or any instance of
so-called spatial form cited by Frank. What is true of literature,
moreover, is equally true of all temporal art, from music through
dance to film. And what is true of analogies on the level of the
fictive world applies in principle to all other levels, from thematic
organization to Jakobson's verbal designs. Whatever the form it
takes—sound pattern, grammatical parallelism, the iteration of a

single word—the verbal equivalence must unfold in sequence; this makes the equivalence subject to the time axis along which the reader traces and integrates it from moment to moment. It is not only that one rhyming word sets up expectations for another, that the reader may be left in temporary suspense about the completion of a parallelism, or that we may be surprised by the twist given to a recurrent word. Frequently, the poetic effect derives less from the imposition of equivalence *on* an inert sequence than from the manipulation of inert equivalence *by* the sequence. Because regular equivalence is a convention of poetry, it may come to assume such stereotyped forms as only temporal deformation and reshaping can infuse with new life. This is precisely what happens when modern poetry displaces rhyming words from their normal position at the end of the line to the middle, or when enjambment disrupts an automatic coincidence between metrical and grammatical parallelism.

Therefore, if the "poetic" function is distinguished by the perceptibility given to the message, then it may be achieved in at least three ways. One, unreasonably granted monopolistic status by Jakobson, consists in patterning sequence into equivalence; another lies in two-way tensions between sequence and equivalence; and still another, in the violence perpetrated by sequence on equivalence. Yet each of the three methods is nothing but a variation on the interplay between the temporal and the spatial dimensions of literary structure—in short, on spatiotemporal dynamics.

All these modes of interdimensional traffic fall outside Aristotle's philosophy of art, in which spatiality plays no role whatever. His is a strictly one-dimensional poetics, with plot as causal sequence forcing itself on nothing except its own recalcitrant materials. Even on its own terms, however, this philosophy hardly justifies the disregard he betrays for the temporal features of the medium outside rhetoric. These features are not just an enabling condition for plot to communicate itself, nor just a link between "means" and "object" in mimetic representation. They also provide the resource for some of Aristotle's most valued poetic maneuvers and effects.

Consider such a key element as *anagorisis*, the discovery or recognition that comes as a surprise to maximize tragic pity and fear. Aristotle himself defines anagorisis as "a change from ignorance to knowledge, producing love or hate between the persons destined by the poet for good or bad fortune" (chap. 11). Accordingly, the change from ignorance to knowledge is supposed to take place within the fictive world—along the object progressing in mimetic time—as a result of new information sprung on the characters. This, however, would explain only their surprise, not ours. Whence the surprise for the reader, in the interests of heightened pity and fear? Surely the surprise does not come from the object of imitation itself, as an action developing in fictive time. If that action appeared before us in its natural sequence, forwarded by the coherent logic of the "whole," then Oedipus's patricide and incest would emerge soon after the beginning, and hence would bring us no discovery and no surprise. So to explain the powerful effect, we have to turn from the represented object to the presentational form imposed on it: from the whole (as an objective order of occurrence) to the plot (as one of numberless orders of unfolding to which the whole is amenable in temporal art). It is the potentialities of the medium that make it possible to dislocate an otherwise straightforward causal sequence into a drama of discovery for the reader as well as for the hero.

Indeed, if presentation in time imposes dynamic shape and working on space itself, little wonder that nothing developing through time, least of all actions, should escape its control. Whether the rendering *of* time makes or breaks the poetic function, therefore, may forever remain in dispute between Aristotelians and Jakobsonians without in the least affecting the main point: that reading *in* time is a universal of poetic communication, and as such must cut across the lines of poetic theory.

Notes

1. Most recently, I have discussed this issue in *Expositional Modes and Temporal Ordering in Fiction* (Baltimore: The Johns Hopkins University Press, 1978); "Ordering the Unordered: Time, Space, and Descriptive Coherence," *Yale French Studies* 61 (1981): 60–88; "Deictic Sequence: Language, World and Convention," in *Essays on Deixis,* ed. Gisa Rauh (Tübingen: Gunter Narr, 1983), 277–316; "Spatiotemporal Art and the Other Henry James," *Poetics Today* 5 (1984): 775–830; *The Poetics of Biblical Narrative: Ideological Literature and the Drama of Reading* (Bloomington: Indiana University Press, 1985) and earlier references there.

2. Aristotle, *Rhetoric* (trans. W. Rhys Roberts). All citations in text for this source refer to this translation.

3. W. K. Wimsatt and Monroe C. Beardsley, themselves opting for cognition, indeed find the *Poetics* guilty of "the affective fallacy" (W. K. Wimsatt, *The Verbal Icon* [New York: The Noonday Press, 1958], 28). Of course, there is no question of guilt here, nor, at least in Aristotle's case, must we push the opposition too far. Note, for example, the reasoning by enthymemes in oratory or the equally mandatory, quasi-philosophical inference about and from causality in literature. Yet the principle holds because even these cognitive operations remain subordinated to the affective (persuasive or cathartic) goals of communication as an affair between author and audience.

4. Aristotle, *Poetics* (trans. S. H. Butcher)

5. According to Aristotle's own theory, "everything that changes changes in time": time is an aspect or dimension of motion, ordering its states into relations of priority and posteriority. See *Physics,* bk. 4, chap. 10ff., and John F. Callahan, *Four Views of Time in Ancient Philosophy* (Cambridge: Harvard University Press, 1948), chap. 2.

6. See, for instance, R. S. Crane, *The Languages of Criticism and the Structure of Poetry* (Toronto: University of Toronto Press, 1953) and the reference to Crane in Wayne C. Booth's *Critical Understanding* (Chicago: University of Chicago Press, 1979), 77–80. The line drawn by Booth himself is far less sharp—whence *The Rhetoric of Fiction*—sometimes to the point of elusiveness. See "*The Rhetoric of Fiction* and the Poetics of Fictions," in his *Now Don't Try To Reason with Me* (Chicago: University of Chicago Press, 1970), 151–69.

7. The background and the exceptions to this tendency, as well as recent developments in general, are reserved for a separate study. Jane P. Tompkins's anthology *Reader-Response Criticism* (Baltimore: The Johns Hopkins University Press, 1981) offers a useful, though partial, selection of relevant theories. (See also n. 10 subsequently.)

8. Gerald F. Else, *Aristotle's Poetics: The Argument* (Cambridge: Harvard University Press, 1957), 217.

9. This observation is also implied by R. S. Crane's "The Concept of Plot and the Plot of *Tom Jones,*" in *Critics and Criticism,* ed. R. S. Crane (University of Chicago Press, 1952), 616–47. His Aristotelian analysis of *Tom Jones* begins in effect (624ff.) by reconstituting the whole, from "Bridget's scheme to provide security for both herself and her illegitimate son" through middle to end, and then goes on (631ff.) to discuss its constitution into the novel's finished plot. Despite Aristotle's failure to spell out this distinction, Crane keeps it admirably stable, though not without terminological discomfort. Other Chicago Aristotelians, however, have plainly been misled by Aristotle's silence. Far from repairing the master's omission by locating such an ordering strategy in the interplay between object and medium—or representation and presentation—they assimilate it to his "manner" of imitation, where it could not possibly belong because "manner" is the sphere of point of view rather than time. Thus Elder Olson, for instance, in "An Outline of Poetic Theory," *Critics and Criticism,* 562–63, or the recent "A Conspectus of Poetry, Part II," *Critical Inquiry* 4 (1977): 383–86; notes the heterogeneous factors subsumed by *manner* here and the interpretation of *plot* as a chronological process.

10. Apart from the neglect of reading time as a universal of literary communication, Aristotle's priorities also show themselves in the equally traditional bias of the references to time toward drama and narrative, both plot-regulated genres. The lively concern for centuries with the unity of time (dramatic versus epic duration) or the plunge *in medias res* (epic versus historical order) are cases in point, and ones, moreover, that have nowadays lost their prescriptive force but neither their relevance nor their partial bearing on action sequences. Even the elaborate classifications in a study like Gérard Genette's *Narrative Discourse,* trans. Jane E. Lewin (Ithaca: Cornell University Press, 1980), hardly venture outside its delimited generic area. A principled exception to this tendency is the work done since the 1960s by Tel-Aviv scholars: its thrust extends to poetry (an early example would be Menakhem Perry and Joseph Haephrati's "On Some Characteristics of the Art of Bialik's Poetry," *Akhshav* 17/18 [1966]: 43–77), to weakly narrative prose (e.g., Benjamin Hrushovski, *Segmentation and Motivation in the Text Continuum of Literary Prose: The First Episode of 'War and Peace'* [Tel-Aviv: The

Porter Institute for Poetics and Semiotics, 1976]), and even to static-looking and spatial representation (my own already-cited "Ordering the Unordered," "Deictic Sequence," and "Spatiotemporal Art," as well as the argument in *Expositional Modes*, e.g., 97–98, 203–35). However variant in approach and special interest, such analyses start from the organizing features of language that cut across the boundaries of genre and object. Another important exception, first generalized in Stanley E. Fish's manifesto "Literature in the Reader: Affective Stylistics," *New Literary History* 2 (1970); 123–62, goes to the extreme opposed to the traditional, for what it demotes is the time axis of plot. These glances at the contemporary scene (which I hope to develop elsewhere) suggest once again the need for bringing the extremes together: the ability to move between world-time and medium-time is a decisive measure of a theory's power and adequacy.

11. Gotthold Ephraim Lessing, *Laocoon*, trans. Ellen Frothingham (1766; reprint, New York: Noonday Press, 1963), 91. Subsequent citations from this work are noted parenthetically in the text.

12. In early drafts of *Laocoon*, Lessing went so far as to exclude simultaneous or juxtaposed actions as well. See Victor Anthony Rudowski, "Action as the Essence of Poetry: A Revaluation of Lessing's Argument," *PMLA* 82 (1967): 333–41.

13. Some aestheticians have even objected to the dictate of the pregnant moment on the ground that it gives fantasy too much latitude. See, for instance, Rudolf Arnheim, *Toward A Psychology of Art* (Berkeley: University of California Press, 1972), 77–78.

14. To this extent, at least, we need to qualify the strong claims recently made for the role of the imagination and imaginative activity in Lessing's aesthetics, whereby poetry supposedly outranks the plastic arts all along the line. See David E. Wellbery, *Lessing's Laocoon: Semiotics and Aesthetics in the Age of Reason* (Cambridge: Cambridge University Press, 1984), e.g., pp. 133–37.

15. As it might well be in principle: see the comparison of the reader- and the writer-oriented approaches in my "Mimesis and Motivation: The Two Faces of Fictional Coherence," in *Literary Criticism and Philosophy*, ed. Joseph P. Strelka (University Park, Pa.: Pennsylvania State University Press, 1983), especially 172–76.

16. As throughout the analysis of Aristotle, it is worth indicating, the point holds no matter whether one subscribes or objects to the model of literary communication outlined earlier in this paragraph. Some may object (e.g., in the name of "representation") to the very claim that literature communicates anything; but this objection amounts to little here, unless carried to the extreme of ruling out not just statement and argument but any transaction between author and reader. Other objectors may wish to replace the anthropomorphic "author" by "text" and readerly "reconstruction" by construction, even to scrap altogether the idea of *communicative* control in favor of anything from *interpretive* code and convention to creativity. This would not much affect the issue either, unless they challenged (and few seriously do) the very directionality along with the other directives of reading. However dead the author, however wild or liberated the interpretation, the rule of time then remains in force, mental process and all. Except for the sake of argument, of course, one need not and I do not grant such objections—least of all in the contexts of the *Poetics* and *Laocoon*, with their authorial reference point, their image of a reasonable reader, and their emphasis on a prestaged encounter with the work that objectively mediates between the two to determinate ends.

17. Nor does he go into such matters elsewhere, though *Hamburg Dramaturgy*,

trans. Helen Zimmern (New York: Dover, 1962), glances at a few interesting side issues. These include the midway position of the actor's art, as visible yet transitory painting, between the plastic arts and literature (19); tempo in language versus music (24) or the advantage of combining the two time-arts (75); and the unity of time in use and abuse (136–39).

18. Etienne Souriau, "Time in the Plastic Arts," in *Reflections on Art,* ed. Susanne K. Langer (Baltimore: The Johns Hopkins University Press, 1958), 122–141; first published in *Journal of Aesthetics and Art Criticism* 7 (1949): 294–307. Subsequent citations from this work are noted parenthetically in the text.

19. Joseph Frank, "Spatial Form in Modern Literature," in *The Widening Gyre* (1945; reprint, Brunswick, N.J.: Rutgers University Press, 1963), 3–62. Subsequent citations from this work are noted parenthetically in the text. See also Frank's recent retrospects "Spatial Form: An Answer to Critics," *Critical Inquiry* 4 (1977): 231–52, and "Spatial Form: Some Further Reflections," *Critical Inauiry* 5 (1978): 275–90.

20. Roman Jakobson, "Linguistics and Poetics," in *Style in Language,* ed. Thomas A. Sebeok (Bloomington: Indiana University Press, 1960), 356.

21. They have no place except as a "transitional linguistic area . . . between strictly poetic and strictly referential language" (374)—obviously a counsel of despair that exposes an irremediable weakness.

22. See my *Expositional Modes,* e.g., 56–128, 153–54, 225–29; "Spatiotemporal Art;" and references therein.

References

Arnheim, Rudolf. *Toward A Psychology of Art.* Berkeley and Los Angeles: University of California Press, 1972.

Booth, Wayne C. *Critical Understanding.* Chicago: University of Chicago Press, 1979.

———. *"The Rhetoric of Fiction* and the Poetics of Fictions." In *Now Don't Try To Reason with Me,* 151–69. Chicago: University of Chicago Press, 1970.

Butcher, S. H. *Aristotle's Theory of Poetry and Fine Art.* New York: Dover, 1951.

Callahan, John F. *Four Views of Time in Ancient Philosophy.* Cambridge: Harvard University Press, 1948.

Crane, R. S. *The Languages of Criticism and the Structure of Poetry.* Toronto: University of Toronto Press, 1953.

———. "The Concept of Plot and the Plot of *Tom Jones.*" In *Critics and Criticism,* edited by R. S. Crane, 616–47. Chicago: University of Chicago Press, 1952.

Else, Gerald F. *Aristotle's Poetics: The Argument.* Cambridge: Harvard University Press, 1957.

Fish, Stanley E. "Literature in the Reader: Affective Stylistics," *New Literary History* 2 (1970): 123–62.

Frank, Joseph. "Spatial Form in Modern Literature." In *The Widening Gyre,* 3–62. New Brunswick, N.J.: Rutgers University Press, 1963. Originally published in 1945.

———. "Spatial Form: An Answer to Critics." *Critical Inquiry* 4, no. 2 (1977): 231–52.

------. "Spatial Form: Some Further Reflections." *Critical Inquiry* 5, no. 2 (1978): 275–90.

Genette, Gerard. *Narrative Discourse*. Translated by Jane E. Lewin. Ithaca: Cornell University Press, 1980.

Hrushovski, Benjamin. *Segmentation and Motivation in the Text Continuum of Literary Prose: The First Episode of 'War and Peace'*. Tel-Aviv: The Porter Institute for Poetics and Semiotics, 1976.

Jakobson, Roman. "Linguistics and Poetics." In *Style in Language,* edited by Thomas A. Sebeok, 350–77. Bloomington: Indiana University Press, 1960.

Lessing, Gotthold Ephraim. *Laocoon*. Translated by Ellen Frothingham. New York: Noonday Press, 1963.

------. *Hamburg Dramaturgy*. Translated by Helen Zimmern. New York: Dover, 1962.

Olson, Elder. "An Outline of Poetic Theory." In *Critics and Criticism,* edited by R.S. Crane, 546–66. Chicago: Chicago University Press, 1952.

------. "A Conspectus of Poetry, Part II." *Critical Inquiry* 4, no. 2 (1977): 373–96.

Perry, Menakhem, and Joseph Haephrati. "On Some Characteristics of the Art of Bialik's Poetry." *Akhshav* 17/18 (1966): 43–77.

Rudowski, Victor Anthony. "Action as the Essence of Poetry: A Revaluation of Lessing's Argument." *PMLA* 82 (1967): 333–41.

Souriau, Etienne. "Time in the Plastic Arts." In *Reflections on Art,* edited by Susanne K. Langer, 122–41. Baltimore and London: The Johns Hopkins University Press, 1958. Reprinted from *Journal of Aesthetics and Art Criticism* 7 (1949): 294–307.

Sternberg, Meir. *The Poetics of Biblical Narrative: Ideological Literature and the Drama of Reading*. Bloomington, Ind.: Indiana University Press, 1985.

------. "Spatiotemporal Art and the Other Henry James." *Poetics Today* 5 (1984): 775–830.

------. "Deictic Sequence: Language, World and Convention." In *Essays on Deixis,* edited by Gisa Rauh, 277–316. Tübingen: Gunter Narr, 1983.

------. "Ordering the Unordered: Time, Space, and Descriptive Coherence." *Yale French Studies* 61 (1981): 60–88.

------. "Mimesis and Motivation: The Two Faces of Fictional Coherence." In *Literary Criticism and Philosophy,* edited by Joseph P. Strelka. University Park: Pennsylvania State University Press, 1983.

------. *Expositional Modes and Temporal Ordering in Fiction*. Baltimore and London: The Johns Hopkins University Press, 1978.

Tompkins, Jane P, ed. *Reader-Response Criticism*. Baltimore and London: The Johns Hopkins University Press, 1981.

Wellbery, David E. *Lessing's Laocoon: Semiotics and Aesthetics in the Age of Reason*. Cambridge: Cambridge University Press, 1984.

Wimsatt, W. K. *The Verbal Icon*. New York: The Noonday Press, 1958.

Master Text and Slave Text: A Hegelian Theory of Writing

Claude Gandelman

The form of this essay was shaped *post factum,* that is, after its oral delivery by a query addressed to me from the audience: "What does Hegel's model buy us?" Indeed, why should it be deemed necessary to bring the rather dusty ideas of a nineteenth-century philosopher to the discussion of recent avant-garde theories concerning the interaction of text and audience?

In the first place, acknowledging Hegel is intellectually honest. To paraphrase Marx and Engels, "a phantom has been going round" during this conference—the phantom of dialectics, and it seems reasonable, when people are talking about contextual communities, communal inferences, the dialogic form of texts, and hermeneutic (re)construction of texts, to return to the inventor of modern dialectics, to the prototype, or original theory of interaction between text and context. Such a model is provided by Hegelian dialectics—specifically by the "dialectics of master and slave" expounded in chapter 3 of the *Phenomenology of Spirit.*[1]

In the second place, Hegel buys us clarity. It was Hegel, not Adorno or Derrida, who was the first to demonstrate how culture advances by negating itself qua culture, thereby gaining access to new artistic and cultural forms.[2] The Hegelian model allows us to understand how a *master* text (i.e., the unread text of a dominant culture or of individual authors successful within the dominant culture) can become the *real* text by negating itself as an authoritative (and authoritarian) text. A cultural text, thus, can become a reader's text, metamorphosed by an actual reader's textual work. Furthermore, rethinking the Hegelian model into a reception model carries further the idea suggested but not developed by Schleiermacher, that a hermeneutics implies dialects, or that the functioning of hermeneutics is, indeed, dialectical.[3]

Central to the Hegelian model is the idea of the pursuit of self-consciousness *(Selbstbewusstsein)* by an individual or a class of individuals. The process through which this self-consciousness is achieved is a process of self-recognition *(Selbsterkennung)* whereby self-consciousness supersedes mere consciousness. I will argue that the reading process is a process of self-recognition.

Self-recognition can only be achieved if it has been preceded by the recognition of the self through another consciousness—this is the point of departure of dialectics. The reason for this is the doubled *(gedoppelt)* character of consciousness, says Hegel. Any subject is the conglomerate of a nature that is both seeing and seen, which is both subject and object. Yet this doubling is not enough for actual self-consciousness to be realized. Self-consciousness is a process of recognition only to be achieved when the seeing consciousness realizes that it is also, at the same time, a consciousness that is seen—and, conversely, when the consciousness as seen experiences the revelation that it, too, sees.

In other words, consciousness is fundamentally split; in order to recapture its unity it must recognize itself, and this self-recognition is only possible through an encounter (some would say a duel) with another consciousness that will provide it with its complementary—though antithetical—components. Hegel asserts that the self-recognition process can only be possible historically—that is, if consciousness externalizes *(entäussert)* and alienates itself into history.[4]

My thesis here is that another type of externalization and incarnation in the world is possible: the self-externalization into a text (i.e., into an artwork that is a text) or into an art object. Indeed, one cannot help wondering why Hegel in his *Aesthetics*[5] did not apply his model to the relation that links creative consciousness and receptive consciousness together during and after the act of producing an art object. The reason for this, however, is obvious: Hegel saw the sphere of art—just as that of religion—as the domain of what he called Absolute Spirit *(absolute Geist),* that is, as a domain beyond dialectics that he reserved for consciousness concretely engaged in the world. This essay, therefore, is a presentation of Hegel and a critique, by which I attempt to further absolutize the Hegelian model.

The first stage of the historical dialectics of master and slave is the stage at which the master aims to establish himself once and for all as a universally recognized master. In terms of the relations between consciousnesses, the process can be described as follows.

First, in order to achieve recognition, a master consciousness aims at establishing itself as pure subject by subjugating an object, that is, a slave consciousness. In order to achieve self-recognition, a master consciousness must become a historical object (or slave) dominated or merely seen by the Other.

In historical reality, however, although recognizing the master consciousness as its master, the slave is the true consciousness of the master: it is the master who is *for* the servant, the slave, and not the opposite. Although being given the status of object, consciousness in its slavish form has become the subject. At the same time the master consciousness has failed to accede to self-recognition: it is only *for* the Other.

Second, the transformation now occurs in reverse order: in order to be recognized, the object must prove that it is not an object. Slavish consciousness that had achieved self-consciousness through slavish work must now endeavor to prove itself the real master.

Third, during this stage, mutual recognition occurs in which a master-slave encounters a slave-master.

Were the dialectics of master and slave not real dialectics but the mere description of a duality, of a never-to-be-overcome splitting within the consciousness, the master would remain forever with his mastery but without self-recognition, whereas the slave, though achieving self-knowledge (or, rather, self-consciousness and class-consciousness) would remain forever a slave without self-recognition.

For a synthesis to be possible a master-slave must encounter its reverse, a slave-master. It is only through being confronted by its own otherness in the actual shape of another being that consciousness can achieve self-consciousness through mutual recognition. The process of recognition that brings about self-consciousness is the encounter of an "I" with an "I" that is "another." The two consciousnesses that enter into dialectic interplay with one another are not only distinct but also antithetical in relation to each other: identity must be recuperated through antagonism. For Hegel, the realm of the encounter is history. In my view, the sphere of aesthetics is another privileged realm in which mutual recognition occurs. Within the text, the mutual confrontation and subsequent mutual recognition of two consciousnesses can also occur.

The aesthetic relationship that links creativity, or the creative artistic consciousness, to receptive consciousness (i.e., the consciousness of the reader) can be understood in terms of a double dialectics. The text is largely the result of a dialectical exchange between consciousnesses. This dueling, actual and virtual, constitutes itself into two subdivisions: the dialectics of creation and appreciation. I shall now proceed with a description of these two text-producing duels.

Dialectics of Artistic Creation

The dialectic first begins between the consciousness of the author and the consciousness of a virtual receptor or destinatory. It is located as an implied reader within the consciousness of the author. This destinatory also represents the overconsciousness[6] or the context that is the artistic or literary tradition, and is intended by the writer as the final receiver of the finished text.

This starting point of the dialectic is the master stage: the future destinatory of the text exists as an object for the artist—as an imagined (i.e., virtual) passive consciousness intended to be absorbed by the text (as a reader can be absorbed in his reading) and held captive or annihilated as a subject. The overconsciousness that is tradition is also destined to undergo destruction. The finished text, although standing out from the backdrop of tradition will exist primarily as a negative (i.e., as not being tradition). Yet, only a subject, a master, can be a true destinatory, a true reader. Therein, precisely, lies the paradox and the irony (some might say the tragedy) of dialectics. Through dialectical irony it is the overconsciousness meant to be enslaved that is the real truth of the master (die Warheit des Herrn)—in other words, is the real, hidden, master. Creative consciousness is master because it aims at enslaving or annihilating the critical consciousness of the Other; it is also master because it strikes the typical attitude described by Hegel: it risks its own death and, indeed, pursues its own death fearlessly. It is ready to externalize and alienate itself, to reify itself, forever, into an art object, into a text.

Yet, through a dialectical movement, it is also a slave because it works in the name of the Overconsciousness that is tradition (even in the case when it works *against* tradition); what makes it a slave is that it looks over its shoulder at tradition in order to shape its text. Thus, creative consciousness is a slave for two reasons: first, because it creates while looking all the time at tradition, and, second, because it is ready to reify itself into an (albeit artistic) object in order to exist for the Other. This, even though, as I said before, it strikes the masterful pose. In short, creative consciousness is ready to become a slave in order to achieve recognition.

Simultaneously, it is the consciousness of the Other that is the true master. First, because of its willingness to reify itself to win recognition, and also because it is the receiver, the Other as reader, who really works in the text.

With the term *work*, I have touched on a concept central to the Hegelian model: *Arbeit,* which ends the dialectics of master and slave. The author did not really work; he manipulated language in order to annihilate a reading consciousness. Or, he deconstructed language to impress a slavish consciousness, that is, he deconstructs the language of tradition. It is the reader, however, who really works and grapples with the text. It is this work that shall be described in detail in the subsequent section on text reconstruction.

Once it is finally reified into a text, creative consciousness is incapable of existing for itself. It can only exist for the Other. The formerly virtual Other, the virtual destinatory or virtual receiver is the true seeing consciousness of the author, this selfsame author who originally started out as a master of what he thought would be the purely receptive consciousness of a passive alter ego. Thus, the creating consciousness that aimed at turning itself into a pure subject by turning the Other into an object has reified itself in order to obtain recognition from an actual Other. Yet, this death, followed by recognition from the Other is the very condition for self-recognition of the creative consciousness, the ultimate aim to be achieved. Indeed, one becomes the author of the book one has written through the recognition of the reader.

The text is now finished. It exists as an artifact in which mastery over a consciousness existing as a virtual object to be dominated and annihilated has crystallized together with a slavish consciousness that has concretely worked *(gearbeitet)* and grappled with a material medium, achieving through this action a reversal of situation, which has left it possessed of true mastery and self-consciousness—but not self-recognition. This is also the point when the text has achieved historical actuality; it is now launched into the historical world, for the appreciation of an Other who is no longer virtual (inside the consciousness of the author) but actual, in the world.

This is the point when a second struggle and synthesis is about to occur: the synthesis of art appreciation. This is actually a virtual recreation of the text but in reverse order, through the hermeneutic activity of the destinatory or receiver.

Dialectics of Art Appreciation

The actual genesis of the text has been accomplished. The virtual genesis of it must now be achieved. The dialectic between reified consciousness—the consciousness of the author that has sunk into the matter of the artifact (the text) and between the consciousness of the Other (originally intended to be objectified)—of the destinatory or observer must now begin.

The seeing consciousness of the actual observer or destinatory behaves as a master who wants to appropriate the art object, the text.[7] As a matter of fact, it has every reason to behave so because the first dialectics—described in the preceding section—has found its mastery: to create a text, to create a work of art is from the outset to demand its hermeneutic reconstruction by a destinatory.

Indeed, the text cannot be merely a typographic presentation of letters on paper, the art object cannot be merely an object. It is only through the recognition of the consciousness reified therein that the receiver or observer (the destinatory) can attain self-consciousness and self-recognition. Thus, the reified consciousness in the artifact, in the text, becomes, for the destinatory, the seeing consciousness that observes him or her. It has reached the status of universal consciousness.

Artistic consciousness, thus, aims at its own death in the form of a text. Only through this self-inflicted death can artistic consciousness hope to achieve self-recognition through being (itself) recognized by the gaze of the Other. Yet, insofar as the text is reified consciousness—that is, insofar as the master has achieved his or her own death—the created object, the text, has become (in its turn) a cause of death for the observing consciousness of the destinatory, the Other. At the end of its hermeneutic reconstruction the consciousness of the destinatory has to dissolve itself (as individual consciousness) into the text that confronts it. The destinatory must also risk his or her own death by willingly absorbing the consciousness of the artist alienated into the text, into the art object. By annihilating his or her own sense of selfness, the destinatory can attain the virtual recognition of a virtual consciousness (the author's) and thus achieve self-recognition. In this double "death" and double self-sinking into the text, into the art object, lies the mutual recognition that causes the self-recognition, and is the ultimate and final aim of the whole process.

In conclusion, I would like to say that Sartre, indeed, was right when he described the created art object (in this case, the text) as the locus of an encounter between artist and destinatory.[8] I think his formula, however, should be rephrased according to a more Hegelian terminology. The encounter that occurs is not merely an encounter between two freedoms, as Sartre likes to say. Were it indeed so, a real synthesis would not occur, but both creative and appreciative aesthetic consciousnesses would remain locked forever in a seesaw situation that would turn them alternately and ceaselessly from slave into master and vice versa. What occurs in the shared text is an encounter between two freedoms that aim at becoming eventually self-conscious and self-recognized. The condition for such an achievement can only be mutual recognition through the dialectical process that was delineated in the preceding lines, a process that implies a double death and a double rebirth.

The preceding may seem terribly speculative—how does one map out in the text, concretely, the several Hegelian moments that were described earlier? When is a masterly discourse in progress, and when a slavish one?

Indeed, the task is a difficult one unless one deals with textual forms that are overtly and outspokenly dialogic. Thus, it is not very difficult to trace the master and slave phases in the discourse of *Le Neveu de Rameau* or *Jacques le Fataliste et son Maître* or in the English novels of the eighteenth century, which preceded and influenced Diderot, and those of Fielding and Sterne. This is precisely the irony in our procedure: it is said that Hegel himself hit on the idea of dialectics of master and slave because of the influence of Diderot.[9] Thus, the first application of the Hegelian model to the study of literary discourse is the very text that gave rise to the Hegelian model.

The dialogic form, however, did not disappear with the eighteenth century. Subsequently, Henry James's "The Novels of George Eliot" also talked dialectics. According to James, "the writer makes the reader," and, if he "makes him well" the master text will be well constructed.[10]

Even closer to us, the Jakobsonian model, too, seems to me to reflect the Hegelian model. Its central couples are dialectical couples. The *émetteur-récepteur* with its emotive versus cognitive functions expresses a dialectical relationship. Similarly, the reference versus self-reference (i.e., poetic) functions, so central to the dynamics of this model, are dialectical. It is through the negating of itself as emotive and through its becoming conative that the *émetteur*-text can become the real, concrete, text—just as it is through its self-negating as reference (to the outside world) that the text becomes the real, concrete, poetic (in Jakobson's terminology) text.

But again, Jakobson's model was only an elaboration of the Mukařovský model, and Mukařovský came overtly and explicitly from Hegel.[11] This too is the proof of the pudding—namely, that an understanding of dialectics, of the Hegelian model, can buy us an understanding of modern semiotics.

Notes

1. Georg Wilhelm Friedrich Hegel, *Phenomenology of Spirit,* trans. A. V. Miller (Oxford: Clarendon Press, 1979).

2. Mikhail Bakhtin, the "inventor" of the "dialogic form" of the novel, would have gained in stature, had he clearly proclaimed himself, as he was, a neo-Hegelian. In Stalinist Russia, however, constraints of a terrible nature existed that Bakhtin had to survive.

3. See, for example, Friedrich Schleiermacher, *Ausgewählte Werke in Vier Bänden* (Leipzig: Meiner Verlag, 1910–13), 240 and 410ff.

4. For an enlightening account of this terminology see A. Kojève, *Introduction à la lecture de Hegel* (Paris: Gallimard, 1974), especially chap. 3, pp. 243–46.

5. Translated as *The Philosophy of Fine Arts* by F. P. B. Osmaston (London: G. Bell and Sons, 1916), 1:53.

6. I use the term as a neologism analogous to Freud's "superego."

7. The appropriation of the art object by the ego of the destinatory is sometimes described as empathy, *Einfühlung,* in nineteenth-century aesthetics. See, for example, F. Th. Vischer, a disciple of Hegel, especially his *Plan zu einer neuen Gliederung der Aesthetik,* first published in 1843 and republished by Robert Vischer in *Kritische Gänge* 4 (1922): 160ff. Also see Robert Vischer, *Das aesthetische Akt und die reine Form* (Leipzig: 1874); Theodor Lipps, *Grundlegung der Aesthetik* (Hamburg / Leipzig: 1903–1906); and Wilhelm Worringer, whose *Abstraktion und Einfühlung* (Munich: 1908) was programmatic for the German Expressionist movement.

8. Jean-Paul Sartre, *L'imaginaire* (Paris: Gallimard, 1966), 362–73.

9. See Jean Hyppolite, *Genèse et Structure de la Phénoménologie de l'Esprit de Hegel* (1939; reprint, Paris: Aubier, 1946), 391–401.

10. Henry James, "The Novels of George Eliot," *Atlantic Monthly,* 28 (1866): 485.

11. On this subject, see my "Mukařovský's Functional Model as a Dialectical Model," in *The Prague School: 1982, A Ben-Gurion University Conference,* ed. Y. Tobin (The Hague: J. Benjamin, 1988), 265–73.

References

Diderot, Denis. *Le Neveu de Rameau* or *Jacques le Fataliste et son Maître.* Paris: Garnier-Flammarion, 1974.

Gandelman, Claude. "Mukařovský's Functional Model as a Dialectical Model." In *The Prague School: 1982, A Ben-Gurion University Conference,* edited by Y. Tobin. The Hague: J. Benjamin, 1988.

Hegel, G. W. F. *Phenomenologie des Geistes*, 1807. 6th ed. Hamburg: Meiner Verlag, 1952.

———. *Aesthetics*. Translated as *The Philosophy of Fine Arts* by F. P. B. Osmaston. London: G. Bell and Sons, 1916.

Hyppolite, Jean. *Genèse et Structure de la Phénoménologie de l'Esprit de Hegel*. Paris, Aubier-Montaigne: Aubier, 1946.

James, Henry. "The Novels of George Eliot." *Atlantic Monthly* 28 (1866).

Kojève, Alexandre. *Introduction à la lecture de Hegel*. Paris: Gallimard, 1947.

Lipps, Theodor. *Grundlegung der Aesthetik*. Hamburg / Leipzig: 1903–1906.

Sartre, J. P. *L'imaginaire*. Paris: Gallimard, 1966.

Schleiermacher, Friedrich. *Ausgewählte Werke in Vier Bänden*. Leipzig: Meiner Verlag, 1910–13.

Vischer, F. Th. *Plan zu einer neuen Gliederung der Aesthetik*, 1843. Republished by Robert Vischer in *Kritische Gänge* 4 (1922): 160ff.

Vischer, Robert. *Das aesthetische Akt und die reine Form*. Leipzig: Kappstein Verlag, 1874.

Worringer, Wilhelm. *Abstraktion und Einfühlung*. Munich: Piper Verlag, 1908.

Part II
Audience Incompetence and Textual Instruction

5

Bible Reading: The Hermeneutic Narrative

Betty Rojtman

The text of the Bible, it is well known, is an open text, one that calls for interpretation. Its narrative modes and mythical models, combined with an ideological rhetoric of reading also make it a source of its own poetics—of idiosyncratic rules for its own interpretation.[1] Through the interlocking of its narratives, it provides an internal model of reading; the biblical text itself is a representation of a hermeneutic process.

My example here will be the episode of the binding of Isaac (Gen. 22). What strikes us is the indeterminacy shown in the initial setting out of the parameters of the narrative: the place is uncertain, as is the nature of the action, and the identity of the protagonists. The narrative, however, I will show, progressively determines the references as it unfolds before us by means of prenarrative elements that are semantically variable and act, on the thematic level, like deictics in language, i.e., they serve as "switches" that may open onto a series of concrete realizations. If we consider the narrative structure and the meanings it takes in traditional Jewish exegesis, we see that the biblical text seems to construct a series of corollary existential realizations around a basic core. From the "deep" undifferentiated structure that emerges in the diegetic fabric, increasingly elaborate narrative formations appear in the complementary phases of the story, through the recurrence of key terms.

The biblical narrative, thus, is first an account of its own making, by the repeated projection of a founding schema on the several particular contexts of experience as lived by the biblical Hebrews. We find that each narrative sequence lays the foundations for the sequence that resumes the story again, prolonging and interpreting it further. A recurrent arrangement occurs, which assures the passage from myth to narrative, then from the narrative to history, in an hermeneutic chain in which each element plays alternately the role of text and context.[2]

Thus, the particularity of the biblical text is that it acts as a context from the outset, repeating a previous, yet implicit account. The text is, in itself, already both repetition and reflection; it testifies to the modification of the meaning throughout the narrative.[3] Initiating thereby the hermeneutic process, it takes the readers into its spiral and renders them responsible for the latest historical realization of the myth.

The account of the binding of Isaac opens with the enunciation of a program: "And it came to pass, after these things, that God did prove Abraham. . . . Take your son, your only son, whom you love,—Isaac; and take yourself to the land of Moriah, and offer him there for a burnt offering upon one of the mountains which I will tell you of"[4] (Gen. 22:1–2).

This appeal both models and initiates the narrative; in the divine order, a basic structure can be read: a micronarrative still open to multiple determinations. Its indicators, here undetermined, are not yet anchored in any precise reality. This underdetermination of reference in the statement, before its implementation in a particular factual context, marks here a founding myth destined to be accomplished in the exploits of biblical heroes throughout the generations. "And it came to pass, after these things, that God proved Abraham."

The Midrash[5] stresses that this "trial" is above all a proof to be given, the translation of a possibility into reality, a testimony of faithfulness expressed in the praxis. "After these things . . .": once He has assured Himself of the spiritual readiness of the patriarchs, says the Midrash, God initiates his project of trial. Listening to the imaginary dialogue of the characters, He considers that the time has come for the test (*Bereshit Rabbah* 55:4):[6] "And it came to pass, *after these things* that God proved Abraham." Abraham and Isaac both agree to perform the Will of the Creator. God appears to Abraham at the conclusion of the narrative to confirm his success: "For *now* I know that you fear God (Gen. 22:12). I know; did He not know before? [asks the Midrash]. But this is a truth which appears in the world. I know: [means] I have made known" (*Bereshit Rabbah* 26:12).

By undergoing the trial, then, Abraham accomplishes the divine Will by actualizing God's intentions, by giving them concrete reality. Taking on himself this trial, Abraham gives body to God's project, determines its worldly parameters, situates it in time and space. Abraham worships God by performing the myth, and by performing it he situates it; by developing it, he reveals himself.

It is Abraham's accomplishment of God's order, his interpretation of it into its existential reality, that makes the narrative possible: the narrative uses the open structure of the myth and determines it referentially in a precise historical context. Abraham's action is thus revealed as an hermeneutic application, by which the narrative relating it develops.

Let us follow its stages, while marking its "blank spaces":[7] "It came to pass, after these things, that God proved Abraham. . . . Take your son, your only son, whom you love,—Isaac" (Gen. 22:1–2).

The Midrash from the outset calls attention to the hesitation that borders the statement, its uncertain progression toward a developing meaning, which readjusts itself at each determination. The dialogue underlying this hesitant injunction is restored by the Midrash as follows: " 'Take your son': 'Which one?' asks Abraham, 'I have two "sons." ' ' 'Your only son': 'Each one is an *only* son for his mother.' 'Whom you love.' 'I love them equally,' says Abraham. And God [specifies]: 'Isaac' " (*Bereshit Rabbah* 55:7).

The appearance of the "proper noun" is deferred, so that the multiple combinations of the possible referential determinations may be released progressively. Throughout the entire narrative a distance is left between "actors" and "actants," between the mythological topoi and their actual crystallization in the process of narration.[8] The unfolding of the trial corresponds, through Abraham's choice, to the determination of a meaning; in the concrete event the "son" resolves into Isaac, the category into individual, the common noun into proper noun.

In the reading, the divine order is expressed thus: "Take yourself to the land of Moriah, and offer him there as a burnt offering on one of the mountains *that I will tell you of*" [emphasis added]. The Midrash seizes on this indeterminacy; it identifies there a characteristic strategy of uncertainty, commonly used in the Bible:

On one of the mountains that I will tell you of: on this verse, Rabbi Huna in the name of Rabbi Eliezer ben Yose Hagalili said: the Holy-One-Blessed-be-He confuses the Just and suspends their perspicacity; only later is the sense of His word revealed to them. [We find for instance the following enigmatic statements, elucidated a posteriori]: "[Get you from your country, and from your birthplace, and from your father's house,] unto *a land which I will show you*": (Gen. 12:1). "On one of the mountains which *I will tell you of*" (Gen. 22:2). Or in Jonah (3:1): "[Arise, go unto Nineveh, that great city and] preach unto it the preaching *that I bid you*." Or again in Ezekiel (3:22): "Arise, go forth into the plain, *and I will there talk with you*" (*Bereshit Rabbah* 55:7).

In all these examples, the meaning emerges slowly within the event. It is thus not by chance that God's summons to Abraham presents this constitutive indeterminacy that awaits humans, awaits an interpretation into which it will be precipitated. Thus Abraham sets out early, "for the place of which God had told him" (Gen. 22:3): an unnamed place—the patriarch does not even know its exact location, and it will be discovered only in the journey leading there. It is only on the "third day" that Abraham raised his eyes and "saw *the place* afar off" (Gen. 22:4). Still anonymous (recognized, but from afar off), the "place" emerges only gradually in the narrative. For Abraham before the trial, it is still a "yonder" to be explored: "Abide here with the ass; and I and the lad will go 'yonder'" (Gen. 22:5).

Only at the end of the journey is the place identified by Abraham, who perceives its profound essence. In fact, the place of the trial receives its name from the design accomplished there: "Abraham called the name of that place: *Adonai Yireh* (shown by God)" (Gen. 22:14).

At the same time that the contours of the place are specified, the distribution of the protagonists is decided. This distribution of roles, which gives a human face to each function of the narrative, is accompanied by a further revelation of identity.

Abraham's abnegation withdraws into a silence of the text, where Isaac's universe, in an abrupt enlightenment, is suddenly overturned: "Isaac said to his father . . . 'Behold the fire and the wood, but *where is the lamb for a burnt offering?*' Abraham replied: 'God will show me a lamb for a burnt offering, my son.' So they went both of them together" (Gen. 22:7–8).

The function of victim has been assured—according to the opening command: "Take" (Gen. 22:2)—but as a blank space. The action of the narrative, its tragic action, begins with the detection of the possible figures that might fill that space. It isn't Ishmael, as Abraham thought. It is not to be even Isaac, as Abraham and Isaac thought at one point of the narrative. It is finally the concrete event of the actual trial, its irreducible present that will decide between these different potentialities and designate the actual victim, the unsuspected term of the paradigm: "And Abraham lifted up his eyes and looked, and behold behind him a ram caught in a thicket by its horns. And Abraham went and took the ram, and offered it up for a burnt offering *in the stead of his son*" (Gen. 22:13).

In view of this final dramatic turn of events, based on a change of "actors," the reader is now led to a reexamination of the design of the myth. This "coup de theatre" affirms, through the existential rereading, that mutation of the key symbols is possible: the "son" is exchanged for the ram, initiating the possibility of substitution. More exactly, the substitution made is integrated henceforth into the original schema and will accompany it in future realizations.[9] For if Isaac comes back down from the altar on which the ram is to be sacrificed instead of him, the very Word of the founding project is called into question.

The Midrash states that this inversion of references, this dynamic translating into a reality in which a different understanding is elaborated, was already inscribed in the Word of God, retrieved as the original, ambivalent intention, introduced in the words of the program:

> R. Achaz said: Abraham was lost: "Your words confuse me" [he said to God]. "Yesterday, you said to me 'for in Isaac shall your seed be called' (Gen. 21:12); then you say to me: 'Take your son . . . ,' (Gen. 22:2) and now you say to me: 'Lay not your hand upon the lad' (Gen. 22:12)—Is this not confusing?" And God replies to him: "Abraham, 'I will not break my covenant' (Ps. 89:34), 'But my covenant will I establish with Isaac' (Gen. 17:21). '*I will not . . . alter the thing which has gone out of my lips*' (Ps. 89); when said I unto you 'Take your son . . .', *I did not say unto you 'slay him*' but '*offer him as a burnt offering*' (*Bereshit Rabbah* 56:8).[10]

Interpreted at first in a conventional framework (where "OLA" is understood as a "burnt offering," i.e., as "sacrifice"), the divine order, when accomplished, reveals its authentic sense, based on the literal meaning of the sign.

The Midrash relates (*Bereshit Rabbah* 56:8) how Isaac was blinded on the altar by the tears of the angels; how in the trauma of the renunciation, Isaac, still a malleable child, vanished—to be reborn in a new dimension after the trial. This passage from one level of being to another, this "raising up" of Isaac through the sacrifice, is indeed the "OLA" in the literal sense of the word referred to in the divine injunction.

This meaning was suspended within the statement and is played out in the trial of the sacrifice. The disqualified sense of a blood sacrifice is discharged in the narrative[11] by the minor figure of the ram. What remains is the elevation, at the specified place, of the beloved son.

What is revealed, at the end of the story, is thus the constitutive polysemy of the programmatic statement, which gives the action its hermeneutic role. The Word, God's injunction, is offered as an enigma; its "prophetic situation"[12] (i.e., its being out of context) favors an ambiguity of expression that has to be resolved in the narrative context. The interpretation of the myth, contained in the actions of the heroes, opens onto a *textual exegesis*. During the actual evolution of the story, the sense of the words is determined. An equivalence takes shape here between the actualizing of the myth at the existential level and its linguistic exegesis. Not only does the story have a hermeneutic function, but, reciprocally, the determination of the meaning is itself an event.

Unlike a Greek-style elucidation of the oracle, however, the ambiguity here is essentially irreducible. Like all open structures, the original formulation sets out a range of possibilities both infinite and ordered. It is, however, Abraham in his free will who decides the sense.[13] Likewise, the translation of the myth into reality takes the form of a narrative. Coming from language, the act that accomplishes its sense returns to language: coiled into the narrative process, it *produces* a new sense, homologous but not identical to the first. Not surprisingly, we find a specifically *performative* value to the words with which the narrative is composed: "Abraham said to his young men: 'Abide here with the ass; and I and the lad will go yonder and worship, and come again to you' (Gen. 22:5). 'We will worship and come again to you': [the word uttered by his mouth] informed him that they would return" (*Bereshit Rabbah* 56:2).

The interpretation of the biblical micronarrative, carried by the narrative of the interpretation, necessarily opens up a space for difference of meaning. The narrative thus contains within itself this dual valence: it is both interpretation *and* language. Although it offers the determination of a specific narrative structure, at the same time, by virtue of its language, it initiates a new intransitiveness: the mythical symbols are modified but not resolved. The opacity of the narrative, its referential indeterminacy continues throughout the very experience of its determination. It calls for new "readings," a rewriting of its symbols in future contexts. Because the original narrative elements are thus delivered over to the narrative itself as the arbiter of meaning, it will always be possible to move on to new possibilities.

Thus the actual text prepares an "afterwards" of the meaning. The place "shown by God," which Abraham finally names in the exercise of the trial (Adonai Yireh), will receive *subsequently* a new designation: *"as it is said to this day,"*[14] in the mount of Adonai Yira'eh'. This appellation is very close to the first, a paronym of it, with the same disposition of consonants; the new mention displaces the sense of the name given by Abraham and modifies its vocalization.[15]

The meaning of the place does not finish with the binding of Isaac. The space is reserved for a fresh narrative. This displacement in the repetition, thus, marks the anticipation of a new contextual setting.

The first account initiated by the patriarchs becomes "myth" in turn, a ritual or a sign for the future generations. After the trials and achievements of the patriarchs, human families are formed: they take up the path traced by the fathers, repeat its cycle collectively. The deeds of the Fathers are a sign for the children:[16] sign as an example, but more profoundly as a prototype, a secret destiny. For the Midrash, Israel's vicissitudes rediscover the trace of an old itinerary: no generation exists, it says, without its Abraham (*Bereshit Rabbah* 56:7). Thus God's summons is repeated, swelled with future investments: "Abraham, Abraham. . . ."

After the story of Abraham a new period of narrative begins, an ambivalent reformulation of the first narrative structures. The acquired experience of the trial is irreversible, the inheritance through Isaac is decided. God renews his blessing to Abraham, engaging the future; the act is indelible: "For because you have done this thing . . . I will surely bless you; I will surely multiply your seed as the stars of the heaven. . . . And in your seed shall all the nations of the earth be blessed, because you have obeyed my voice" (Gen. 22:16–18).

At the same time, however, the reproduction of the pattern that is always *different* in its performance through history, brings out fresh ambiguities. In the new event, an original linguistic sense is always revealed—a sense deciphered through the words or rites used to express it, which germinates a recurrent ambiguity.

The deeds of the heroes never reoccur in their entirety. It is the Midrash that recognizes and thus retrieves the continuity of the episodes, distinguishing complete narrative cycles in the text of the Bible. Each generation performs an episode, conferring on it its epic and national dimension. Thus the traditional elements of the narrative—time, place, protagonists, acts and words (the foundations of the myth)—are dispersed as so many symbols (or signifiers), integrated into the fabric of new narratives. The Midrash traces their return, marked by a recurrence of expression: the narrative motifs reappear in the linguistic mold into which they were originally cast. The linearity of the biblical account is thus restructured by the Midrash[17] and its repetitive character comes to light, filtered through the traditional exegesis.

Thus the three days preceding the trail reappear in new episodes: Joseph's brothers' three days of anguish in prison; the three days of

preparation for the revelation on Mount Sinai; the three days spent
by the spies in Canaan; the three days spent by Jonah in the belly of
the fish; and, later in history, the three days preceding the return
from exile, and those of Queen Esther confronting Ahasuerus. In
addition we could include, according to the Midrash, beyond the
dimension of time in the eschatological extension of the theme, the
future third day of the final resurrection (*Bereshit Rabbah* 56:1).
The recurring motif involves a semantic recurrence, the anticipation of a revelation.

As for the place of the trial, it is the place recognized later by
Jacob in his flight to Haran: "And he lighted upon a certain place,
and tarried there all night, because the sun was set" (Gen. 28:11).
" 'The place, it is this very place,' says the Midrash (as quoted by
Rashi), that Abraham had seen 'afar off,' the place of the revelation:
'And Jacob awakened out of his sleep, and he said, Surely the Lord
is *in this place* and I knew it not' " (Gen. 28:16).

As for the protagonists, father, son, and ram,[18] they will merge in
the same embodiment, in the collective destiny of Israel as a
people, reliving the trial, alternately in the fashion of Abraham,
Isaac, or the ram.

In the Midrash, the victim of the burnt offering—the ram sacrificed represents the salvation of Isaac, the sacrificed part of Isaac
that makes possible his raising up—is explicitly the symbol of
Israel, caught in the web of their own sins, their horns tangled in the
exile of the nations, and destined to be saved by the sounding of the
shofar[19] (*Bereshit Rabbah* 56:9).

Repetition of the theme, then, is not identity. It comes later, is
recognized as repetition: the path of the heirs prolongs the action of
the fathers, bears its irreversible mark, not as fate, but as progression, as imitation and metamorphosis of a theme seeking its
resolution. Like the ram, Israel is caught in the thicket of its
destiny; the image of an Isaac led to the sacrifice. Abraham, however, has already followed the path toward the trial, and the sense of
the narrative has already changed: Isaac will not be sacrificed. This
ram, which played only the role of substitute, has become, by the
merit of Abraham who first lived out the drama, the ram of redemption.

Thus all the events return as if they were reoccurring but defused
by Abraham's merit: for each act of the father, a parallel event will
come to save the children. As it is performed, the myth is transformed. As the wood was *split* by Abraham, the Red Sea will split
before the Hebrews (*Bereshit Rabbah* 55:8); because of the *knife*

raised by Abraham, Israel will be saved from Pharoah's sword (*Bereshit Rabbah* 55:8).

These transformations show us the fundamental ambiguity of the myth: lost like the ram, Israel will be saved by the ram's horn. Fall and Redemption merge in the same symbol. This multiplicity of valences is a function of the extension of the paradigm into history; in its praxis it describes new hermeneutic circles. For the Midrash does not limit itself to the biblical frontiers of the theme; once initiated, the process extends beyond the narrative itself and opens a contemporary perspective: "And Abraham lifted up his eyes, and looked, and behold a ram behind him [or "another ram," or a "ram, afterwards"] caught in a thicket by its horns" (Gen. 22:13). In literal expression "a ram afterwards" is a solicism which the Midrash reads as a temporal indication: "After all these events . . ." (*Bereshit Rabbah* 56:9). The ram is heralding History: "Abraham saw the ram wandering from one bush to another, freeing itself from one only to become entangled in another. And God said to him: "Thus your children will be entangled in one exile after the other, from Babylon to Persia and from Persia to Greece, and from Greece to Rome,—and they are destined to be saved finally by the ram's horn; as it is said (Zechariah 9:14): 'And the Lord God shall blow the shofar'" (*Bereshit Rabbah* 56:9).

For the Midrash, the corpus of the Bible is not a closed universe. The mythical schema is there experienced but in order to allow extension: multiple indications in the text inform the midrashist of a permanent or repetitive existential reality, throughout the entire progress of Jewish history. In the view of the Midrash, for example, God permanently provides Israel with its daily bread only through the merit of the sacrificed ram (*Bereshit Rabbah* 56:3). Similarly, in the historical perspective, the trial of exile is repeated until the day when, like that ass saddled by Abraham on the morning of the trial ("And Abraham rose up early in the morning, and saddled his ass" [Gen. 22:3]), another ass will return bearing the saviour (*Bereshit Rabbah* 56:2).[20] The span of history is thus embraced until the Last Judgment. The myth, tapped throughout the biblical narrative, continues to be performed in history. Spiral history repeats and modifies its basic structure, its rhythm being ordered by an internal meaning.[21]

This postbiblical meaning, without a linguistic substratum on which to build, still finds its incarnation in the symbolic form of ritual. The epic of Abraham founds history, but at the same time it institutes the Law given as a new language. The law is a symbolic repetition of a first ceremony, but each time with a new meaning. Law is made to act, in the event, as parallel repetition of the myth, as a hidden meaning in history, which the narrative can no longer express.

It is mainly the ritual of the sacrifices that is shaped by Abraham's accomplishment: two lambs will be sacrificed daily in the Temple, in remembrance of the ram (*Vayikra Rabba* 2:11). Further, the Talmud draws from the account of Abraham's burnt offering a series of teachings on the laws of the sacrifices. We have already mentioned the reminder of the ram as the burnt offering in the (commemorative) rite of the sounding of the *shofar* on the first day of the Jewish New Year *(Rosh Hashana)*.[22]

Thus ritual becomes a symbolic form of actualization, parallel to the narrative. It duplicates the historical event, casting it in the mold of an already known sense. By ritual, the symbolic openness of the myth is perpetuated and the profound, repetitive structure of history is revealed. Its commemorative value merges with its performative force, which pledges the future.

"Rabbi Chanina ben Yitzhak said: Throughout the year, the children of Israel succumb to their own faults, and they become entangled in their misfortunes. But on the day of the New Year (Rosh Hashana), they sound the shofar and recall themselves to the Holy-One-Blessed-Be-He; and finally, they will be saved by the ram's horn,—as it is said: 'And the Lord God will sound the Shofar' " (*Bereshit Rabbah* 56:9).

The sounding of the shofar thus is both ritual and event; as ritual, it recalls the event of the binding of Isaac and repeats it symbolically. This symbolic repetition acts in history, however, because on the merit of the enactment of this event, Israel will be saved in the final realization of the symbol. Rite will become history in the ultimate and unique sounding of the Shofar of the Redemption. It is by the ceremonial act of commemoration that history advances. The exchanges between myth and narrative are transmuted, beyond the narrative, in a bivalence of ritual and history.

In conclusion, we should note the paradoxical principle of history: its cyclical structure, coupled with a generative myth, is also (through the Law or the narrative) symbolic: it is intransitive and polysemous. Recognition of the myth in an event is, in fact, the mainspring of midrashic thought. "In the beginning, God created the heaven and the earth" (Gen. 1:1). "In the beginning: towards the beginning . . ." (*Bereshit Rabbah* 1:1). The world develops from a project, a scheme that reality implements. The "beginning," the original structure that marks the beginning of history, reveals itself, only *after* its enactment, through the identity of the act that has borne its mark: "For the divine dimension is as if suspended and awaiting he who will show himself apt to assume it" (Yehudah Halevi, *The Kuzari* 2:14). The end is contained as if coiled into the beginning—but as a hollow, a possibility. It is the human figure that gives Time a name and a trajectory. The revelation is brought about from an initial design that stamps its rhythm on the future.

The dynamic is assured, furthermore, by the relay of the narrative that discovers the symbolic value of the real in order to project it toward new meanings and developments. The realization of the project in the world goes through the detour of its representation: it is the symbolic mediation that guarantees the opening up of the paradigm. Thus, it converts this paradigm into a "floating signifier" (Lacan, 1966):[23] history's vocation is to fill the myth, and it takes place by the very fact of the hermeneutic awareness of its function, which is the ultimate measure of its historicity. History, thereby, frees itself from the constraint of the myth. The myth, as we have seen, is modified through the signification that it assumes in history and which conditions its perpetuation. Here we recognize a dialectic of the fixed and the undetermined that situates human activity between model and liberty. This fluctuation is founded on the ambiguity of the sign (e.g., narrative or ritual) between motivation and arbitrariness.

The question can never be resolved whether it is the myth that determined history or vice versa. Is Abraham summoned to the "place" that, according to tradition (*Bereshit Rabbah* 55:7), marks the future site of the Temple *because* of its sanctity? Or is it the patriarch who by his burnt offering consecrates the place of the sacrifice as a holy mountain? Humans both reveal and initiate the sign in history. This uncertainty casts the very origin of the sense back into the unknown. For the founding myth, assumed to be functionally original, maintains this same ambiguous character. It may itself be only the projection of an already constituted historical structure.[24]

Could the account have been written in a different way? Perhaps a different version would have involved another Abraham, in another place and another time. . . . Behind this system of ambiguity lies the ethical responsibility of interpretation, which is the responsibility for ethical conduct. Against the voice from heaven affirming an absolute truth of the text, the rabbinical consciousness revolts: "the Torah is not in heaven" (*Baba Metzia* 59) but caught up in the weave of history that embraces it. Everyone must read this text and decide whether 'OLA' is an exaltation or a sacrifice.

Notes

1. See Meir Sternberg's comprehensive and detailed study, *The Poetics of Biblical Narrative: Ideological Literature and the Drama of Reading* (Bloomington: Indiana University Press, 1985).

2. From a different vantage point, Harold Fisch confronts the same issue, introducing the paradoxical and fruitful concept of "historical myth" in *A Remembered Future: A Study in Literary Mythology*" (Bloomington: Indiana University Press, 1984). In particular, see chapter 1, "Historical Archetypes," 1–19.

3. For a discussion of recurring patterns and their possible modification, see Sternberg, *Biblical Narrative*, 269–72. For a more general analysis of repetition, see chapter 11, "The Structure of Repetition: Strategies of Informational Redundancy," 365–440.

4. Citations from the Bible have been rendered into English by the author with the aid of the British and Foreign Bible Society's English translation.

5. *Midrash Aggadah* is the general term used for the traditional exegetic texts of a parabolic or homiletic nature. These midrashim appear in the Talmud and in other collections.

6. The *Midrash Rabbah* including *Bereshit Rabbah* represents one of the most important corpora of commentaries of *Midrash Aggadah*.

7. For a study of the notion of gap filling, see Sternberg, *Biblical Narrative*, 187ff., 267.

8. The distinction is taken from A. J. Greimas, differentiating a structural role (actant) from the person who fills it (actor). *Sémantique structurale* (Paris: Larousse, 1966).

9. "R. Bebaia said: Abraham says to God: 'Lord of the Universe, consider this ram's blood as representing the blood of my son Isaac, and these organs as those of my son Isaac'" (*Bereshit Rabbah* 56:9). From Abraham onward, every ritual sacrifice retains this substitutive sense of compensation.

10. The subtlety of the Midrash is clearer in the Hebrew in which the same root OLA (The root consists of the Hebrew letters ayn lamed hay), meaning "raising up," serves to designate both the Levitical term for one kind of sacrifice (burnt offering) and the spiritual elevation that accompanies the sacrifice.

11. The Midrash considers this possibility, stressing that it is stated nowhere in the text that Isaac *came down* from the mount again. Perhaps Abraham goes back to his traveling companions alone (*Bereshit Rabbah* 56:19 and *Vayikra Rabbah* 20:2).

12. The expression is coined by Roland Barthes in *Critique et Vérité* (Paris: Seuil, 1966).

13. The Midrash tells us that God had presented a request to Abraham: "Take, please, your son . . ." (*Bereshit Rabbah* 55:7 and Sanhedrin 89b). God gives to humans the keys and responsibility of the meaning.

14. "Today" is the day of the utterance of the statement. It announces the broadening, if not the breaking out, of the narrative frame.

15. In Hebrew, only consonants are written. The text is thus an open structure, actualized by a reader's choice of one vocalic interpretation or another.

16. See Ramban on Gen. 12:6, and *Tanhuma, Leh Leha* 9.

17. Cf. restructuration in columns, as Claude Lévi-Strauss does with the Oedipus myth in *Anthropologie structurale* (Paris: Plon, 1958).

18. The account of Moses' vocation is initiated with the theme of the lamb. The recurrence of the motif with the paschal lamb suggests a continuity, from Abraham to Moses, from the individual trial to the collective redemption.

19. The ram's horn sounded by the Jews on the Day of Judgment.

20. Thus the three days journey toward the "place" also heralded the three days of the final resurrection.

21. See Fisch, chapter 5, "The Binding of Isaac," 81–101. In particular, see the historical recapitulation of the myth during the Holocaust (92–93).

22. The ritual of the ram's horn is stipulated by the biblical text itself (Num. 19:1). The parallel with the sacrifice of Isaac is established by the Midrash.

23. Jacques Lacan, *Ecrits* (Paris: Seuil, 1966).

24. For each gesture of Abraham binding his son on the altar, says the Midrash, the Holy-One-Blessed-Be-He reproduces its sign in the antehistoric or ahistoric, celestial universe, in the world of the "project" (*Bereshit Rabbah* 56:5).

References

Barthes, Roland. *Critique et Vérité*. Paris: Seuil, 1966.

Fisch, Harold. *A Remembered Future: A Study in Literary Mythology*. Bloomington, Ind.: Indiana University Press, 1984.

Halevi, Yehudah. *The Kuzari,* art. 2, para. 14.

Lévi-Strauss, Claude. "La Structure des mythes." In *Anthropologie structurale*. Paris: Plon, 1958.

Mirkin, A. M. *Bereshit Rabbah*. Tel-Aviv: Yavneh, 1968.

Ramban on Gen. 12, 6.

Greimas, A. J. *Sémantique structurale*. Paris: Larousse, 1966.

Sternberg, Meir. *The Poetics of Biblical Narrative: Ideological Literature and the Drama of Reading*. Bloomington, Ind.: Indiana University Press, 1985.

Tanhuma Leh Leha, 9. Sota 34a.

6

Prophet versus Audience

Harold Fisch

Ezekiel describes the setting for his prophetic utterances in several different passages: 8:1; 14:1; 20:1; and 33:31. We see the elders of the people sitting around him, perhaps in a circle, waiting for him to begin. Ezekiel needs his audience to witness his symbolic actions and to hear his oracles and yet we see him rebuking them for their eagerness. What, we may wonder, was the kind of gratification they expected and why do they merit rebuke? The clearest glimpse of the scene is given in the following passage.

> As for thee, son of man, the children of thy people, who talk against thee by the walls and in the doors of the houses, speak one to another, everyone to his brother, saying, Come, I pray you, and hear what is the word that comes from the Lord. And they come to thee as the people come, and they sit before thee, my people, and they hear thy words, but they do not carry them out; for it is become love songs in their mouths, whilst their heart is set on unjust gain. And, lo, thou art to them like a love song [or perhaps: a flute song] by one who has a pleasant voice and can play the instrument well: for they hear thy words, but they do them not. (Ezek. 33:30–32)[1]

Clearly, the people who have gathered themselves together are hoping for something like an artistic performance. At about this same time Homer's poetry would be chanted, if not to the flute then to the lyre or cythara, before a duly appreciative audience in Athens or Smyrna. The people around Ezekiel in Tel-Abib in the sixth century had similar expectations. They had settled down rather comfortably in Babylon and had acquired a taste for fine words and allegories. "Does he not speak in allegories?" (better,

---

This essay forms chapter 4 of my book, *Poetry with a Purpose: Biblical Poetics and Interpretation* (Bloomington: Indiana University Press, 1988); reprinted with permission.

metaphors) they said of Ezekiel (Ezek. 20:49). The prophet is their bard and minstrel and the beauty of his language only confirms them in their way of relating to him as to one who sings love songs. Some examples include his marvelous vision of the valley of dry bones (chapter 37), the mighty armies of Gog storming in epic style out of the land of Magog (chapter 38), and his romantic tale of the foundling girl who becomes the beautiful bride of her foster father (chapter 16). Ezekiel is claiming to speak here of matters more important to his audience than those spoken of in Homer's epics, because he speaks the word of God; if, however, it is God himself who prompts Ezekiel to tell the tale of "a great eagle with great wings and long pinions, rich in plumage of many colors" (Ezek. 17:3), that does not make the telling of such a tale a less powerful literary event.

The audience, we should remember, has a part in determining the nature of the genre to which a particular piece of writing or speaking belongs. Novels are novels because the reader agrees that this is what they are. A different contract between reader and writer would make *Robinson Crusoe*, for instance, something else—for example, a newspaper account of a remarkable voyage, a report to the Royal Society of conditions in the South Atlantic, or a tract written to support the aims of The Society for the Propagation of the Gospel. Such a contract always exists. A priest or rabbi in a church or synagogue knows he is there to "preach," and the audience agrees to react according to the nature of the occasion. Abstracted from that occasion and agreement, the words could add up to something different—for example, a contribution to the gossip column of a weekly paper or an exercise offered in partial fulfillment of a bachelor of divinity degree. In the case of Ezekiel, we seem to have a failed contract. He rejects the role of minstrel that has been assigned to him by his audience with some violence—he will not be like one who sings flute songs, he tells them—whereas the audience rejects what he has determined as his mode of speech (i.e., the prophetic word as command): "they hear thy words, but they do them not." Or as we might say in our modern jargon, "They read thy words, but they write a different text."

It is not only the reader, however, who is enticed by the fascination of artistic speech. The prophet himself has a struggle. Remember, he is a poet as well as a prophet: that other kind of relation between text and reader, text and author (i.e., the artistic relation), cannot be avoided.[2] The more strongly Ezekiel protests against the role of poet, the richer does his language become, the more vivid his imagery. He would banish his audience, and yet without their presence, his words will echo in the vacant air. He needs to fascinate them with words. More than that, he himself cannot escape the fascination of words. After saying with disgust, "Ah Lord God! they say of me, / Does he not speak in allegories?" (Ezek. 20:49)—he proceeds to his great oracle about the sharpened sword: "A sword, a sword is sharpened / and also polished, / it is sharpened to make a sore slaughter: / it is polished that it may glitter" (Ezek. 21:9–10).

He then breaks off with the question, "Or do we make mirth?" Perhaps he has noticed his audience nudging one another and smiling with pleasure at this "Song of the Sword" as some editors have termed these verses. He rebukes members of the audience by telling them that they had better stop enjoying the poetry, for the sword is intended for *them*. "Cry and howl, son of man, for it is against my people; / it is against all the princes of Israel" (Ezek. 21:12). But if and when that sword manifests itself against the princes of the people, it will put a stop to the very *Sitz im Leben* of the prophecy itself, as in this scene in which the people sit around him waiting for their entertainment. It is no wonder that the prophet is bidden to cry and howl; his prophecy is a self-destroying prophecy that announces the doom of its own language, the coming of silence.

Earlier on, in chapter 20, Ezekiel had turned angrily on the elders and said to them: "Are you come to inquire of me? As I live, says the Lord God, I will not be inquired of by you" (Ezek. 20:3). He is asking the elders whether they want oracles but says there will be no more oracles. A passionate and moving speaker, Ezekiel here anathematizes the very art of speech itself. He enacts a drama in which he performs symbolic signs and explains them to a delighted audience, but then, somewhat in the manner of the cynical philosopher Diogenes, he excoriates them for having come to the play.

We may pause to consider the verb *dāraš* in the last quotation, here translated as "to inquire of." It is this inquiring of him like an oracle that Ezekiel spurns. A further overtone of meaning emerges, however. The term with its cognate noun *midraš*, as in 2 Chron. 13:22 and 24:27, also suggests "imaginative exposition" or "interpretive discourse,"[3] pointing evidently to the verbal aspect of prophecy. To be a prophet is to be a master of words that invite interpretation. The people come to *lidĕrōš* and he, by the power of his language, submits to *lĕhiddārĕš* (i.e., to being inquired of or interpreted). At the heart of this mode of communication is the play of words, the use in particular of paronomasia for assonance, explication, or antithesis. The prophet savagely abjures any more *midraš*. The very verse that says this, however, is in its paratactic sequence of the two forms of *dāraš*—"Are you come to inquire of me? As I live . . . I will not be inquired of by you"—a perfect example of the verbal play that is being proscribed here.

The verse that follows introduces for contrast a different verbal double: "Wilt thou judge them, son of man, wilt thou judge them? / Let them know the abominations of their fathers" (Ezek. 20:4). (A better rendering, perhaps, is Moffatt's "Arraign them, son of man, arraign them.") Instead of the *dāraš,* or verbal function of the prophet, here we have him in his judgmental role, that denoted by the verb *šāpaṭ.* No more words, he is saying; instead of that, you will get from me the sword of chastisement. I will be Moses, he seems to say, but not the Moses who speaks to the rock—rather the Moses who strikes the rock. The image, six times repeated, which governs the whole powerful discourse that follows (Ezek. 20:5–44) is that of the raised hand. God raises his hand to take Israel out of Egypt and declare himself to the people (verses 5–6), and he raises his hand to punish them in the wilderness and scatter them among the nations (Ezek. 15:23). The gesture suggests an oath but also a blow, thus ambiguously combining promise and punishment. Eventually, the raised hand is transmuted (34) into the well-known figure of the mighty hand and outstretched arm of the God who judges both his people and their enemies.

A metonymic term for judgment, the uplifted arm of God (or of his prophetic messenger) had been originally introduced, as noted earlier, for a sign of the nonverbal (indeed, antiverbal) function of the prophet, but it has now become the focus of a sinuous play of language whereby all the various possibilities of the trope are explored. Instead of discourse, he says, you will have the arm, a kinesics of pure gesture. But even as the gesture is performed, it becomes an eloquent utterance, one made richer by the multiple repetition of the phrase and its variants. Anaphora constitutes the basic rhetoric of chapter 20. In verses 35–36, the verb *šāpaṭ,* to judge or remonstrate, returns to be thrice repeated. Indeed, the accumulation of words by the device of anaphora is the very medium of this prophecy. The prophet is saying that he does not offer words but acts or judgments, however ironic and however defeated the claim is in the very moment of saying it. In verse 37 that claim resolves itself into another image of violence, perhaps one associated with and suggested by, the raised arm. It is the image of the rod: "I will cause you to pass under the rod, and I will bring you into the discipline of the covenant: and I will purge out from among you the rebels, and them that transgress against me" (Ezek. 20:37–38).[4] The punitive force of the "rod" is intensified by the sequel that speaks of the bond or discipline of the covenant by the term *māsōret,* suggesting binding or imprisoning but perhaps also chastising and (as in later Hebrew) handing down (from the verb *māsōr*), that is, the handing down of a verbal tradition.

The whole paradox we have been discussing is compressed in the three words bridging verses 37 and 38: *māsōret habbĕrît ûbārôtî*— "the discipline: the convenant: I will purge." The covenant, in its original essence a verbal exchange or contract, here becomes a physical bonding or chastisement (linked to the "rod" of the first half of verse 37). The word *bĕrît* (covenant) then yields by paronomasia to the following word, *ûbārôtî* here translated "I will purge"[5] but perhaps suggesting also the sharpening of an arrow (as in Isa. 49:2). A contrast sealed in words changes into a cleansing agency or a sharpened arrow but does so actually through a play on words—that very same wordplay that is supposed to be banished so as not to obtrude on the direct, judgmental role that the prophet has assumed. Language here undoes itself at the same time as it knits its marvelous web. The audience is enchanted at the same time as all such enchantment is condemned as flute music to be silenced by the sword of judgment.

We may consider the special relationship between the prophet and his audience as a kind of "covenant." Clearly from the phrase just quoted the covenant, or *bĕrît,* suggests a bond or partnership but also suggests a measure of constraint on both sides. "I will cause you to pass under the rod, and I will bring you into the discipline of the covenant. I will purge out from among you the rebels, and them that transgress against me." As well as referring to the drama being played out between God and Israel, this sentence viewed metapoetically—as it demands to be viewed—also refers to the drama being played out between the prophet and his audience. They are bound together by a common destiny and common obligation; yet the audience is being coerced, the prophet in effect saying to them, "I will make you read the words my way." They in their turn are rebelling and insisting that they hear a different word, see a different vision; they are as it were writing a different text. "Covenant" signifies relationality, even a mode of relationality that neither side can abrogate—for they are bound to one another—and yet it is an uneasy, even an antithetical relation, one full of tension and recalcitrance on both sides.

Chapters 3 and 4 of this prophet are full of dreadful images of constraint. In chapter 3 it is said that the people will put him in bonds, they will rebel against him; but to match their refusal to hear him, his own power of speech will be paralyzed—he will be struck dumb: "But thou, O son of man, behold, they shall put cords upon thee, and shall bind thee with them, and thou shalt not go out among them: and I will make thy tongue cleave to the roof of thy mouth, that thou shalt be dumb, and shalt not be able to reprove them: for they are a rebellious house" (Ezek. 3:25–26). If they will not obey the voice of command, they will not have fine words either—the prophet will become speechless. The irony, however, is that in the sequel the speechless acts become themselves an eloquent language of signs. The prophet acts out the drama of coercion: he lies on his side for forty days bound with cords "so that thou shalt not be able to turn thyself from one side to the other" (Ezek. 4:8). No doubt the audience was as fascinated, however, by that vivid performance as they were by his fine speeches. The audience is not eliminated: they are bound to him, and he is bound to them—evidently by those very same ropes that bind him to his task.

The biblical text as a whole is founded in relationality. It demands an audience, actively participating not merely in understanding but even in constituting the text. This position is classic Jewish doctrine. The written law, *tôrâ šebbiktāb* cannot stand alone; it is validated by the *tôrâ šebbĕ'al-peh* (i.e., the oral Torah), or continuing tradition of interpretation. This "community of interpreters" gives meaning and generic character to the written text.[6] This concept is possibly also what is meant in Ezekiel's term *māsōret habbĕrît*—the bond or tradition of the covenant. Relationality continues, a living "bond" of continuing interpretation in which the text is constituted from age to age by the dialectical relation subsisting between the written and the unwritten scripture, between a community of interpreters and a text that is constantly reinterpreted by them. The "text" does not exist anywhere except in the tension-laden space between that community of interpreters and the words that they have received by tradition.

Such relationality is not an invention of rabbinic Judaism. It is already asserted in some of the most notable passages of scripture. "Hear O Israel: the Lord our God, the Lord is one" (Deut. 6:4). This is not a simple proclamation, a *kerygma,* nor is it a simply prescriptive statement; instead, it is an invitation, a summons to "Israel" to hear, to apprehend, to interpret. What it tells us is that the divine unity is realized only when a community of hearers exists to achieve that perception, to make that affirmation; it is a perception that has to be striven for, created in the act of reading, hearing, and understanding. Nor are the words *šĕma' yiśrā'ēl* a form of apostrophe, a mere rhetorical gesture: they imply rather a genuine partnership, the invocation, as a necessary presence, of a hearing ear and a perceiving intelligence in the constitution of meaning. We have in short a covenantal encounter in which the very mode of the utterance is governed by the categories of covenant. The willingness to hear, to understand, to cooperate is here declared to be a prior condition for the affirmation to which the sentence moves. It is that willingness that the sentence solicits. Relationality, in short, precedes pronouncement and precedes command. Relationality—the presence within that discourse which we call Torah of the hearing ear and the perceiving mind—is the theme of this sentence. In addition, a question arises as to where to situate these words in the dramatic pattern of the relationship. Who speaks them and to whom? In their deuteronomic context they seem to be words spoken by Moses to Israel in the name of God and are from this viewpoint parallel to the sentence that precedes it: "Hear therefore, O Israel, and take care to do them [i.e., the commandments]: that it may be well with thee" (Ezek. 6:3). This meaning, however, is not how they have been construed by the interpreting community in practice. The words "Hear, O Israel: the Lord our God, the Lord is one" have become much rather a passionate cry from the hearer to whom they are ostensibly addressed! In fact, their direction has been exactly reversed. In the daily repetition of that sentence it becomes the sign of the acceptance of the "yoke of the commandments." The interpreting community now takes the words that summoned it into existence and makes them its own. What had seemed to be a cross between an invitation, a summons, and a command in the original signification now becomes a speech act of a very different kind—a passionate acceptance of the hearer's own role in the discourse and a cry to the fellowship of Israel to share in his or her discovery and affirmation. Thus, an exchange of roles in the process of communication from speaker to reader occurs. The reader becomes speaker by accepting an active role as a full covenanting partner without whom the sentence cannot achieve its meaning.

We should not underestimate, however, the strain involved, the sense of difficulties to be overcome—what I have previously termed "recalcitrance" on the part of the audience. The same verb *šĕmaʿ* occurs in the phrase *naʿăśeh wĕnišmaʿ*, "we will do and we will hear," in connection with the acceptance of the Law at Mount Sinai (Exod. 24:7). Commenting on that phrase, the rabbis say that the willingness to both do and hear—the latter implying also perceiving, obeying, and understanding, as in the present context of "Hear

O Israel"—was only achieved after God had inverted Mount Sinai over the heads of the people like a great barrel and threatened them with destruction.[7] To accept the role of "hearer" in the sense understood by "Hear O Israel" is to accept an almost overpowering responsibility. It is not a simple act of response that is required of us as though we were readers of a novel called on to assist in the creating of a fictional illusion; rather we are called on to commit ourselves, to accept an obligation. For the word *šĕma‘* implies not only reading but also obeying; the text seizes us even against our will.

One element in that contract that determines the manner of reading biblical texts deserves to be emphasized. The words "Hear O Israel" do not only say something about relationality in the present; they affirm a continuing relationality—a community of interpreters that carries perceptions (in this case the perception of the divine unity) derived from the past into the present and future. The example of the eleventh-century commentator, Rashi, following the Sifre links our sentence with Zech. 14:19—"And the Lord shall be king over all the earth; on that day the Lord shall be one, and his name one." According to this perception, a time dimension, a future reference, is implied in the *šema‘*. The hearer in the *šema‘* affirms a continuity of which he or she is the guarantor. In other words, the verb *šĕma‘* implies not only hearing, perceiving, and interpreting but also *remembering*. Past occasions are linked by memory to present occasions—the true hermeneutic circle of interpretation. "Hear O Israel" in fact says something about history: the word that has been heard validates itself in the historical present as it did in the past; it continues to resound. The words "Hear O Israel" can thus be glossed: "*Continue* to hear, O Israel; a living word is carried into the future by a living people constituting an undying community of auditors. I declare myself to be part of that community."

Such historical continuity must, accordingly, be distinguished from the relativism that some modern theorists have maintained, according to which the hearer or reader, situated in a particular historical context, can never reach the same perception of the text as a predecessor or successor. No essential continuity of meaning exists.[8] This position is not the one taken by the sentence we are considering, nor can it be supported by biblical poetics. "Hear, O Israel: The Lord our God, the Lord is one" may further be glossed: "Hear, O Israel at all times and you will hear that the same Lord is still our God, the same one Lord." The hearing itself becomes, in short, the affirmation of a unity of perception, a covenantal bonding of the generations. Each reader becomes a witness to that continuity, firmly placing himself or herself in a context that includes the witnesses who have preceded and those who will follow. Again, this unifying perception has to be striven for, recalcitrance has to be overcome. It is easier to slip into total relativism, to assume that the generations of readers are not bound to each other. We are enjoined, however, not to let this happen.

The demand made of readers that they become witnesses, guarantors of continuity, is central to the Bible's own definition of poetry. I now wish to consider this definition occurring in Deuteronomy (chapter 31) briefly. Moses is instructed to write a poem before he dies, a poem that will live unforgotten in the mouths and minds of the people. The poem, itself usually known by its opening word *ha᾽ ăzînû,* is in chapter 32. In chapter 31, however, is part of the programmatic introduction (or instruction) to the poem:

> Now therefore, write you this poem, and teach it to the children of Israel: put it in their mouths, that this poem may be a witness for me against the children of Israel. For when I shall have brought them into the land of which I swore to their fathers, one flowing with milk and honey; and they shall have eaten and filled themselves, and are grown fat; then will they turn to other gods, and serve them, and provoke me, and break my covenant. And it shall come to pass, when many evils and troubles have befallen them, that this poem shall answer them as a witness, for it shall not be forgotten out of the mouths of their seed: for I know their inclination, and what they do, even now, before I have brought them into the land of which I swore. (Deut. 31:19–21)

A rather complex time scheme is used in this passage. The poem takes us back to a time of origins, to the sojourn in the wilderness "before I have brought them into the land of which I swore," but it is designed for a future time after the land has been settled and has become flourishing and fertile ("a land flowing with milk and honey"). It will then act as a mnemonic device, an aid to memory, because during the intervening period it will have lived unforgotten in the mouth of the reader or hearer, ready to come to mind when needed. Poetry is thus a kind of time bomb; it awaits its hour and then it springs forward into harsh remembrance. If the sequence of the sentences in the quoted passage is attended to, it will be seen that the poem will come as a warning,even a kind of punishment, to a people which has broken the covenant. It will live in their minds and mouths, bringing them back, whether they like it or not, to the harsh memory of the desert sojourn. Once learned it will not easily be forgotten. The words will stick, they will be importunate, they will not let us alone.

It is worth pausing on the word *ʿēd*, "witness," a key word twice repeated in the quoted passage and twice again in the continuation (verses 26 and 28). As in Lam. 2:13, it seems to connote the actual process of poetic imagining. It is evidently related to the root *ʿûd* with the sense of "persistent repetition." It enters into the definition here as an aspect of the process of learning, of lodging the words in the memory (meaning "teach it to the children of Israel ... put it in their mouths, that this poem may be an *ʿēd*, or 'witness' "). It also seems to refer, however, to the process of the poem's evocation in the future time; it will then become a nagging presence, returning on those who have learned it with a disturbing constancy, like a revenant (for "this poem shall answer them as a witness, for it shall not be forgotten out of the mouths of their seed.")

The poem as a revenant is a concept not easily accommodated to modern poetics. It calls to mind the romantic poets' interest in the action of memory (Wordsworth, for instance, remembering the daffodils or remembering his earlier visit to Tintern Abbey, but on the whole such poetry dealt with pleasurable memories; if pain existed, the poem would help to ease that pain. The *ʿēdût* or witness function of the poem has nothing to do with the easing of pain. We have instead a disturbing shock of recognition as a remembered text comes to us charged with a new historical urgency. The *ʿēd* function means that texts from the past do not simply echo; they invade us, they demand attention. We discover that *ʿēdût* is a covenant word, a synonym for *bĕrît* itself as in the phrase *ʾărôn hāʿēdût*, "ark of the covenant." It signifies a dynamic of relationships, a bond between hearer and utterer constantly reimposed, sometimes even on an unwilling hearer. It takes the hearer back to earlier sayings, earlier encounters, recalling obligations he or she would rather forget. Like a revenant, it arrests the hearer as though to say: "You know me, I come to remind you of what you know." There is a call to remember in the following lines of the "Song of Moses": "Remember the days of old, / consider the years of many generations: / ask thy father, and he will recount it to thee / thy elders, and they will tell thee" (Deut. 32:7). In addition, a condemnation of forgetfulness is expressed: "Thou hast forgotten God that formed thee" (Deut. 32:18). The memory forced on the reader is not exactly pleasurable; it is the memory of an encounter in the wilderness: "He found him in a desert land, / and in the waste howling wilderness" (Deut. 32:10). The wilderness was the setting for the fundamental exchange of words on which the covenant was founded. Future poems will bear witness to this scene, or, rather, readers of those future poems will themselves have to bear witness to this scene.

One further implication of the notion of the reader as witness may be noted. A relationality between text and reader founded on the term *ʿēd* or *ʿēdût* suggests the relationship of litigants in a lawsuit. The reader is cast in the role alternately of witness and defendant; he or she is called on to "respond" in the special sense of a witness or litigant responding to a charge or a piece of evidence in a court of law. This is "audience response" of a particular kind.

Many images relating to justice and the administration of justice are to be found in the "Song of Moses." In Deuteronomy 32:4, we are told that "all his ways are justice." In verse 36 we are told that God will judge his people: in verse 41 his hand "takes hold on judgment"—there he is, as it were, giving sentence. Some modern students of the form-critical school have in fact related the opening verse of the poem to the *Gattung* of the lawsuit.[9] In the formula with which the poem opens, heaven and earth are called to bear witness against the people of Israel: "Give ear, O heavens, and I will speak; / and hear, O earth, the words of my mouth" (Deut. 32:1). "Hear" in the second half of that verse gives us the same stem *šĕmaʿ*, which we have already considered. The antithetical relation of text and audience is here gathered again into the root *šĕmaʿ* with a strong additional sense of "bearing witness against." To hear or read is to be confronted with such testimony. The concept of witnessing against had already been announced as part of the poem's function in the programmatic introduction of chapter 31 that we considered earlier. A later continuation of that passage reads: "Gather to me all the elders of your tribes, and your officers, that I may speak these words in their ears, and call heaven and earth to witness against them" (Deut. 31:28). The first verse of the poem represents the fulfillment of that announcement. Heaven and earth bear witness against Israel,[10] to which one must "respond." The reading of the poem thus becomes a struggle for vindication. The notion of a trial or a court of law is not a pleasing trope here as in Shakespeare's sonnet: "When to the sessions of sweet silent thought, / I summon up remembrance of things past." Instead, the words from Deuteronomy are a way of structuring the relationship between the text and the reader, or more correctly between the reader and the God who is seen to stand behind the words of the text. The *Haʾăzînû* poem, from this viewpoint, attacks and challenges the reader. Here again, however, an exchange of roles occurs. To adapt a phrase of Milton (also spoken with reference to the covenanting God of the Old Testament) the reader "judges and is judged."[11] He is a defendant, but he is also, as the poem proceeds, a "witness for the Crown." He is not only rebuked; he is also caught up in the majesty of the impeachment itself. He becomes as it were God's witness (as in Isa. 43:10) as the poem mounts to its triumphant conclusion:

> See now that I, even I, am he,
> and there is no god with me;
> I kill, and I make alive;
> I wound, and I heal;
> neither is there any that can deliver out of my hand.
> For I lift up my hand to heaven,
> and swear, as I live for ever,
> if I whet my glittering sword,
> and my hand take hold on judgment;
> I will render vengeance to my enemies,
> and will reward those who hate me. (Deut. 32:39–41).

It will be seen that in these final sentences we have not left behind the *Gattung* of the lawsuit. God is here seen raising his hand to take an oath. The reader has become a witness to that oath taking. In the oath, judgment is promised on "my enemies"—the enemies of the people who have also become God's enemies. Readers are promised that (as with Job) their judge will become their vindicator, bearing witness on their behalf in a future that is "laid up in store with me, sealed up among my treasures" (Deut. 32:34). Readers for their part will testify to the oath that they have witnessed. The poem has now become a testimony in the sense of a saving word, an affidavit, to which readers themselves are the witness. This is the sense that the verb *'ûd,* "to testify," finally comes to bear. It occurs for the last time in the short prose passage that follows the song at the end of chapter 32. There Moses says to the people: "Set your hearts to all the words which I testify *(mē'îd)* among you today . . . for it is not a vain thing for you; because it is your life: and through this word you shall prolong your days in the land, which you are going over the Jordan to possess" (Deut. 32:46–47).

Notes

1. Unless otherwise specified, the translations of the Hebrew text are taken from *The Holy Scriptures* (Koren: Jerusalem, 1969), the English text revised and edited by Harold Fisch.

2. Meir Sternberg has written perceptively of the tension between the aes-

thetic and nonaesthetic modes, or rhetoric and ideology in biblical discourse, in *The Poetics of Biblical Narrative* (Bloomington: Indiana University Press, 1985), 42 and 483–89. Although he mentions the "rough handling of the audience" by the prophet Jeremiah, his examples are almost always drawn from narrative (for instance, the story of Saul's fall in 1 Sam. 15). I am concerned here with an equal if not greater tension to be discerned in prophecy. For some apt remarks on audience-speaker conflicts in Isaiah, see also Y. Gitay, "Isaiah and His Audience," *Prooftexts* 3 (1983): 227–28.

3. Cf. S. R. Driver, *Introduction to the Literature of the Old Testament* (New York: Scribners, 1891), 497.

4. The revised standard version here, leaning on the Greek version, renders 37b as "I will let you go in by number." With a sounder instinct, the translators of New English Bible revert to the Hebrew and render the phrase as "I will . . . bring you within the bond of the covenant." It is not merely that the Hebrew original has greater authority but, in this case, the reading is supported by the wordplay *(habberit ubaroti)*, which is so essential a feature of the prophet's discourse.

5. Editors are generally insensitive to such wordplay. W. Eichrodt and W. Zimmerli consider our text here to be the result of confusion and dittography. With a finer literary instinct, the most recent editor, M. Greenberg, *Ezekiel I: The Anchor Bible* (New York: Doubleday, 1983), 373) supports the masoretic text by reference to "the high incidence of repetition and alliteration in verses 33–40."

6. Cf. Stanley E. Fish, *Is There a Text in This Class?* (Cambridge: Harvard University Press, 1980), 11.

7. Cf. Babylonian Talmud *Shabbat* 88a and parallels.

8. Such radical relativism, for instance, characterizes the hermeneutic philosophy of Hans-Georg Gadamer. (See his *Wahrheit und Methode* [Tübingen: Mohr, 1960], 159f.). He believes that no unchanging core of meaning exists, for we are inevitably caught in the historicity of our being, which is conceived not as continuity but as flux. Gadamer was arguing against the assumption of the earlier philological-historical school of German criticism, which believed in the possibility of recovering some absolute starting point (Anknüpfungspunkt) by which meaning was permanently governed. This is not what is meant here by continuity either. Moses would not have grasped Rabbi Akiba's interpretations of his book, but one would like to argue for a continuity between them nevertheless.

9. Cf. G. E. Wright, "The Lawsuit of God: A Form-Critical Study of Deuteronomy 32" in *Israel's Prophetic Heritage,* ed. B. W. Anderson and Walter Harrelson (London: SCM Press, 1962), 26–67; and G. E. Mendenhall, *Law and Covenant in Israel and the Ancient Near East* (Biblical Colloquium: Pittsburgh, 1955) 34. S. R. Driver, *The International Critical Commentary . . . On Deuteronomy* (Edinburgh: T. and T. Clark, 1895), 349, argues, however, that in Deuteronomy, chapter 32, "heavens and earth are invoked, not as witnesses, but as forming an audience."

10. In their comment on these verses, the rabbis had actually anticipated this notion of the calling of heaven and earth to witness as though in a court of law. See *Sifre,* "Haazinu," section 306.

"Give ear O heavens." R. Banaah was wont to say, when you are found guilty, only the witnesses raise their hand against him (i.e. the guilty party) as it is said, "The hand of the witnesses shall be first upon him to put him to death," (Deuteronomy 17:7), and then the others come on afterwards, as it is said, "and afterwards the hand of all the people." (ibid.). When Israel fails to carry out the will of the Omnipresent, what is said of them? "And the anger of the Lord [will] be inflamed against you, and he [will] shut up the heavens, that there be no rain." (Deuteronomy 11:17) and the rest of the punishment will come on afterwards as it said, "and you [will] perish quickly from off the good land." (ibid.). And when, conversely, Israel carries out the will of the Omnipresent, what is said of them? "And in that day, says the Lord, I will answer the heavens . . . and the earth shall answer the grain . . . and I will sow him for myself in the land." (Hosea 2:21–23)

11. J. Milton, *The Doctrine and Discipline of Divorce* in *Works,* vol. 3 (Columbia edition: New York, 1931), 440.

References

Fish, Stanely E. *Is There a Text in This Class?* Cambridge: Harvard University Press, 1980.

Gadamer, Hans-Georg. *Wahrheit und Methode.* Tübingen: Mohr, 1960.

Gitay, Y. "Isaiah and His Audience." *Prooftexts* 3 (September 1983): 223–30.

Greenberg, Moshe. Ezekiel 1. *The Anchor Bible.* New York: Doubleday, 1983.

Driver, S. R. *The International Critical Commentary: Deuteronomy.* Edinburgh: T. and T. Clark, 1895.

Mendenhall, George E. *Law and Covenant in Israel and the Ancient Near East.* Pittsburgh, Pa.: The Bible Colloquium, 1955.

Milton, John. *The Works of John Milton.* Edited by Frank A. Patterson. Vol. 3, *The Doctrine and Discipline of Divorce.* New York: Columbia University Press, 1931.

Sternberg, Meir. *The Poetics of Biblical Narrative.* Bloomington, Ind.: Indiana University Press, 1985.

The Holy Bible: Revised Standard Version. New York: Thomas Nelson, 1953.

The Holy Scriptures. The English text revised and edited by Harold Fisch. Jerusalem: Koren, 1977.

Wright, G. Ernest. "The Lawsuit of God: A Form-Critical Study of Deuteronomy 32." In *Israel's Prophetic Heritage,* edited by B. W. Anderson and Walter Harrelson, 26–67. London: SCM Press, 1962.

7

Simultaneous Reading in Hebrew Poetry: An Interpretive Strategy

Tova Cohen

The purpose of this essay is to illustrate the way in which Stanley Fish's theory of the "interpretive community" and its strategies might explain changes in modes of reception of a specific group of nineteenth-century Hebrew poems. Fish defines interpretive strategies as "the shape of reading" shared by members of specific interpretive communities. "These strategies exist prior to the act of reading and therefore determine the shape of what is read." What is significant about them, moreover, is that they "are not natural or universal, but learned." Once acquired, those same ways of interpreting "can also be forgotten or supplanted, or complicated or dropped from favor."[1]

The possibility of such changes in interpretive strategies, it will be argued here, is particularly important for an understanding of the modern perception (or misperception) of nineteenth-century Hebrew *haskalah* (Enlightenment) poetry.[2] As originally composed, that poetry demanded the activation of a particular interpretive strategy that was conventional to the interpretive community for which it was written. Subsequent extraliterary influences, however, brought about a neglect of those interpretive strategies and a consequent failure to understand the demands of the texts themselves.

In order to illustrate this argument, a particular study will be made here of the writings of two of the most important Hebrew poets of the early *haskalah* period: *Shirei Tiferet* (1789–1802), an epos describing the life of Moses composed by Naftali Herz Wessely; and a group of "philosophical poems" incorporated in *Shirei Sefat Kodesh* by Adam Ha-Kohen.[3]

Each of the poems included in this corpus opens with a reference to a biblical text. Thus, each section of *Shirei Tiferet* commences with precise references (chapter and verse) to specific passages in the Book of Exodus, whose content is parallel to that in the poem. The method employed by Adam Ha-Kohen in many of his philosophical poems is somewhat different. Almost every one of those compositions commences with a distinctive biblical epigraph, to which is appended a precise textual citation.

Notwithstanding the consistency with which both poets thus employ biblical references, their purpose in so doing has never been clarified. Probably for that reason, the purpose of the biblical texts referred to by these poets has been almost completely ignored in the standard criticisms. The biblical references, however, supplied by Wessely and Adam Ha-Kohen did not merely reflect the dry pedantry said to be typical of the *maskilim* (the enlightened). Rather, their appearances were motivated by the poets' deliberate and conscious desire to direct their audiences to the cited biblical passage in order that those passages be read simultaneously with the poems themselves. In other words, the poem calls on the reader to activate a precise interpretive strategy, which I refer to as "simultaneous reading." What have to be compared are two separate compositions: a central literary work (in this case, the poem); and a supplementary text, usually canonical (in this case, a biblical passage). The simultaneous activation of these two texts creates new intertextual patterns.[4]

What distinguishes this method from the more common use of literary allusion is the degree to which it insists on a close comparison of the poem with the parallel biblical passage. A literary allusion provides only hints of other texts, whereas simultaneous reading specifies the particular analogical passage, thus insisting that the two texts be read simultaneously. The requirement is expressed in the fact that the discovery of the supplementary text is not left to the reader's volition or made dependent on his or her education.[5] Rather, references are provided in the "reading instructions" with which each of the poems commences.

Thus placed in context, the "reading instructions" provided in the poems analyzed here can be seen to have served a distinct purpose: they were designed to activate an interpretive strategy shared by the interpretive community for which the poems were intended. Essentially, that community consisted of late eighteenth- and early nineteenth-century "enlightened" Jews living in central and eastern Europe, all of whom read Hebrew (even if they did not speak the language). This was not an entirely homogeneous group. Dividing its members were various gradations of secular education, different attitudes toward religion and the observance of religious rituals, various perceptions of the Christian and Jewish societies in

which they lived, and contrasting degrees of affiliation to the conflicting camps and parties in contemporary Jewry. Nevertheless,
what all members of this literary community shared was their
common use of the interpretive strategies that they activated when
reading a particular text. Compounded of an intense familiarity with
the Bible and its traditional Jewish commentaries, this strategy had
been imbibed at the most formative stage of their personal educa-
tions. Consequently, its essence remained with them throughout
their later lives, notwithstanding the fact that they had meanwhile
rebelled (ideologically, if not practically) against the religious dis-
positions in which it had taken root and on which they had been
reared.

In traditional Jewish society, both elementary and advanced education (as conducted first in the *heder* [Jewish elementary school]
and then in the *yeshivah* [Jewish academy for secondary or higher
learning] was based on a close reading and exegesis of two principal
religious works: the *Torah* (Pentateuch), divided into weekly por-
tions; and, above all, the *Talmud*. The study of both of these
canonical texts employed the technique of simultaneous reading.
At different stages in the educational process, the weekly
Torah-reading was studied through two such systems: the younger
children read and repeated each verse, twice in its original Hebrew
and once in its (Yiddish) translation;[6] slightly older children studied each individual verse in conjunction with its accompanying
exegesis—specifically, the commentary composed by the twelfth-
century French exegete, Rashi. From the present perspective, the
most important result of this system was that the biblical text was
never assimilated in isolation; it was always read simultaneously
with another, either a translation or a commentary. Such was also
the case with regard to the *Talmud*. Indeed, the very physical
appearance of every page of the standard editions of that work (in
which the original text is surrounded on both sides by differentiated
classes of traditional commentary) illustrates and emphasizes the
degree to which these materials are considered to be intrinsically
interdependent. Multiple "texts" are to be read simultaneously; the
understanding of one is dependent on the others.

The interpretive strategy thus deeply embedded in traditional
Jewish culture was not immediately cast aside by enlightened Jews.
On the contrary, it was transferred—even if unconsciously—to the
newer areas of intellectual endeavor, which became their principal
concerns in the period after the late eighteenth century. For members of this literary community, simultaneous reading remained
the accepted technique whereby all texts could be approached and

understood. By extension, then, it was transferred to the modern phenomenon of Hebrew poetry.

The requirement for simultaneous reading demanded by Wessely and Adam Ha-Kohen reveals some of the intertextual patterns essential to an understanding of their content. Certain layers of meaning are only hinted at in the poetic texts themselves. Indeed, a single reading of the poem, one in which the biblical parallel is not simultaneously read, would miss them altogether. Invariably, it is only when the poems are placed side by side with the biblical passages referred to in the citations that their true import is fully understood. Thus, an appreciation of the reading strategy of this particular interpretive community provides a key to the inner code of the poems and thus helps to uncover a deeper layer of their meaning.

In *Shirei Tiferet,* Wessely usually employs the technique of simultaneous reading in order to highlight the structural differences between his own modern, epic description of the life of Moses and the biblical biographical portrait. The reader is thus invited to contrast the former's plenitude of similies, together with its detailed descriptions of the thoughts of the heroes and numerous quotations from their conversations, with the laconic biblical depictions, from which such characteristically epic manifestations are notably absent.[7] Similarly, the poem also posits the possibility of the exegetical interpretation of certain tricky passages in the original text. Wessely was quite frank about his desire to provide "supplements" such as these to the biblical version of the life of Moses; indeed, he states as much in the introduction to his work.[8]

It is the activation of the technique of simultaneous reading of the two texts, however, that clarifies certain less obvious differences between them, differences that are important for an understanding of the distinctively modern character of *Shirei Tiferet* as a whole. For example, only by a close comparison of that poem with Exod. 4:24–26 can the reader appreciate the extent to which Wessely altered the biblical description of the circumcision of Moses' son. He does not explicitly criticize the violence of the account in Exodus even though, enlightened and rational, he was almost certainly offended by that aspect of the incident. Instead, he attempted to create a different, more correct, understanding of the story by composing a new version of the tale that he requires his audience to contrast with the original text. Exod. 4:24–26 relates:

At a night encampment on the way, the Lord encountered him and sought to kill him. So Zipporah took a flint and cut off her son's

foreskin, and touched his legs with it, saying, "You are truly a bridegroom of blood to me!" And when He let him alone, she added, "A
bridegroom of blood because of the circumcision."[9]

Wessely's version is:

> They came to an inn where they sought to lodge
> And to meet him the Lord sent His angel
> Who stood at the side and sought to kill him.
> Zipporah, a sensible woman, considered what to do;
> Hurried and took a sharp stone and circumcised the boy.
> At the feet of the angel as a ransom offering
> His foreskin she cast and crying out, she said:
> "For a bridegroom of blood art thou to me, O angel from above!
> Look at this blood of the Covenant, O God, and forgive me
> And on an angel on earth lay not thy hand."
> And the Lord heard, commanded, and released him.
> Then she said: "God has commanded you not to shed blood.
> To be a bridegroom of blood for circumcision you came here."[10]

The severely condensed nature of the passage from Exodus has
given rise to several attempts to explain it, differing in detail. It is
agreed, however, that the short narrative refers to an incident that
occurred on Moses' return to Egypt, on God's orders, to confront
Pharaoh. Moses is suddenly confronted by the Lord (or by an angel
of the Lord) who seeks to kill him. (Some say the child is near
death because of the father's failure.) Zipporah, realizing that the
guilt for which her husband (or her son) is in danger of his life is his
(Moses') failure to circumcise his son, promptly performs the circumcision. She then casts the foreskin at the feet of (or touches it to
the feet of) either her husband, or the angel, or the child, declaring
her understanding of what has happened. Whichever interpretation
one accepts, the three verses relate three violent acts—the sudden
seizing of Moses (or the child) who is brought to the brink of death,
Zipporah's grasping of the flintstone and swift circumcising of the
child, and her symbolic gesture of touching (or casting) the foreskin. In addition, her taunt, or accusation, is another violent act.

The extent to which Wessely transmuted the original scriptural
account is not at all apparent from a straightforward reading of his
poem (on the contrary, what then becomes most apparent is the
verbal consonance with the biblical original). It is only a close
textual comparison that reveals the degree to which Wessely's
poem alters the entire atmosphere of the Exodus passage by ex-
panding the narration from three verses to thirteen lines. This

seems to cushion, as it were, the sharpness of the act of circumcision itself. He also, by choosing one interpretation over others, modulates the story. Entirely absent is the dramatic confrontation between Zipporah and Moses, centering on the possibility that either he or the child might die. Instead, by using almost the very same words as the biblical account, Wessely transforms the scene into a moral tirade by the mother against the angel.

Adam Ha-Kohen considerably extended the application of this technique; indeed, he transformed it into an essential basis for the literary understanding of his philosophical uncertainty. Roughly one half of his "philosophical" poems (which themselves constitute one third of his entire corpus of 120 poems), open with a reference to a biblical text.[11] In each case, a comparison of the poem with the biblical passage brings into focus details whose significance could not otherwise have been appreciated. In so doing, it also clarifies the poem's confrontation with the biblical text. As much is apparent from a reading of his *Shir Ha-Ma'alot* ("Song of Degrees") with psalm 130, the biblical passage that is cited (in full) as the epigraph to that poem. It then becomes plain that the entire poem is at odds with the basic thrust of the scriptural text; it expresses the poet's opposition to the biblical outlook on the world and articulates his skepticism with regards to the possibility of untarnished religious belief. What needs to be stressed, however, is that Adam Ha-Kohen is not forthright in his manifestation of this confrontation. Indeed, its full extent does not become apparent until the two texts are systematically compared through a process of close and simultaneous reading.

At first sight, for instance, the poem *Shir Ha-Ma'alot* (Song of Degrees) has the appearance of a traditional expression of uncomplicated religious faith.[12]

1

"Out of the depths of my heart, out of depths of earth
I will call unto thee, God most high who rides upon heavens.
Hearken you who are lofty and high, attend your ears
To listen to the voice of my supplication. Spare me.

2

If God on high will mark every sin and iniquity
Can man, who has been compared to dust, stand and rise?
Can he reach your throne and heavenly circuit!
If you mark and inscribe the sins
Of man whom you have created from earth's dust
How can you declare: "Like me, he will be pure."

3

O fearful and very terrible! Can man stand before you?
Could he hear God? Could he have the strength?
That is why, O fearful one, forgiveness is with you.
And so that you may be feared, do indeed forgive.
You are fearful, but forgiving; terrible but full of mercy!
In your forgiveness, God, your awe will be established.

4

How awesome is your majesty my God! Grant me knowledge.
More than any fear known to me, you are awesome.
How merciful and gracious you are, teach me.
More than any mercy known to me, you are elevated.
Teach me to fear you to the extent of your honor
Or grant your servant your forgiveness.

5

Not you O God will mark transgression and iniquity
But my soul will watch—like those who watch
for the mornings—it will watch for salvation
It will watch and hope for your unfathomable words.
For your forgiveness my soul hopes
For with you is mercy and plenteous redemption, Selah.

6

Let Israel hope, my soul too will hope!
Have hope, my people! Together with me, God's word we shall await.
From all sins, O my soul, may you be redeemed.
He will redeem His people for foolishly they have acted.
We have hoped O God! Every spirit has hoped
And in you, O God of mercies, my heart trusts."

Adam Ha-Kohen does not expect his reader to approach this
poem as an independent text. By preceding his poem with a complete citation of psalm 130, he clearly indicates that his own work is
to be regarded as but one portion of a compounded literary system.
His "instruction" is that the audience systematically compare the
biblical and modern compositions, thereby noting the points at
which they differ in intent and meaning.
Here is the psalm in English:[13]

A song of ascents.
Out of the depths I call You, O Lord.
O Lord, Listen to my cry; let Your ears be attentive to my plea for
mercy.

If You keep account of sins, O Lord,
    Lord, who will survive?
Yours is the power to forgive so that You may be held in awe.
I look to the Lord; I look to Him; I await His word.
I am more eager for the Lord
    than watchmen for the morning,
    watchmen for the morning.
O Israel, wait for the Lord; for with the Lord is steadfast love and
    great power to redeem.
It is He who will redeem Israel from all their iniquities.

When read side by side with the biblical text, Adam Ha-Kohen's poem does indeed take on a new meaning. The psalmist version stresses the ties that bind him to his Maker, whereas the modern poet is at pains to emphasize the chasm between humans and God. Quite contrary to first impressions, his opening lines do not simply paraphrase the biblical verse ("Out of the depths I call You, O Lord"); on the contrary, he contrives to invert their meaning. He attains this effect, throughout the first stanzas, by the systematic use of contrasting physical metaphors. These emphasize the fact that although God is situated somewhere on high ("God most high"; "who rides upon heavens"), humans are confined to the lowest physical plain of existence ("the depths of the earth"; "dust of the earth"). In the original psalm, the metaphor is used in order to express the strength of the psalmist's attachment to God, with whom contact is possible even from "the depths." The modern poem, however, conveys quite the opposite feeling. Here, the physical and unbridgeable distance between humans and God becomes a metaphor for the human inability to reach, to believe in God. Only when the two texts are compared word by word does it become possible to appreciate that the biblical phrases have now become a medium for the implicit expression of the poet's crisis of faith in a deity of whose distance he is ever conscious.

A similar effect is attained at the end of the poem. Superficially, its concluding lines can be read as an expression of a simple "biblical" faith. Here too, however, a close comparison with the signposted biblical passage reveals the considerable distance in meaning separating the two texts. Psalm 130 concludes with an exhortation deeply rooted in religious certainty:

"O Israel, wait for Lord; for with the Lord is steadfast love and great
    power to redeem.
It is He who will redeem Israel from all their iniquities."

Adam Ha-Kohen's faith is far more questionable. Particularly
significant in this context is his hope (the word *yahel*, "he will hope
or await," is repeated three times) for Divine redemption. Read by
themselves, the lines that express that sentiment seem to convey a
conventional religious aspiration. That this is not the case, however,
becomes apparent when the poet's form of expression is compared
with that of the psalmist. The latter feels no need to articulate his
hope more than once; moreover, the concluding verse—the summa-
tion of the entire psalm—treats that aspiration as itself the cause of
its realization. Adam Ha-Kohen's position, by comparison, is far
more ambivalent. As we have seen, at the beginning of his poem, he
has already intimated his sense of distance from God; his concluding stanza also communicates his doubts concerning the immi-
nence of redemption. In both instances, the poet employs precisely
the same technique to convey his feelings. He shares them with his
reader by composing a poem that, although superficially congruent
with the biblical text, turns out—on closer examination—to be
entirely contrary to it in thrust and meaning. It is his biblical
epigraph, itself constituting an instruction to simultaneous reading,
which invites the reader to make precisely such a close
examination and thus to appreciate the poet's distance from the
psalm.

The argument presented here is thus twofold. First, the biblical
citations supplied by these poets constitute reading instructions
that are essential keys to the complete understanding of their compositions. Second, the choice of this distinctive method was determined by the prior existence of an interpretive strategy of
simultaneous reading shared by the interpretive community of enlightened Jews and, for that matter, by the entire interpretive community of Jewry at that time. It follows, therefore, that the reader
who would wish to appreciate the original meaning of these poems
must adopt the strategy intended by the poets themselves.

On the basis of our general knowledge of their literary habits and
conventions, we can probably presume that Wessely's and Adam
Ha-Kohen's contemporaries did indeed acknowledge the demand
for simultaneous reading. Moreover, because those readers
shared the interpretive strategy on which that demand was based, it
might also be assumed that they also activated the method when
reading the poems themselves, specifically by implementing the
signposted instructions. What subsequently transpired, however,
seems to present an outstanding example of the effect of extraliterary influences on the composition of an interpretive community
and on the reading strategies that a particular community employs.

The fact that recent generations of critics do not seem to have appreciated the importance of the reading instructions supplied by Wessely and Adam Ha-Kohen must, it seems, be attributed to the crucial shifts that during the past century have transformed the cultural ambience of their putative audiences. During the course of that period, the education of the average Hebrew reader became progressively less dependent on the system of instruction traditionally employed by eastern European Jewry. Instead, Hebrew schooling was largely based on western European approaches and methods, in which the strategy of simultaneous reading is not conventionally employed. For that reason, the particular demands required by that strategy have become less easily assimilated and, specifically, have also become less frequently adhered to in the reading of the corpus of Hebrew Enlightenment poetry.

Hebrew speaking audiences have become less sensitive to the reading strategies adopted by the interpretive community in which Hebrew Enlightenment poetry was written. Perhaps the most obvious consequence of this process is that modern Hebrew readers have failed to appreciate the full meaning of the poems. Within the contemporary world of Hebrew literary criticism it has also generated a further misperception regarding the general character of these poems. Both Wessely and Adam Ha-Kohen, it has been suggested, adopted a "naive" (or, at least, uncritical) attitude toward the Bible.[14]

This essay has attempted to demonstrate the extent to which that generalization is out of place. An analysis of *Shirei Tiferet* and of *Shir ha-Ma'alot* (to which can be added many other examples), does not reveal the existence of a naive attitude toward the Bible; on the contrary, those poems posit a distinct confrontational posture, which becomes explicit once a textual comparison is made of the contrasts between the poems themselves and the scriptural passages with which they are meant to be compared. Furthermore, a study of these writings reveals that they do contain a distinct ideological message. Its essence consists of a perception of the gulf separating the biblical from the modern person and an emphasis on the problems of faith that confront the latter. The poems of Wessely and Adam Ha-Kohen do not, in sum, constitute an extension of the traditional Jewish approach to the Bible. On the contrary, their confrontation with Scripture deserves to be considered the opening salvo in the Enlightenment's campaign against the thrust of that text, a campaign that was to reach its apogee in the militantly antireligious poems composed by Y. L. Gordon during the last third of the nineteenth century.

The ways in which Wessely and Adam Ha-Kohen differed from later Enlightenment poets, it has been suggested here, was less in the matter of their writings than in the manner in which they encoded their messages and provided instructions for its understanding. Like all enlightened Jews of their generation, they found themselves situated in the dangerous borderlands between the old and the new. Possibly for that reason, they sought a means of conveying a revolutionary message without needing to articulate it explicitly. In the technique of simultaneous reading they found a sophisticated manner of doing so. By placing those poets within the context of their own specific interpretive community, the modern reader can appreciate both the origins of their demand for the technique and the purpose of that requirement.

Notes

1. S. Fish, "Interpreting the 'Variorum,'" in *Is There A Text in This Class?* (Boston: Harvard University Press, 1980), 168–73. Fish himself provided an analysis of the means whereby change occurs in the perceptions and strategies of "interpretive communities" in his lecture to the Bar-Ilan conference. There he noted that change "cannot be formalized, but neither is it mysterious. One can at least attempt to understand it case by case, that is, by the patient historical reconstruction of its conditions." This essay attempts to provide one such illustration.

2. The term is used to describe a major movement in Hebrew literature and thought, mainly in Germany, Austria, and Russia, dating from 1780 until 1880. Principal among the ideological features of the *haskalah* were the composition of secular literature, the demand for a change in internal Jewish life, and the effort to attain political emancipation. The poets discussed in this essay are the principal figures of the first, "neoclassical" phase of the movement.

3. Naftali Herz Wessely (1725–1805) is conventionally regarded as the *haskalah*'s first major poet. He was a member of a literary circle that gathered around Moses Mendelssohn in Berlin during the 1870s. He was principally famous as a Hebrew linguist, exegete, and essayist. He did not publish the first part of *Shirei Tiferet* until he was almost 60 years old.

Adam (short for Avraham Dov Mikaelishuk [Lebenson]) ha-Kohen was the principal *haskalah* poet in Lithuania during the first half of the nineteenth century. He was no less famous as a linguist than as a poet.

4. For a fuller discussion of this concept see my article, "Ha-Keriyah ha-Simultanit—Tekhnikat mafteah le-havenat ha-imut im ha-tanakh be-shirat Adam Ha-Kohen," in *Mekhkerei Yerushalaim Be Sifrut Ivrit* (Jerusalem: 1985), 71–89.

5. My definition of allusion is based on Z. Ben-Porat, "The Poetics of Literary Allusion," *PTL* 1 (January 1976). In that article, the "activations" generated by allusions are classified in four phases, of which the first two depend on the reader's volition and education: phase 1—"recognition of a marker in a given text"; and phase 2—"identification of the evoked text."

6. This method was a European adaptation of the older injunction, originally

formulated in the third century of the common era: *shenayim mikra ve-echad targum,* with the translation being given in Aramaic.

7. For a discussion of the contrasts between the epic and biblical styles, see: E. Auerbach, "Odysseus' Scar," in *Mimesis: The Representation of Reality in Western Literature* (Princeton: Princeton University Press, 1953), 3–23.

8. In his introduction (entitled *"Petihat Ha-Meshorer"*), Wessely defines "good poetry" and its foundations, and also sets out his own aims in *Shirei Tiferet.* Among the latter, he specifies the exegesis of the biblical text and the addition to it of conversations that are not explicitly cited in Scriptures.

9. The Jewish Publication Society translation, 1962.

10. "The Sixth Poem," in *Shirei Tiferet* (Lemberg, 1844), 51–52, my translation.

11. See, e.g., the poems: "Higayon La-Erev" (compare with Ps. 104); "La-Boker Rinah" (cf. Job 38); "Ha-Aviv" (cf. Ps. 104); "Yom Ha-Shem Ha-Gadol" (Gen. 29); Ha-meshorer" (Ps. 5, Eccles. 3).

12. *Shirei Sefat Kodesh* (Vilna, 1870), part 2, 39–41. The translation is my own. As far as possible, an attempt has been made to adhere to the biblical language the poet purposely used in order to relate his poem to the biblical source. In several places it has been necessary to give a concrete meaning to language that is deliberately obscure.

13. The Jewish Publication Society translation, 1962.

14. Y. Klausner, *Historiyah Shel ha-Sifrut ha-Ivrit ha-Hadashah* (Jerusalem, 1952), 1:145. See also N. H. Rosenblum, *Ha-Epos ha-Mikra'ie me-Idan ha-Haskalah ve-ha-Parshanut* (Jerusalem, 1983), 13–16.

References

Auerbach, Erich. *Mimesis: The Representation of Reality in Western Literature.* Princeton: Princeton University Press, 1971.

Ben-Porat, Z. "The Poetics of Literary Allusion." *PTL* 1, (January 1976): 105–28.

Cohen, Tova. "Ha-Keri'ah ha-Simultanit—Tekhnikat mafteah le-havenat ha-imut im ha-tanakh be-shirat Adam Ha-Kohen." *Mekhkerei Yerushalaim Be-Sifrut Ivrit* 7. (Jerusalem: 1985): 71–89.

Fish, Stanley. *Is There a Text in This Class?* Cambridge: Harvard University Press, 1980.

Ha-Kohen, Adam. *Shirei Sefat Kodesh.* Vilna, 1870.

Wessely, Naftali Herz. *Shirei Tiferet.* Lemberg, 1844.

Part III
Resistance to Reading: Case Studies

8

Hebraisms as Metaphor in Kadya Molodowsky's "Froyen-lider I"

Kathryn Hellerstein

Reader-response theories have shown how a reader helps to create meaning in a text and how authors shape a reader's participation in the creation of meaning.[1] A common means by which an author will urge the reader to participate is by placing gaps or signals in the text to interrupt the process of reading. The Yiddish poet, Kadya Molodowsky (1894–1975),[2] by interrupting one linguistic pattern with another, creates a metaphor that bears thematically on an essential interpretation of her text. In this essay I will explore the disruptive power of a series of Hebraic words set crucially into one of her Yiddish poems.

In themselves, Hebraisms in Yiddish are neither rare nor unusual. Yiddish is a Germanic language with a rich vocabulary from Hebrew and Aramaic, the Slavic and Romance languages, and others; approximately 15 percent of Yiddish words have Hebraic roots. Many of these Hebraisms are integrated into common Yiddish usage, and certainly were part of the ordinary vocabulary of Yiddish speakers in Vilna and Warsaw, where Molodowsky's poem was published in 1927.[3] Despite their commonness, Molodowsky selects and places Hebraisms in a significant configuration so that, in one particular poem, they appear to the reader as signposts calling attention to themselves. In this poem, language itself becomes a metaphor.

"Froyen-lider [Songs of women] I" is the first in a sequence of eight poems in which a young Jewish woman, troubled by her modernity—Molodowsky's persona—speaks about her visions in the night. I will quote the poem in its entirety, first in transliteration, then in my translation:

es veln di froyen fun unzer mishpokhe baynakht in khaloymes mir
    kumen un zogn:

mir hobn in tsnies a loytere blut iber doyres getrogn,
tsu dir es gebrakht vi a vayn a gehitn in koshere kelers
fun unzere hertser.

un eyne vet zogn:
ikh bin an agune geblibn ven s'zenen di bakn
tsvey roytlekhe epl af boym nokh geshtanen,
un kh'hob mayne tseyner di vayse tsekritst in di aynzame nekht fun
        dervartung.

un ikh vel di bobes ankegn geyn zogn:
vi herbstike vintn yogn nokh mir zikh
nigunem farvelkte fun ayere lebns.
un ir kumt mir ankegn,
vu id gas iz nor tunkl,
un vu s'ligt nor a shotn.

un tsu vos ot dos blut on a tumah
s'zol zayn mayn gevisn, vi a zaydener fodim
af mayn moyekh farbundn,
un mayn lebn an oygeflikt blat fun a seyfer
un di shure di ershte farrisn?

The women of our family will come to me in dreams at night and say:
In virtue we carried a pure blood through the generations,
We brought it to you, like a guarded wine in the kosher cellars
Of our hearts.

And one will say:
I was left an abandoned wife when my cheeks were
Two reddish apples still on the tree
And I clenched my white teeth in the lonely nights of expectation.

And I will go to meet the grandmothers, saying:
The withered melodies of your lives
Chase after me like autumn winds.
And you come to meet me
Wherever the street is dark,
And wherever there's a shadow.

And why shall this blood without impurity
Be my conscience, like a silken thread
Bound on my brain,
And my life a page plucked from a holy book,
The first line torn?

"Froyen-lider I" is divided into two parts: an account of a vision and the seer's refusal to accept it. In the first part (lines 1–8), the speaker sees a vision of her female ancestors who come to her exhorting her to keep her virtue. The last of these women is an *agune,* a woman whose husband has abandoned her or disappeared without granting her a divorce. Because it is unknown whether or not her husband is alive (in which case the woman is still married to him), and because, according to Jewish law, a woman cannot initiate a divorce, the *agune* is caught in the bind of being unable to remarry and yet husbandless. Jewish law traditionally defines a woman by her marital and reproductive status. The *agune,* then, has come to symbolize the most extreme helplessness of a Jewish woman. In this poem, the *agune* comes to the speaker to tell her how she has adhered to her helplessness, thereby exemplifying the victimization of a woman by Jewish law. In the second part of the poem (lines 9–19), the speaker goes forth to confront her female ancestors, in order to challenge the applicability of these laws and the precedent of their adherence to these laws to her own life. In sum, then, "Froyen-lider I" presents a young woman who feels burdened by Jewish restriction of women, a tradition that she angrily confronts but from which she cannot shake herself loose. The poem ends on a question, offering neither closure nor resolution. Like an *agune,* the speaker seems caught in a bind; she is suspended between adhering to and relinquishing tradition.

How does one characterize the pattern that the Hebraic words form in relation to the "plot" of the poem that I have sketched? What does this pattern add to the reading of the poem? The following analysis of the Hebraic words will show how, although the poem is left "open" or unresolved on the existential level or "plot," it finds resolution and closure on the poetic level. Through the extended metaphor of Hebraisms, the crisis of the woman—a dramatized narrator—becomes the crisis of the poet—a dramatized author.[4] By conflating the drama of sexuality with a pattern of textuality, Molodowsky brings the poem to a close linguistically, and opens the way for the remaining poems in the sequence to address the problem of women and poems.

In dreams at night, the speaker's female forebears announce to her across the generations the inheritance they have bequeathed her (lines 1–4). This inheritance is "the pure blood" of family lineage, preserved and passed on like wines prepared according to the laws of *kashrut* (the Jewish dietary laws). In the first two lines, four Hebraic words appear: *mishpokhe* (family), *kholomes* (dreams), *tsnies* (virtue), and *doyres* (generations). *Kholomes* provides the occasion for the poem, the speaker's dreams of her female ancestors. *Mishpokhe* and *doyres* set up the linear, temporal relations of the speaker to these women through her family in the present and past generations. *Tsnies* introduces the central issue of the poem. This last word has a range of meanings: modesty, virtue, chastity, which in Yiddish, is applied almost exclusively in reference to women. The connotations of sexual purity in *tsnies* are important to acknowledge here, for these "songs of women" present the lives of women defined sexually by both nature and by Jewish law, as well as the conflicts these definitions create for the poet.

The word *koshere* appears in line 3, modifying *kelers* (cellars) in a simile that develops over the enjambment to the fourth lines: "in the kosher cellars / Of our hearts." Through the word *koshere,* the pure blood of generations connotes the blood of animals slaughtered according to Jewish law, in a *kosher* way, and is compared through a simile to wine prepared and stored in observance of the law as well. Molodowsky's way is to compound metaphor with simile to charge the speaker's voice with the tension of aggregate figures that work against each other, forcing the poem onward while barring its progress.

"Blood" develops in these lines from the abstract blood of pure lineage into a sexually charged image of bodily blood, which leads synecdochically to the blood of the heart, the blood of pure womanhood. Through this developing figure, blood itself is likened to the virtue inherent in a ritually correct way of living. The word "blood" suggests here the blood of menstruation, which, according to Jewish law, is impure. A *niddah,* or a menstruant woman, is literally "excluded" from sexual and other physical contact until she undergoes the ritual purification.[5] These laws of prohibition and purification, initially stated in Lev. 15:19–30, are elaborated extensively in the *Mishnah* and in subsequent rabbinic law.[6] Molodowsky's image of blood conveyed through the bodies of women conflates the pure blood of *tsnies,* a symbol of modest virtue that a woman deliberately maintains, with the inherent quality of impurity in the actual blood of menstruation, over which a woman has no control. Implied here is a contradiction between what a woman does and what she is. The female ancestors euphemize their adherence to the laws by describing their blood as kept *"in tsnies,"* in virtue; later in the poem, the speaker refers in a derisive tone to their blood *"on a tumah"* (line 15), without an impurity. The Hebraic word *tumah,* denoting the many kinds of Levitical uncleanness,[7] calls to mind in this context the laws restricting the *niddah.*[8]

The ritual cleanness and chastity of the speaker's female progenitors place a burden on the speaker of the poem to continue in their virtuous ways (lines 5–8). The Hebraism, *agune,* exemplifies the extremity of that burden (line 6). According to Jewish law, which values and commands the sexual productivity of a woman in marriage, the *agune* is in the worst dilemma of the tradition, a woman who is legally prohibited from functioning as a woman.[9] Because the Hebrew root of the word *agune* means literally "bound" or "anchored," a woman designated by this word is literally in a bind, and must remain chaste, despite her youth, need, or desire. The untenable position of this faithful woman is the strongest occasion for the poet's outrage. What provokes outrage in these lines is how the *agune* epitomizes sexual frustration: her cheeks are like ripe apples, but her teeth are clenched in the nights of expectation.

The metaphor of the *agune's* cheeks as unbitten fruit makes her an object of desire, seen from without. Those cheeks are reddened by the flush or flux of blood beneath the skin. Within them, the image of her own teeth closed rather than opened in expectation, reveals the subject's experiential bind of desiring. The apples are ripe; she cannot bite. The question arises, what is she unable to bite, herself? As this figure of speech unfolds syntactically, it comes to refer disturbingly to the *agune* as both object and subject of desire. Moreover, with her teeth clenched, the *agune* cannot talk to protest her situation in words. Molodowsky's device encapsulates in language the tension between what was expected externally of the generations of women in Judaism and what women themselves, represented by the extreme situation of the *agune,* experienced as a consequence of that tradition. This tension is the culmination of the vision in the first part of the poem.

In the second part of the poem, the speaker goes out to meet the vision (lines 9–19). She resists the *agune's* example of virtuous adherence, of silence, by initiating an accusation. The first Hebraic word here, *nigunem,* denotes holy songs, melodies that joyously rejuvenate a singer who voices belief. Yet in these lines, *nigunem* are a metaphor for the lives of old women, withered like autumn leaves. This figure of speech (lines 10–11) opens into a reading of articulation. The *nigunem farvelkte,* "withered melodies," bring together culture and nature, song and silence. In this metaphor, the melodies of Jewish culture sing, but devastatingly for the lives of women. The women wither away, according to the rhythms of the natural world beyond Jewish tradition. Those rhythms of nature are both outward—the chronology of the seasons—and inward—the biological rhythms of the female body.

In the phrase in line 9, *ankegn geyn zogn,* "go against/opposite to say," the speaker will confront the generations of the past that try to restrict her in the present. This confrontation however, is undermined by the dynamics of what she goes on to say (lines 10–14): the lives of the grandmothers *yogn nokh mir zikh,* chase after her into the dark places. Withered melodies, autumn winds, and shadows are the meager legacy of obedient chastity. Yet this heritage takes on a peculiar power against the active, seeking, unchaste modern woman. It transforms her initial accusation into an accusing question.

This question gathers force over the last five lines. These lines (15–19) contain a cluster of Hebraisms that have special significance. The first of these is *tumah,* in the phrase, *on a tumah,* without impurity. The meaning of this word can be further refined. Specifically, in Hebrew and Yiddish, *tumah* denotes the Levitical ritual impurities, of which the blood of a *niddah* is one. In Yiddish, *tumah* also refers to a larger, more general sense of impurity or blemish. Initially, my translation "without impurity" alludes to the first lines of the poem. The phrase, *blut on a tumah,* blood without impurity, redesignates, with an emphasis on the negative, the pure blood of lineage in the generations of women in the past, evoked in line 2. Such blood defined as pure must be other than the impure blood of menses and childbirth. How, though, can a lineage of women not include the blood of the womb? Perhaps this phrase for blood without a blemish suggests women who do not menstruate, who, according to the Levitical definition, are sexually not women. We might be tempted to think of these "unwomanly" women as the *alte bobes,* old grandmothers whose fecundity has passed. Molodowsky, however, keeps this figure general, impersonal, and unspecified. *Blut on a tumah* connotes more ambiguous feelings on the part of the speaker than the derogatory reference in previous lines to old women. Her empathy for the young *agune* disallows the speaker a simple dismissal of women who were once young. The speaker herself cannot shake off the old ways. The power of nature's blood and the cultural concept of impurity hold her. Subsequently, the Levitical sense of *tumah,* impurity, refers to the *agune*'s silent submission to and the poet's articulate rebellion against the traditional laws that govern or constrict a woman's sexuality.

The next word in this culminating question is *moyekh,* the brain bound by a silken thread. The *fodem,* or thread, is a contradictory hidden metaphor for the assonant *odern,* or veins conducting blood in the brain; the silken thread constricts or "binds" *(farbundn)* the brain. To follow out the logic of these figures, if blood is a thread and life is a book, then the cutting of the silken thread looses the page from its binding and lets the blood from the body. This double release should imply deracination and death. Instead, the letting of *tsniesdike blut* allows for the desires of the body to assert themselves against the text that has restrained them. At once the speaker experiences loss and freedom.

The thread bound on the brain also suggests the *t'fillin,* small boxes enclosing handwritten verses from the Bible on parchment, which a man binds to his brow and left forearm with leather thongs. If *t'fillin* bind a man to God as he prays, the silken thread binds this woman restrictively to a tradition written by men. The next Hebraic word, *seyfer,* a religious book from which one studies, carries the metaphor of binding still further. In the penultimate line of the poem, *seyfer* establishes two significant patterns. First, the Hebraic word refers the reader back to the other Hebraic words in the poem, *koshere, agune, tsnies, nigunem, tumah,* which denote or connote the holy books interpreting the biblical and talmudic laws by which the generations of women preceding the speaker lived. The *seyfer* itself is the book from which the words of sexual restriction come, the text to which the *nigun* or melody of the women's lives is set. Second, in the likening of life and book, the speaker's life, still composed of the traditional text, has been ripped from its context. The first line of the holy writing is *farrisn,* damaged, made impure, perhaps obscured, but still intact. The ambiguity of the word *farrisn* in this context (which means to lift with a jerk, smudge, or, loosely, to tear)[10] can be tentatively understood from its sound and the rhythm of the line, which echo the sound *(tsekritst)* and rhythms in lines 7–8, conveying the clenched teeth of the *agune.* The sounds establish a correspondence between the closed mouth of the *agune* and the opened page of the speaker. Although the speaker's life has been severed from the holy book of tradition and laws that bound the preceding generations of women, the substance of her life consists of that book's language.

On the existential level, then, the poem ends with a paradox. Ironically, though, the paradox of the speaker's situation is resolved in the poem's figurative language. The disparity between the situational and linguistic closures is seen in the last Hebraic word, *shure* (line 19). This word denotes a line or row, here a line of writing, and forms a figure for the speaker's life that includes a verse from both a traditional Hebrew text and a modern Yiddish poem. In Hebrew, from the rabbinic period on, *shure* refers to a row or line (of objects or men, for example) and also occurs in a context of law and justice, as in *kashurah* (according to rule or rule of conduct) or *shurat ha-*

din (the strict law, justice), as well as to lines of words or print.[11] In modern Yiddish, *shure* is defined neutrally as a row or line, and can refer to a line of print in a book or to a line of a poem.[12] Occurring in the final line of Molodowsky's poem, the word *shure* points the reader toward both the charged Hebrew connotations of law and the neutral Yiddish denotation of a line of print. This duality directs the reader simultaneously to follow the opposing texts of the law and the heart, and, in doing so, catches the reader in the same dilemma as the *agune*, the dramatized narrator of the poem and the implied author herself. The line of the holy book and the line of the poem are joined in the word *shure*, and together they serve as a figurative representation of the divided life of the speaker, who is both *froy* and *lid*, a woman and a text.

Even on the poetic level, this closure might not be worked out entirely to a reader's satisfaction. In the subsequent poems of the sequence, Molodowsky attempts to address the speaker's question, yet she never actually settles the ambivalent exchange between tradition and modernity in "Froyen-lider." This very issue gave her poetry impetus throughout Molodowsky's long career. Although, as I have shown, the first and second parts of this poem—the speaker's vision and her accusation—are parallel, they never really "talk" to each other. Readers, though, can find a point at which to settle, returning to the word *shure*, if they take it to refer to the string of Hebraisms that Molodowsky has set out in the poem. This vertical line of words establishes an internal continuity for readers, a linguistic metaphor. We usually think of metaphors in poems as new, unusual, and original figures. Clichés, after all, are "dead" metaphors. In this poem, however, the Hebraisms that lend themselves to a metaphorical reading are ordinary words in the Yiddish language. Simply through their Hebraic etymology in the Yiddish context, they extend a metaphor that draws attention to the clash of values within which this poet endeavored to write.

Notes

1. This essay, first presented at the Conference on Figurative and Visionary Language, Lechter Institute for Literary Research, Bar-Ilan University, May 22–25, 1986, expands on one section of my longer essay, " 'A Word for My Blood': A Reading of Kadya Molodowsky's 'Froyen-lider' (Vilna, 1927)."

2. Molodowsky, an extraordinary writer of poetry and prose in Yiddish, was best known to her contemporaries for her children's poems and the journal she edited in New York for two decades, *Sviva*.

3. "Froyen-lider, I–VIII," in *Kheshvandike Nekht: Lider* (Vilna: B. Kletskin, 1927), 11–19. All translations are mine.

4. Wallace Martin, *Recent Theories of Narrative* (Ithaca: Cornell University Press, 1986), 154.

5. For a clear explication of the laws of the menstruant, see Rachel Biale, *Women and Jewish Law: An Exploration of Women's Issues in Halakhic Sources* (New York: Schocken, 1984), 147–74.

6. Herbert Danby, trans., *Mishnah*, 12th ed. (Oxford: Oxford University Press, 1977), 745–57. (Niddah, Tohoroth.)

7. Marcus Jastrow, *Sefer Milim: A Dictionary of the Targum, the Talmud Babli and Yerushalmi, the Midrashic Literature*, 2 vols. (reprint, Israel: 1970), 1:524.

8. For a controversial semiotic reading from a feminist perspective of the biblical ideas of impurity as "subordinating maternal power . . . to symbolic order as pure logical order regulating social performance, as divine Law attended to in the Temple," see Julia Kristeva, "Semiotics of Biblical Abomination," in *Powers of Horror: An Essay on Abjection,* trans. Leon S. Roudiez (New York: Columbia University Press, 1982), 90–112.

9. *Women and Jewish Law,* Biale, 102–13. *Mishnah,* Yebamoth 15:1–10 and 3–4, "Sisters-in-law."

10. Uriel Weinreich, *Modern English-Yiddish Yiddish-English Dictionary* (New York: YIVO and McGraw-Hill, 1968), 468. The verb *farraysn* (past participle *farrisn*) means to lift (with a jerk) or to perk up (nose). The verb *farrisn* means to smudge with soot. The adjective *farrisn* means haughty, stuck up. The exact nature of the damage done to the *shure* is ambiguous in Molodowsky's choice of words. Adrienne Rich translates *farrisn* very freely, though onomatopoetically, as "and part of the first line is missing." See Kadya Molodowsky, "Women Songs 1," in *A Treasury of Yiddish Poetry,* ed. Irving Howe and Eliezer Greenberg (New York: Holt Rinehart and Winston, 1972) 284.

11. See Reuben Alcalay, *The Complete Hebrew-English Dictionary* (Jerusalem: Massada, 1975), 2575. Also see Even-Shoshan, *Hamilon hehadash* (Jerusalem: Kiryat Sefer, 1981); and Jastrow, *Sefer Milim,* Jastrow defines *shure* as chain, line, or row, and notes the idiom, *lifn in mishurat hadin,* beyond strict law, an exception to the rule.

12. See Weinreich, *Modern Dictionary,* 468; and Alexander Harkavay, *Yidish-english hebreyisher verterbukh,* 3d ed. (New York: Hebrew Publishing Company, 1928), Weinreich and Harkavy do not specify the usage of *shure* (row or line) for written or printed texts. Yehoash and Khayim Spivak, *Yidish verterbukh: ale hebreyishe (un khaldeyishe) verter . . .* (New York: Farlag Veker, 1926), however, give one definition, *a tseyle fun a bukh* (a line from a book). In the late 1970s, I heard the Yiddish poet Malka Heifetz Tussman use the word *shure* frequently to refer to a line of poetry or a verse.

References

Alcalay, Reuben. *The Complete Hebrew-English Dictionary.* Jerusalem: Massada, 1975.

Biale, Rachel. *Women and Jewish Law: An Exploration of Women's Issues in Halakhic Sources.* New York: Schocken, 1984.

Even-Shoshan. *Hamilon he-hadash.* Jerusalem: Kiryat Sefer, 1981.

Harkavy, Alexander. *Yidish-english-hebreyisher verterbukh* (Yiddish-English-Hebrew dictionary). 3rd ed. New York: Hebrew Publishing Company, 1928.

Hellerstein, Kathryn. "A Word for my Blood: A Reading of Kadya Molodowsky's *'Froyen-lider'* (Vilna, 1927)." *Association for Jewish Studies Review* 13 (Fall, 1988).

Jastrow, Marcus. *A Dictionary of the Targumim, etc.* New York: (n.p.), 1903.

Jastrow, Marcus. *Sefer Milim: A Dictionary of the Targum, the Talmud Babli and Yerushalmi, the Midrashic Literature.* Israel: (n.p., n.d.); reprint, 1970.

Kristeva, Julia. "Semiotics of Biblical Abomination." In *Powers of Horror: An Essay on Abjection,* translated by Leon S. Roudiez, 90–112. New York: Columbia University Press, 1982.

Martin, Wallace. *Recent Theories of Narrative.* Ithaca: Cornell University Press, 1986.

Mishnah, 12th ed. Translated by Herbert Danby. D. D. Oxford: Oxford University Press, 1977.

Molodowsky, Kadya. *"Froyen-lider,* I-VIII" (Songs of women). In *Kheshvndike nekht: lider* (Nights of Heshvan: poems), 11–19. Vilna: B. Kletskin, 1927.

Molodowsky, Kadya. "Women Songs 1," translated by Adrienne Rich. In *A Treasury of Yiddish Poetry,* edited by Irving Howe and Eliezer Greenberg, 284. New York: Holt Rinehart and Winston, 1972.

Weinreich, Uriel. *Modern English-Yiddish Yiddish-English Dictionary.* New York: YIVO and McGraw Hill, 1968.

Yehoash and Dr. Khayim Spivak. *Yidish verterbukh: ale hebreyishe (un khaldeyishe) verter . . .* (Yiddish dictionary: all the Hebrew [and Chaldean] words . . .). New York: Farlag Veker, 1926.

9

Melville's Dansker: The Absent Daniel in *Billy Budd*

Sharon Baris

Beginning with the hero of *Typee* and on through the adventurers of *Redburn, Israel Potter,* and the main characters of *Benito Cereno* and of *Moby-Dick,* Melville's seekers are fascinated by odd languages, symbols, knots, guidebooks, and hieroglyphics that demand deciphering. Even landlocked Bartleby and the lawyer share a concern with proofreading the world they know. Pierre is the ultimate quester for meanings of signs or portraits, and *The Confidence Man* presents a veritable mute whose hand writes on the slate, for all to understand. So it is that in Melville's early novel *Mardi,* when Taji and others set out on a journey, Taji enacts a prototypical scene as he discovers a sailors' chest that is covered "all over" with "inscriptions and carving . . . mystic diagrams . . . and prophecies." Faced with this object, Taji expresses the mood of all those wanderers and questers in Melville's fictions who are intrigued to know the "signs and wonders" of the universe: "Your old tars are all Daniels!" Taji exuberantly exclaims.[1]

The handsome sailor at the center of Melville's last novel *Billy Budd, Sailor (An Inside Narrative)* is not, however, engaged by the problem of signs; Billy is a central figure who is not a Melvillian quester for meanings.[2] He is a tar who distinctly is not a Daniel. Although Billy seems puzzled by Claggart's attitude toward him, and although Billy wonders "What could it mean?" when he talks to the wise Dansker, Billy learns nothing at all about hidden meanings, and the narrator then comments: "Experience is a teacher indeed; yet did Billy's years make his experience small" (86). The world of *Billy Budd,* nevertheless, is full of significances that the other characters do try to unravel. Responses, reactions, reports are prevailing activities for the other sailors in this story, and everyone else from Vere to Albert participates in a widespread system of shared significations. Billy's insensitivity to polysemy thus makes him different, and when the narrator comments, "To deal in double meanings and insinuations of any sort was quite foreign to his nature" (49), we are apprised of a major distinction between Billy and the questing Daniels in Melville's fiction.

Billy Budd as a novel does require the action of an interpretive Daniel, as I will argue. For although Billy himself cannot deal in meanings, this inside narrative dramatizes the disturbing and contradictory demands interpreters must face within Melville's story, as actions of exegesis are widely dispersed among many characters. Because Billy cannot be a judgmental figure, we wonder who will fill that role instead; if Billy is not a Daniel, moreover, we may also wonder why. Finally, although Melville's fiction foregrounds problems of interpretive strategy that are challenging and pertinent to modern study of critical theory, the novel's ragged edges may provide Melville's own painful message about that most difficult and uncertain process of reading texts, signs, and wonders, the universe.

To begin, one can recognize two contrasting reasons within this story for Billy's famous verbal lack; two discrete and fundamental arguments can be mounted for understanding Billy. On the one hand Billy serves as the text or "signal object" (43) the sailors are moved to read; he becomes a kind of hieroglyphic device to arouse the others' Daniel-like curiosity. Presented as voiceless, Billy is not required to enter into the interpretive activity shared by the others. Any weaknesses are accorded to their responses; so if Billy dies, it is their fault for having misread him.

Billy, on the other hand, is not only an object at which the others look. Melville presents Billy as a young man with volitions, fears, and secrets of his own. Unlike a voiceless whale, Billy is a person who can speak out; this is the problem behind Billy's stutter. Charles Olson has claimed, "The stutter is the plot" of this novel,[3] and accordingly it is possible to see Billy not only as a text but also as an interpreter whose will and actions matter. If Billy fails, then it may be that he is a kind of imperfect reader.

Melville's performance in presenting Billy as a character who both reads and is read seems modern. If we consider the strategies allegorized among the fictional readers of Billy, we see how some characters employ methods that consume the text, whereas Billy's illiteracy shows quite the opposite attitude: his insistence on some unmediated truth allows for no reading process at all. Between these two stances, then, Melville recognizes a quarrel embedded in all acts of interpretation, and I will argue that similarities exist between the strategies *Billy Budd* dramatizes, and those approaches to texts and readers explored in theoretical essays of the 1980s. Stanley Fish, for example, has provided a convenient survey of problems recently considered. Fish's essay, entitled "With the Compliments of the Author: Reflections on Austin and Derrida," was published in 1982, just about ninety years after *Billy Budd;* yet the theories presented by Fish are remarkably parallel to those worked out in Melville's fiction. I suggest, therefore, that Fish's essay serve as a useful reference point for our discussion of Melville's insights challengingly expressed nearly a century before.[4]

Tracing the outlines of the novel with the premises stated in this *Critical Inquiry* essay in mind, we see that both begin by positing some ideal interpretive condition. Melville's story opens in a kind of Golden Age, a prior world where the signal object—the Handsome Sailor or sculptured Bull—is an admired or even adored object before whom "the faithful prostrated themselves" (43, 44). The mood of silent worship is carried over throughout section 1 to Billy himself aboard the first ship, *Rights-of-Man*. Here Billy is encircled by the others as they flock to him like "hornets to treacle" (47). He is the peacemaker for whom all show their kinds of honest homage, as they express their adoration by ceremonies of washing, darning, and almost sacramental rites of tribute.

But what is the excellence of this Golden Era in terms of reading Billy? Modern theorists, too, discuss some optimal context that is risk free for communication; this world would be a place where interpretation would not be necessary, as noted in Derrida's critique of the Western philosophy of "presence." Arguing his case, indeed (as Fish's survey observes), Derrida uses such words as "centered" or "anchored" to convey some hypothetical sense of fixed and determined meanings.[5] With uncanny similarity, the first part of *Billy Budd* shows similar felicitous preinterpretive conditions. The first ship is a homeward-bound vessel, moving toward an anchored condition. On that ship Billy is literally centered, because he is circled about by an admiring crew. Language is scarcely needed, as Captain Graveling observes: "Not that he preached to them or said or did anything in particular; but a virtue went out of him, sugaring the sour ones" (47). The sailors on their side, in Graveling's words, take to him; they express their reactions in a total, communal worship.

The only interfering character, Red Whiskers, provides a significant disturbance. Whiskers tries to poke, jab, or approach Billy-the-text in an overly familiar, even extremely responsive method (47). Whiskers's cutting and digging, his butcherlike aspects, are important, and they later are echoed in more drastic ways throughout the book. If Billy is to be worshipped single, whole, absolute, then Billy is not subject to what Derrida calls iterations or versions of the original. For to repeat, inevitably, is to render in part, or to cut up. Melville probes the theological essence of Billy's first self-presence or privileged position when he gives Whiskers a dumb-show drama in which to act the role of a New Testament figure, a Doubting Thomas. As Thomas wished to lay hands on the holy savior, so Whiskers similarly tries to make contact by jabbing Billy's side. He attempts to violate Billy's theoretical absolute identity, even as Thomas doubted Christ's inviolate self.[6] Billy's retributive strike, like Christ's rebuke, is against such doubt because he must be known, in Fish's terms, "directly, simply" as himself. Citing Derrida's "logic that ties repetition to alterity," Fish goes on to quote another modern theorist, Samuel Weber, using words that now seem especially appropriate to Melville's presentation of Billy's case: "If something must be iterable in order to become an object of consciousness, then it can never be entirely grasped, having already been split in and by its being repeated."[7]

It is this link between interpretation, doubt, and butchery as argued by Derrida and Weber, then, that Melville so powerfully, if enigmatically, dramatizes in the opening scene: iteration as attempted by Whiskers is elegantly rejected by Billy in this first-posited, Golden optimal setting. Derrida's claim that language—the text—"may fall prey to interpretation rather than being anchored . . . interpretation . . . is the 'risk' "[8] and, moreover, continues to be relevant when Billy is captured by an outward-bound warship. Its agent, Ratcliffe, avidly pounces on Billy, and like his name, Ratcliffe is characterized by all kinds of predatory habits as a preview to the numerous devouring images of this novel. Such stress on capture and prey serves to predict Billy's danger on the new vessel to which he is forcefully conveyed in "abrupt transition" (50), as Melville says, and we realize that although the first ship had dealt in peaceful matters, the second, named *Bellipotent,* is a ship of war.

Immediately upon Billy's arrival in this new risk-ridden world, therefore, Melville emphasizes Billy's orphaned condition. Billy's singularity, which once made him self-contained or total, now becomes a subject of inquiry. The catechism that Billy must undergo plays on Billy's lack of father, author, origin, and Billy himself suggests the theological-critical crisis: "God knows, sir," he exclaims about his origin (51). The threat for this orphan is forcefully demonstrated in the terrible flogging that he sees, as again the imagery of cutting is used. The "culprit's naked back under the scourge, gridironed with red welts and worse" (68) is reminiscent of Whiskers' butchery, and it is also adumbrative of Claggart's later "tap" with the rattan for Billy and his "sharp cut with the rattan" administered immediately thereafter (73).

Once a text is considered in an interpretive context, it becomes an artifact ready, like spilled soup, to be consumed by reading strategies. The two ship worlds dramatized in *Billy Budd* represent the categories theoretically established between some dreamed-of situation where meanings cannot go astray, and another orphaned instance where messages must be read into being. It is Fish's purpose, however, to declare that in the world of language there never can be such a distinction; he argues that all texts are always equally orphaned. There can be no kind of reading, he would argue, that is not "detached from a centering origin and abandoned to an 'essential drift.' "[9] *Billy Budd* is enacted in such a drift at sea. Yet does Melville agree that the first ship world must be an impossible dream, and that Billy's transcendent meaning be consumed and die? Aside from Claggart, who else might possibly read and save this text? "One person excepted, the master-at-arms was perhaps the only man in the ship intellectually capable of adequately appreciating the moral phenomenon presented in Billy Budd" (78). Melville does make room for "some one person excepted" to negotiate between these two worlds for Billy; he senses the powerful need for some figure who could perform the deciphering in the one world while maintaining some ideal of the other. He allows, that is, for the figure of a Daniel, who can read the signs yet sense the wonder.

Captain Vere presents such a possibility. In many ways his understanding of Billy expresses idealist tendencies appropriate to the first scene's worship. Vere, as his name indicates, seeks absolutes, verities, categorical facts untouched by surrounding circumstances. "Verify it," the captain demands when he wants the truth (100). Moreover, Vere, who seems always so "unmindful of the circumstance" (63), may be called Starry because of his penchant for abstract guidances. In the court case before him he rejects what he calls consideration of "any conceivable motive," and later, confining his attention to the blow's consequence alone, he declares in the courtroom: "The prisoner's deed—with that alone we have to do" (108). Not heeding intentions, that is, Vere treats this young text as a self-enclosed verbal icon, and as these reminders of the first scene's worship pile up, Billy's hopes for safety seem promising under Vere's strong gaze.

Yet oddly enough, Vere does touch Billy: "Going close up to the young sailor, and laying a soothing hand on his shoulder, [Vere] said, 'There is no hurry, my boy. Take your time, take your time.' Contrary to the effect intended, these words so fatherly in tone, doubtless touching Billy's heart to the quick, prompted yet more violent efforts at utterance" (99). When Vere lays his hand on Billy, he also demands some performance from the text he seems so abstractly to consider. Though Vere claims no hurry, Billy surely feels Vere's touch as a call for response. Vere assumes that a text or deed, like Billy, ultimately must "speak for itself" (117). Melville suggests what recent students of critical theory have begun to suspect: Claggart in his too devouring, overly reader-responsive attitude and Vere in his formalist New Critical stance may not be that far apart. They both are powerful figures on this ship, and both are, we realize, commanding officers in Meville's scheme. The similarity between Vere and Claggart is based on the status of the text each presumes. When Claggart blurts out: "And handsome is as handsome did it, too!" (72) he, like Vere, means that Billy can be understood only in performance. By extension we may say that according to both, Billy in himself is emptied of meaning. He is as he does according to readers' requirements that he make sense.

Such perceptions do violence to the text, therefore, for the locus of Billy's meaning is placed within his readers. Any powerful reading will consume its text by insisting that sense is served up according to the commands of the onlooking spectator. Hence the appropriate intrusion in Melville's story of the soup; this food is suggestively spilled as a signal for the commanding officer's devouring interpretive action. While "pointing down to the streaming soup," Claggart, like Whiskers before him, "playfully" taps Billy (72); the young sailor's soup may not itself be devoured, but Billy is intimately approached, consumed—and threatened. Vere, conversely, in denying explanatory circumstances has also as much as declared that no inherent sense to Billy's movement exists. Billy's violent gesture, read by Vere like a poem, is judged not for what it means, but simply is, without intent.

In comparing the dangers of both reader-response and New Critical thinking, therefore, we may find another assessment of the situation helpful: Gerald Graff, in discussing recent trends in literary theory puts the problem succinctly:

> It often follows that the *content* of a literary work . . . has no interest in itself but serves merely as a pretext, the "bit of nice meat," according to Eliot that the burglar holds out to the house dog while going about his

real work. . . . From the position that the literary symbol means no more than itself . . . it is only a step to the position that literature has *no* meaning . . . or that its meaning is totally indeterminate and "open" to interpretation.[10]

Vere, no less than Claggart, devours the object before him. Such an insight provides a cruelly ironic explanation for the Abraham-Isaac reference in the story: in the name of abstract reading or absolute worship, Vere as the father can end by slaying his son. The minute Vere translates a timeless, formalist theory of some text or Billy into the demands for meaning, he demonstrates what Fish cites as the risks for Billy in his new world of representations.

The problem becomes broad, then, as Meville puts it. Billy moves in "abrupt transition from his former and simpler sphere to the ampler and more knowing world of a great warship" (50); but can Billy endure such a rupture? Billy's transition enacts the problematics of communication. If he first represents, in Derrida's terms, "an origin which is free from freeplay"[11] and is transferred to the world of the order of the sign, then again as Derrida would claim, these two interpretations of interpretation seem absolutely irreconcilable, and language is at an impasse. Billy's inside narrative—as in the book's subtitle—thus probes impossibilities within language and by extension at the heart of all narratives. Billy's trauma, moreover, emphasizes deep-felt tensions in a narrative that Melville casts in specifically American terms as well. This broader cultural dimension may now be more fully considered.

Billy's life depends on his remaining intact, even as he had been in the first Golden-world scene of this novel. That first world in its preinterpretive innocence had carried clear Edenic implications, as many critics have observed.[12] If only God knows Billy's origin then Billy like Adam may by the truly unhampered creature whose features combine to equate a sense of his potential with that of the whole New World Garden itself. The story of this young Billy—who in the summer of 1797 is twenty-one (44, 54), thus sharing his 1776 birthdate with that of America—suggests a veritable New Earth adventure, and he personifies what Sacvan Bercovitch has called "the spirit of America's baby and budding age."[13] While Billy's case exemplifies the problematics of reading in general, it also provides an illuminating demonstration of issues raised in reading the American story. In *Billy Budd* Melville probes the inside narrative of America itself.

Stated in American terms that relate to the larger critical concerns we have developed, we may say that Billy as text represents the dream implicit in the American myth. He is first imagined as the object of worship on the idealist decks of a homeward-bound or security-oriented ship, named appropriately in a more abstract, ideal or theoretical way, the *Rights-of-Man*. The American experience, however, also requires what Melville rightly calls the ampler knowing world. The implications of America as a New Earth promised in Daniel and Revelations must be worked out in action, time, iterated versions—which all together become the facts of national history. Such versions can be produced only on the second ship that is outward bound, struggle-oriented, and thus also appropriately named *Bellipotent*. On such a ship American history is acted out as the conflict of powerful opinions, when security, land, or origins, are lost from sight; here Vere's formalist reading of Billy's meaning proves no less violent for Billy than does Claggart's. When Billy is threatened in the fray, therefore, Melville seeks some other critical approach that might save the American text, Billy.

In short, the problem becomes that of relating the first golden scene of primal wonder to the second knowing world; it is the problem of the dream and also its deciphering. Melville questions how, if at all, some single ideal—Billy, myth, or America—can be played out on the pluralist decks of this man-of-war world where significances must always contend. This dilemma is the drama described in the modern theoretical issues we have followed, and the problem in a sense parallels Lawrance Thompson's argument, which he once posed as Melville's quarrel with God.[14] We may now rephrase the issue for Melville by suggesting that in *Billy Budd* Melville challenges the concept of what one Puritan had called "God's plot, America,"[15] when Melville shows in this story how an American plot or ideal cannot be successfully transferred to the decks of a man-of-war world; Melville stages his inquiry on the *Bellipotent* in contrast to the *Rights-of-Man* precisely because he recognizes the terrible rupture between some promised dream of America and the daily possibilities of living out that transcendent ideal in the drift of high seas, through systems deploying conflicting and risky strategies.

Melville seeks an answer to a question that underlies the comment of an officer of the courtroom who murmurs before passing judgment on Billy: "Nobody is present—none of the ship's company, I mean—who might shed lateral light, if any is to be had, upon what remains mysterious in this matter" (108). Is nobody present in the *Bellipotent* who may yet offer a view for saving Billy Budd? There seems to be a lack in this book—not only in Billy's performing abilities but within Melville's story itself.

The story has, however, made room for more information yet to emerge: "But something more, or rather something else than mere shrewdness is perhaps needful for the due understanding of such a character as Billy Budd's" (90). Describing Claggart, too, Melville had used the strange phrase of a "deadly space between" to comprehend such a nature (74). The nagging lack or deadly space implanted within this novel itself is almost palpable, even as it is among the men who watch the final scene of Billy's death in "silence . . . a silence but emphasized . . . this emphasized silence" (125–26). In a novel devoted to varieties of responsiveness, such calls for something more, such silences, spaces are all the more salient. We look for that somebody present needful for understanding Billy. Claggart and Vere have been excepted; there must be someone else in this novel to fill that gaping void.

Most readers have passed easily over the problem of identifying the major figures of this book; they have decided that these major characters unquestionably must be Billy, Vere, and Claggart.[16] If Billy earlier has seemed to be the central figure of attention for critics of the novel, more recently, perhaps with a shift to interest in reader responsiveness, however, the focus has turned toward Vere and Claggart. Yet I would argue that reading *Billy Budd* in terms of these three characters alone itself enforces a lack. The time has come to recognize the Dansker as a major figure of importance in understanding further implications of Melville's program for discussing Billy, texts, and America. It is the Dansker's silence that lies at the core of our pain felt in reading this work; his is the version that might help Billy negotiate between the dream and its lively versions. Aside from Melville's own probing questions directing our attention toward that other one who might have understood Billy, I suggest that certain verbal patterns, images, and contrasts embedded within the text ought to alert us to the importance of the Dansker. This old salt-seer's argument, or, better, his lack of argument for or against Billy, is important to the problematic situation Melville examines.

The case for understanding the Dansker proceeds first of all from an awareness of his place in the design of *Billy Budd* itself. This work, as several critics have noticed, is based on a series of balances and contrasts.[17] Some of these counterforces have already been noted, such as two opposite ships with their differing directions or contradictions. Billy's clear innocence once on the second ship shines in opposition to Claggart's innate depravity. Furthermore, Claggart's personal reading of Billy seems contrary to Vere's approach, which is so implacably abstract. Running throughout the various scenes is the fundamental opposition of Billy as a text others confront and variously read.

An awareness of this last fundamental textual principle, on further scrutiny, however, causes all the other oppositions somehow to shift, weaken, and dissolve. If Billy is read, then Claggart *and* Vere both confront him; then, as we have seen, Claggart's and Vere's positions oddly coincide: the two equally cause Billy's death, both are similar when opposed to Billy. Still further argued, the very opposition they enact between the text and reader also becomes doubtful. For the essential point shared by their two readings becomes their ability to command Billy—to annihilate the difference between his text and their insistent views of him. Emptied of intrinsic meanings, Billy becomes theirs to overcome, as together they manage to impale Billy by the "paralyzing lurch" from Claggart (98) and an equally potent form of "suffocation" by Vere (99). Together their powerful demands thus work to devour him, and the very expectation of oppositions in this novel is thwarted. What will save Billy, we must realize, is precisely some "space between" (74); what is required is some other who will, at last, distance Billy while still reading him.

Our expectations that such a powerful counterbalancing criticism be given by the Dansker have been aroused on many levels. In terms of the configurative patterns of the novel the Dansker ought repeatedly to have drawn our attention. One of the devices Melville uses to emphasize the perceptive attitudes of Vere, Claggart, and the others, is a discussion of their eyes. The various boat readers have focused intently on Billy with "violet orbs," a "ferret glance," or "gray eyes," which are said to "light upon" their subject. But the Dansker's eyes, too, have been repeatedly described: his are notably "small" and "weasel," and he is called the old salt-seer (69, 71). He, too, is fascinated by Billy, "slyly studying him at intervals . . . [in] an expression of speculative query." Dansker's eyes, like the others, also "light on" Billy (70, 87). In presenting his primary characters, moreover, Melville has in each case provided some biographical background, feats, even nicknames. We are told about Vere's and Claggart's prior histories, fame, or rumored habits. The same information is provided for the Dansker, as his noteworthiness, like theirs, is established by reports given at length about his former deeds; his nickname "Board-Her-in-the-Smoke," too, is supplied and colorfully explained.

On the purely textual level, evidence has been brought by the editors of the earliest manuscripts of *Billy Budd* to show that as a character in the book the Dansker in fact preceded the development of the one who would later become Vere in Melville's several tentative drafts. It was, as Hayford and Sealts have shown, only in a third reworking of the text that Captain Vere was at all brought into focus: "In the third and final phase of development, another radical shift of focus occurred when Captain Vere was for the first time brought into the foreground." By contrast, we may note that in the prior stages additions had already been made, as the editors' study details: "One class of these new additions amounted to a program of dramatizing Claggart's campaign against Billy and included such other dramatized material as the . . . development of the Dansker as observer and confidant, the soup-spilling episode witnessed by Claggart, and—slightly later—the encounters between Billy and the Dansker."[18] In the light of his earlier importance in the manuscripts, as well as in the light of the suggestive patterns within the novel we now read, the Dansker's position ought to be more apparently and forcefully felt.

The Dansker's responses, limited as they are in this text, seem precisely those required to grant Billy the distance that can save his very life. "Jemmey Leggs is *down* on you" (85), this Chiron repeatedly declares, and he will offer no more comment. Dansker's negatives are repeated with "that bitter prudence which *never* interferes in *aught* and *never* gives advice" (86). He will "commit himself to *nothing*" (71).[19] Such negations bring out an important cleavage in this novel of contrasts. Although some would all too readily offer, even impose, their versions on Billy, a powerful contingent of figures in this schematic work refuses to speak. We may align the two sides as follows: Vere and Claggart lead their forces of assertive readers, ferreting out meanings, and using Squeak and Albert as undercover agents who join these ranks. Here, too, we may include Whiskers, the newspaper reporter, and the late, lone attendant on Vere at his deathbed, who reports hearing one last version of "Billy Budd, Billy Budd" (129). Finally, we may add, the narrator himself, with his asides and comments, belongs in the column of these outspoken reporters, affording ready versions of Billy.

The side of silence, in opposition, is captained by the Dansker in his refusals and pithy ways. The guarded quality of Dansker implies what Billy himself suspects: this old salt-seer could say more, but he checks himself. The surgeon, with similar self-limitation, dares not argue and will not speak out about Billy Budd. Such enforced silence is at the very heart of this narrative, since the whole story is told in the context of mutinies and uprisings that, like the sailors' murmurs at the end, are either quelled or never fully dare to arise. These silences are willful efforts *not* to read nor to react to given stimuli. In contrast to the overly assertive readings, this emphatic controlled silence directs attention toward some other way of understanding Billy.

The most ominous figure in the novel remains to be introduced and aligned according to these contending modes of silence or response: the chaplain. When Billy is incarcerated, the "good chaplain" at first speaks at length to him about ideas of death and salvation. The glib narrator then describes the minister's "good sense" and "good heart" (121). Melville, however, allows the chaplain to enact one last gesture: "Stooping over, he kissed on the fair cheek his fellow man" (121). In the book's overall network of silence the chaplain's action radiates with troubling implications. The minister of Christ may have wanted to be Christ-like in his behavior, even as Jesus had maintained his silence in Matt. 26:63; 27:14: "But Jesus was silent, . . . he gave him no answer." Yet when the chaplain kisses Billy, he surely evokes the image of a closely related scene, the silent kiss of Judas. Melville emphasizes the possible anomalies of silence. This minister's inability to speak out against Vere's position, or his refusal to question and thus interpret edicts on this ship, may ultimately become just as destructive as the various aggressive renditions have proved.

Moreover, as we consider the forces of interpretive action or of repressed reaction once again, certain problems within Billy Budd himself emerge with troubling clarity. On the one hand, Billy's original innocence and his willing, peaceful submission to the second ship's conditions arouse in Melville's readers expectations of his becoming a New Adam, or a Christ-like figure on the decks of this ship. Yet, as the silence of the chaplain now suggests, Billy's own silent action, conversely, may appear in a more suspect light. We realize that Billy Budd has acted to thwart his own performance; he has stifled his own reports. Billy ought to have warned the captain beforehand. He fails to tell his complete story to the Dansker, too. His innocent silence, like his harmless blow on the first ship, has, on this second one, serious results. Thus, if he is to be a New Adam or Christ, we wonder, ought he like Adam be capable of giving names, and fruitfully iterating, multiplying—as the Midrash suggests—language and life, in this broader world? Like Christ ought he speak out according to the world's usage?

Melville has made this second ship-world rich with names and naming everywhere—"Jemmey Leggs," "Board-Her-in-the-Smoke," "Beauty," and so on—as multiple, even ironic significations abound. A ship itself operates according to titles such as Captain or Lieutenant; efficiency demands this usage. Conflict is inherent in such structures or denominations because free-floating terms work only according to meanings whose validity depends on circumstances as they develop. An awareness of this inherent instability of titles presumably would explain Vere's jealous guarding of his own granted authority. That same awareness lies at the heart of this story's plot, based on threats of insurrection, with new power lurking always in the bulwarks and margins. Billy, however, will not participate in these systems; he cannot understand any doubleness or "sinister dexterity" in language. Uncomprehendingly he says of Claggart: "Why, he calls me 'the sweet and pleasant fellow'" (71), and we sense, perhaps with Vere, the dangerous incongruity of a failure to participate in these significations. Arguing that Billy ought to speak, I would say that his repression is his evil; his stutter, indeed, is the marplot working within him.

If Billy-as-a-text is at fault and this failure causes his shipmate readers to be repulsed, or most drastically, in Claggart's case, to be killed off, we may have a new case against Billy. Barbara Johnson raises the issue of what I thus call a possible second premise within the book for understanding Billy. Johnson, in fact, offers Billy as a reader and not as a text, commenting that in eliminating equivocation Billy eliminates the text he reads—Claggart—with the deadly blow.[20] Johnson, however, misplaces the emphasis here; Billy in killing Claggart is killing off readers, not texts, and the most emphatic reader he knows is his own accuser. In eliminating him, Billy is eradicating the reading or lingual process especially within himself—hence, Billy's paroxysm. Billy's is the struggle to suppress iterations.

Billy will not participate in multiplying versions. A perverted New Adam, he does not name the creatures nor participate in proliferating systems. This perpetual Baby Budd simply will *not* be fruitful, in life or in language, despite the suggestions of his bud-name, or his Adamic connotations. So he stutters and falls silent when like Jesus he insists that his "yea be yea" and his "nay be nay" in absolute terms, and he will not "deal in double meanings and insinuations" (49). In denying the insinuations of speech Billy denies his Adamic role and paradoxically fails to bring God's sense into relation with this world when, Christ-like, he says nothing.

The Dansker, thus, becomes all the more important. Is this guarded seer similarly to be blamed for his refusal to speak? Melville passes no judgment on the Dansker. As "lateral light" we know that in his developing manuscript versions of *Billy Budd,* as Hayford and Sealts have shown in their study of Melville's revisions of this text, Melville reduced the centrality of the Dansker and increased the focus on Vere. In another work he wrote at that same time—*Daniel Orme*—Melville introduced a major figure similar to the Dansker, a hero who was in fact named Daniel.[21] Melville abandoned that tale, however, and by using in *Billy Budd* a similar figure with a foreign name, a man no longer the titular hero, Melville seems to have sought ever more insistently to deny the need, or even the desirability, of focusing on a Daniel who speaks out. The Dansker here is only a watchful sage who offers no dream and no judgment. Melville never challenges this salt-seer, and I would argue that in this authorial refusal, we may have Melville's own Dansker-like vision. The narrator gives his views in frequent, often obtuse, commentary, whereas the author himself, like the enigmatic Dansker, conveys his attitude in a powerfully different way. Although the narrator serves as one of this story's aggressive readers, neither the Dansker nor Melville shares that function. They are not outspoken interpreters; yet they are also not to be aligned with the Judas-Billy-Chaplain frustrators of all readings.

The Dansker does make some puzzling comments, and Melville does write this fictional commentary on reading and American interpretive assumptions. But how can one speak yet maintain emphasized silences? Or, like Daniel, how can one both affirm the wonder of some absolute dream or transcendent text, and yet participate in an experiential and unstable deciphering of worldly signs? These are the demands Billy places before this seer, and Melville thus presents the Dansker's difficult answer. The Dansker's odd statements to Billy show that he knows not so much what Claggart says, but that he tends, generally, to make such comments. Thus he knows the name Jemmey Leggs, and he readily uses the expression "down on you" for Claggart, because he presumably has noticed this habit of, and description for, being down on someone in Claggart before.

If these sparse comments and clues show the Dansker's "pithy guarded cynicism" (71), they also serve as an excellent, though strange, "summing up of the case submitted" (72). This salt-seer, as Melville presents him, seems to avoid specific interpretive endeavors and prefers, instead, to highlight the conditions or critical processes that make meanings possible. His program, that is to say, sounds remarkably like a statement originally made by Jonathan Culler in 1976 in an essay entitled, appropriately, "Beyond Interpretation." Culler argues in this essay much the same approach that the Dansker at first exemplifies:

> In this critical climate it is therefore important, if only as a means of
> loosening the grip which interpretation has on critical consciousness,

. . . to maintain that . . . the interpretation of individual works is only tangentially related to the understanding of literature. To engage in the study of literature is not to produce yet another interpretation of *King Lear* but to advance one's understanding of the conventions and operations of an institution, a mode of discourse.[22]

Culler's reference to "this critical climate" seems especially appropriate to Billy's surrounding second ship scene; Claggart, Vere, the surgeon, and the newspaper reporter are all engaged in finding and producing hidden meanings and yet another interpretation of the texts about them—and especially Billy. The Dansker's reticent attitude toward explanations might suggest his agreement with Culler's view that if there is one thing we do not need it is more interpretations. Rather, this thoughtful Chiron Dansker will provide a theory of those operations that are in practice. If at first he is struck by the anomaly that a univocal Billy presents on the decks of the *Bellipotent,* then the Dansker, like Culler, strives to find some framework as a summing up of the operations of the inside of the American narrative.

Although the Dansker does not wish to participate in interpretations, perhaps he slowly discovers as the situation becomes more complex that even such summing up cannot help but slide into revisions once again. Dansker's very choice of language conveys a certain derivative stance; the meaning even in cognomens like Jemmey Leggs or expressions such as "down on you" seems innocent of bias but nevertheless is in place for him—living and functioning as he does on this ship-world—already there for his use, defined by their very availability in his lexicon. Whatever structures the Dansker chooses to see will betray a judgmental preconditioning. So the Dansker desists. Such an insight into this seer's final silences—and even his ultimate disappearance from the text, however—leads to surprising further revelations about the consequences of the textual strategies presented in *Billy Budd.* This novel claims no symmetry of form and insists on truth's "ragged edges" (128). Yet *Billy Budd's* own less finished truth may lie in the rough symmetry of the novel's silent beginning and ending scenes.

We have noted that Billy's position as he begins this book—repressing iterations within a scene of peaceful worship—is one of silent stasis. What also can be acknowledged, however, is the way that at the novel's conclusion—in the second world of struggling, active, even tumultuous renditions—the final scene after all is no less repressive, and no less muted or immobilized. When the silence of the first ship scene is repeated in awful solemnity at the concluding moments of the second, we may see the fullest implications

of the drama, as Melville—and as Stanley Fish, ninety years later—
would have it. The novel draws to a suffocating close, and what had
seemed the freer world of personally determined approaches to
texts or to Billy, in contrast to the static submissiveness of the first-
posited condition, then appears in quite another light.

If all the meanings in this world of shared systems are situational,
then even the most abstracted critics (like the Dansker who seeks
to remain aloof from the dictates of the attitudes around him and
merely to observe how they function) ultimately must face their
own limitations because of those very attitudes and systems that
are at work, always and already there. Even such an analyst finds
that choices are governed by situation, and thus in a sense, all agree
with those critics who have argued on behalf of Claggart or Vere as
sincere believers in their views. Claggart cannot help seeing the
spilled soup in his own way any more than can Vere, Squeak, or
Albert in theirs; working together in this man-of-war enterprise we
do thus, variously, agree on the notion of devouring versions. Although Culler has spoken of avoiding the critical climate of gripping
interpretations, Melville yet suggests through the Dansker that
even an "understanding of the conventions and operations of an
institution, a mode of discourse," as Culler puts it, will invoke the
very terms whose hold the person engaged in study seeks to release. Fish, recognizing such a problem, argues, indeed, that there
can be none of Culler's loosening the grip of interpretations because
they are built in to the systems that govern our thought or situation.
Melville's second ship's environment, then, it would seem, cannot
permit the neutral terms desired by a noncommittal Dansker, and
such a world resembles, more closely, the situation that Fish describes as a community of interpreters.[23] Yet when Dansker withdraws from the final scenes of *Billy Budd,* in his absence we may
have a comment on the interpretive drama, and we may recognize
in that very space Melville's wise critique of those same views that
Fish would expound nearly a century later.

As the novel ends Melville increases the tensions felt on all sides.
Billy hangs from the yardarm, and repressions seem everywhere in
force; Melville in a brief description highlights the drive toward
powerful outbursts and the contrasting forces of silence: "The
silence at the moment of execution and for a moment or two
continuing thereafter, a silence but emphasized by the regular wash
of the sea against the hull or the flutter of a sail caused by the
helmsman's eyes being tempted astray, this emphasized silence was
gradually disturbed by a sound" (125–26). The sound heard in
distinction to the emphasized silence is like that of a "freshet wave
of a torrent suddenly swelled by pouring showers" (126). The mur-

mur of the men, however, cannot naturally "wax into clamor" because it is immediately met by a strange command by Vere: "Pipe down the starboard watch, Boatswain, and see that they go." The silver whistles instantly thin the throng and quell the sounds, even as the yards are trimmed in the course of the ship's business. Reaction once again threatens to arise, but Vere then turns on the drummers, in "measured forms" (128) to dissolve the protesting sounds. The subtle point of Vere's knowledge of whistles, drums and forms—all customs and usages on his ship—is this: he knows the reactions that are built into the systems, and he recognizes the way that in such a ship-community responses are automatic and preconditioned. At the given signal, despite all other seemingly powerfully willed reactions to the contrary, the sailors simply cannot help obeying the signals. These men, that is, obey not Vere, but more truly themselves, as they go about the business of the ship, with its sign systems that allow it to function.

It is important to remember at this point, however, that the very plot of this story is based on awareness of the drive toward change, revolution, or disruptive political action in our world.[24] In a sense when Melville makes the central figure a child born in 1776, he places at the very heart of this story the fact of both American history and of the Revolution. Yet, too, we are forced to acknowledge, if the community of interpreters regnant on this ship holds totalitarian sway according to Fish's theory that "noticeability is a function of what it is *possible* to notice given a particular set of assumptions,"[25] then revolt, genuine reaction, or purposeful rebellion—all terms of regeneration in the sense of new thought, change, or progress—will be quelled; the very course of history will be shunted, and, like Billy, America would be nipped in the bud.

Vere's whistles and drums ominously demonstrate the fact that even as Billy's promise is denied, so, too, are the voices of his interpreters when they are as much as gagged and bound by their context and condition. Stanley Fish might not acknowledge such an ending to this tale of interpretations; he might want to argue that interpreters can be open to an argument or an influence that causes them to learn and thus to change their assumptions. But again, could one *hear* that which one was not already able to notice? Not so, if in Fish's words, "that which is noticeable is always the product" of that which has been decided or interpreted.[26] Melville, in his dire ending for *Billy Budd,* perceives an impasse that Fish—nearly a century later—must consider; Melville's own silences differentiate him therefore not only from the narrator of his tale but also from the modern theorist of *Critical Inquiry.*

It is in the Dansker's aborted role that Melville offers his answer to his quarrels with Billy, texts, and readers. The Dansker, who might have been a Daniel or a seer of Billy in idealistic vision, and who could also have judged and saved him through interpretive revision, finally falls silent, and Melville leaves blank a space between the positions held by the two ship-worlds of his novel. When both the text and the readers have each failed, then the incompatibility of both—though bound in systems of unresolvable tensions—poignantly suggests that absent power of the whole that might have been. Following the Dansker's example that fails to provide any Daniel-like interpretation as well as any absolutist dream, Melville's readers appreciate Melville's own withdrawal and silence. Such readers know the despair involved in the lost hope of a Billy who could, as a new Adam, or Christ, have used his power to intercede in this world and bring to it some promise of wonder, in transcendent truth. They also recognize the dangerous, even suffocating possibilities inherent in reading signs, making their own interpretations. Melville presents in this story in the best way possible, his own recognition of a great and painful impasse when he allows no other comments than these, as this reader's own strange summing up of a powerful case submitted.

Notes

1. Herman Melville, *Mardi and a Voyage Thither* (New York: Capricorn, 1964), 55. Maxine Moore sees *Mardi* as a huge puzzle made up of diagrams, charts, hidden allusions to games, and almanacs, in *That Lonely Game: Melville, "Mardi," and the Almanac* (Columbia: University of Missouri Press, 1975).

2. Herman Melville, *Billy Budd, Sailor: (An Inside Narrative)*, edited from the manuscript with introduction and notes by Harrison Hayford and Merton M. Sealts, Jr. (Chicago: University of Chicago Press, 1962). Subsequent citations are noted parenthetically in the text.

3. Charles Olson, *Call Me Ishmael* (New York: Grove Press, 1947), 104.

4. Stanley E. Fish, "With the Compliments of the Author: Reflections on Austin and Derrida," *Critical Inquiry* 8, no. 4 (1982): 693–721.

5. Ibid., 703–4.

6. "Unless I . . . place my hand in his side, I will not believe" (John 20:24–29). It is interesting to note that in *The Confidence Man* written more than thirty years earlier, Melville is, as Hershel Parker has suggested, "alluding obliquely" to this same passage about the doubting Thomas. See *The Confidence Man: His Masquerade*, ed. Hershel Parker (New York: W. W. Norton, 1971), 25.

7. Fish, "Austin and Derrida," 703. Fish cites Derrida, "Signature Event Context," *Glyph* 1 (1977): 180, and Samuel Weber, "It," *Glyph* 4 (1978): 7.

8. Fish, "Austin and Derrida," 701.

9. Ibid., 707.

10. Gerald Graff, *Literature Against Itself: Literary Ideas in Modern Society* (Chicago: University of Chicago Press, 1979), 49.

11. Jacques Derrida, "Structure, Sign and Play in the Discourse of the Human Sciences, in *The Structuralist Controversy: The Languages of Criticism and the Sciences of Man,* ed. Richard Macksey (Baltimore: Johns Hopkins University Press, 1970), 264.

12. Some examples of "American" readings would include R. W. B. Lewis, *The American Adam* (Chicago: University of Chicago Press, 1953), chapter 7; Ursula Brumm, *American Thought and Religious Typology* (New Brunswick: Rutgers University Press, 1970); Milton R. Stern, *The Fine Hammered Steel of Herman Melville* (Urbana: University of Illinois Press, 1957).

13. Sacvan Bercovitch, "Melville's Search for National Identity: Son and Father in *Redburn, Pierre* and *Billy Budd,*" *College Language Association Journal,* 10 (1967): 226. R. Evan Davis, "An Allegory of America in Melville's *Billy Budd,*" *Journal of Narrative Technique,* 14 (1984): 179, shows that Billy, like America, was born in 1776.

14. Lawrance Thompson, *Melville's Quarrel With God* (Princeton: Princeton University Press, 1952).

15. Thomas Shepard, "Autobiography" and "Journal," in *God's Plot: The Paradoxes of Puritan Piety: Being the Autobiography and Journal of Thomas Shepard,* edited with an introduction by Michael McGiffert (Amherst: The University of Massachusetts Press, 1972), 3. In the "Journal," Shepard also speaks of "God's main plot" and "God's deep plot" (119, 141).

16. Barbara Johnson, for example, says: "It is a tale of three men in a boat," *The Critical Difference: Essays in the Contemporary Rhetoric of Reading* (Baltimore: The Johns Hopkins University Press, 1980), 79.

17. John D. Seeyle speaks of *Billy Budd* as Melville's "final balance." See *"Melville the Ironic Diagram."* Evanston, Ill.: Northwestern University Press, 1970, 159ff. But see Edgar Dryden: "truth is revealed only when formal order is destroyed." *Melville's Thematics of Form: The Great Art of Telling the Truth* (Baltimore: Johns Hopkins University Press, 1968), 209.

18. Hayford and Sealts, editors' introduction to *Billy Budd,* 8, 7.

19. The emphasis in this quotation is mine.

20. Johnston, *The Critical Difference*, 97–98.

21. See F. Barron Freeman, "The Enigma of Melville's 'Daniel Orme,' " *American Literature* 16 (1944): 208–11. Hayford and Sealts have shown that *Daniel Orme* was not a fragment intended for inclusion in *Billy Budd,* but they do acknowledge significant similarities in the two works. See also H. Bruce Franklin, *The Wake of the Gods: Melville's Mythology* (Stanford: Stanford University Press, 1963), 220.

22. Jonathan Culler, "Beyond Interpretation: The Prospects of Contemporary Criticism," *Comparative Literature* 28 (1976): 244, 246.

23. Fish, "Austin and Derrida," 716. See also Fish, "Interpreting the *Variorum,*" *Critical Inquiry* vol. 2, no. 3 (1976): 483–85.

24. Hannah Arendt, *On Revolution* (New York: Viking Press, 1965); and "Reflections on Violence," *New York Review of Books* 12 (February 27, 1969): 28. Both Arendt works are cited by Kingsley Widmer, *The Ways of Nihilism: A Study of Herman Melville's Short Novels* (San Diego: University of California State Colleges, 1970), 18, 19. Norman Holmes Pearson in 1951 pointed out that mutiny is "the ubiquitous metaphor in *Billy Budd.*" Billy Budd: The King's Yarn," *American Quarterly* 3 (1951): 111.

25. Fish, "One More Time," *Critical Inquiry* no. 6, 4 (1980): 750.

26. Ibid.

References

Bercovitch, Sacvan. "Melville's Search for National Identity: Son and Father in *Redburn, Pierre* and *Billy Budd.*" *College Language Association Journal* 10 (1967): 226.

Brumm, Ursula. *American Thought and Religious Typology.* New Brunswick, N.J.: Rutgers University Press, 1970.

Culler, Jonathan. "Beyond Interpretation: The Prospects of Contemporary Criticism." *Comparative Literature* 28 (1976): 244 and 246.

Davis, R. Evan. "An Allegory of America in Melville's *Billy Budd.*" *Journal of Narrative Technique* 14 (1984): 179.

Derrida, Jacques. "Structure, Sign and Play in the Discourse of the Human Sciences." In *The Structuralist Controversy: The Languages of Criticism and the Sciences of Man,* edited by Richard Macksey. Baltimore: The Johns Hopkins University Press, 1970.

Derrida, Jacques. "Signature Event Context," *Glyph* 1 (1977): 172–97.

Dryden, Edgar. *Melville's Thematics of Form: The Great Art of Telling the Truth.* Baltimore: The Johns Hopkins University Press, 1968.

Fish, Stanley E. "One More Time." *Critical Inquiry* 6, no. 4 (1980): 749–75.

———. "With the Compliments of the Author: Reflections on Austin and Derrida." *Critical Inquiry* 8, no. 4 (1982): 693–721.

———. "Interpreting the *Variorum*," *Critical Inquiry* 2, no. 3 (1976): 465–85.

Franklin, H. Bruce. *The Wake of the Gods: Melville's Mythology.* Stanford, Calif.: Stanford University Press, 1963.

Freeman, F. Barron. "The Enigma of Melville's 'Daniel Orme.' " *American Literature* 16 (1944): 208–11.

Graff, Gerald. *Literature Against Itself: Literary Ideas in Modern Society.* Chicago: University of Chicago Press, 1979.

Johnson, Barbara. *The Critical Difference: Essays in the Contemporary Rhetoric of Reading.* Baltimore: Johns Hopkins University Press, 1980.

Kingsley, Widmer. *The Ways of Nihilism: A Study of Herman Melville's Short Novels.* San Diego: Publication of University of California State Colleges, 1970.

Lewis, R. W. B. *The American Adam.* Chicago: University of Chicago Press, 1953.

Melville, Herman. *Billy Budd, Sailor (An Inside Narrative).* Edited by Harrison Hayford and Merton M. Sealts, Jr. Chicago: University of Chicago Press, 1962.

Melville, Herman. *Mardi and a Voyage Thither.* New York: Capricorn, 1964.

Moore, Maxine. *That Lonely Game: Melville, "Mardi," and the Almanac.* Columbia, MO.: University of Missouri Press, 1975.

Olson, Charles. *Call Me Ishmael.* New York: Grove Press, 1947.

Pearson, Norman Holmes. "Billy Budd: The King's Yarn." *American Quarterly* 3 (1951): 111.

Seegle, John D. *Melville: The Ironic Diagram.* Evanston, Ill.: Northwestern University Press, 1970.

Shepard, Thomas. "Autobiography" and "Journal." In *God's Plot: The Paradoxes of Puritan Piety: Being the Autobiography and Journal of Thomas Shepard,* edited by Michael McGiffert. Amherst, Mass.: University of Massachusetts Press, 1972.

Stern, Milton R. *The Fine Hammered Steel of Herman Melville*. Urbana, Ill.: University of Illinois Press, 1957.

Thompson, Lawrance. *Melville's Quarrel With God*. Princeton: Princeton University Press. 1952.

Weber, Samuel. "It," *Glyph* 4 (1978): 7 and 1–31.

10

W. B. Yeats: Poet as Reader

Kinereth Meyer

In reaction to the valorization of the text practiced by the New Critics and other formalists, critical attention has recently shifted to the reader's participation in the literary text and to an examination of the reader's central position as active revealer rather than passive observer. The reader is seen as the actualizer of the text's complexities and convolutions, without which the text cannot fully exist. The poetry of W. B. Yeats overtly invites such participation and actualization. In the poem "The Phases of the Moon," (18) for example, we find not a private mythological edifice that allows entry only to the initiated, but a gateway into the world of Yeats's poetry, and, perhaps, into the poetic process as a whole.

> . . . that shadow is the tower
> And the light proves that he is reading still.
> He has found, after the manner of his kind,
> Mere images; chosen this place to live in
> Because, it may be, of the candle-light
> From the far tower where Milton's Platonist
> Sat late, or Shelley's visionary prince:
> The lonely light that Samuel Palmer engraved,
> An image of mysterious wisdom won by toil;
> And now he seeks in book or manuscript
> What he shall never find.[1]

It may be, says Michael Robartes (one of Yeats's more famous masks), that the poet searches for a final key—a complete and perfect deciphering. Ultimately, however, the poet "shall never find"; he can only "seek," repeat the quest, and intensify the search. Yeats, in short, saw the poet as engaged in an activity—an activity that echoes and condenses the larger activity of man—"All things fall and are built again / And those that build them again are gay" (292).

What is the nature of this activity in Yeats? In order to suggest an answer to this question, I would like to begin with a rather strange comment that Yeats made, late in life, in an essay entitled "A General Introduction for My Work." "I must choose a traditional stanza. Even what I alter must seem traditional. I commit my emotion to shepherds, herdsmen, camel-drivers, learned men, Milton's or Shelley's Platonist, the tower Palmer drew. Talk to me of originality and I will turn on you with rage. I am a crowd, I am a lonely man, I am nothing. Ancient salt is best packing."[2]

Yeats "commits his emotion" to the nomads of the world—to shepherds, camel-drivers, herdsmen—and to poets and artists who must also continually search for the best watering ground for the soul.[3] His violent rejection of originality in his own work—"Talk to me of originality and I will turn on you with rage"—in fact presages the present critical concern with "literature as a topos of writing" and with texts as setting other texts "in motion."[4] Ours is an age in which attention has shifted to the author as a figure conscious of the act of repetition, conscious of echoes, parallels; an age of the text's awareness of itself as text and of writers' awareness of themselves as readers of former texts. One critic has even called the present era an age of "artistic recycling," and in a recent novel with the artistically recycled title, *The Prick of Noon*, the central character characterizes writers and readers as "pickpockets," and calls personal development a "long process of learning by example." In other words, as he succinctly puts it, "plagiarism." Indeed, in both literature and criticism, originality has given way to intertextuality, "anteriority" to "hermeneutic perplexity," and the need to be new to the need to decipher the old.[5]

In this context, Harold Bloom has characterized the poet as a "wrestling Jacob," a strong creative figure who wrestles with the great and emerges from the struggle only after "receiving a new name all his own." Bloom's choice of the biblical metaphor vividly and graphically concentrates his theory of the "anxiety of influence": every poet, if he is to be truly great, must grapple with an inevitable "foe"—his literary and historical inheritance. The work that the poet consequently produces becomes an "achieved anxiety," or a record of his struggle to achieve priority even as he ineluctably repeats the past. For Bloom, the anxiety of influence is the conflict between originality—or the poet's desire to be self-generating, to construct his own origins—and repetition—his inevitable indebtedness to others.[6]

Bloom's theory of influence elicits particularly interesting questions when applied to a self-consciously eclectic and syncretistic poet like W. B. Yeats. Does the theory of the "anxiety of influence" aid us in our reading of a poet who apparently denies his own "priority," glories in "influence," and embraces, rather than wrestles, the angel?

We will discover that Yeats's originality lies in an interesting observation of Bloom's idea: Yeats's poetry is characterized by a kind of "anxiety of noninfluence"—a continued attempt to assimilate, and thus affirm, prior expressions of his ideas and language. Yeats consistently rejected his own priority and affirmed his own "belatedness."[7] He was delighted whenever he found echoes of his ideas and language in previous (and therefore, to Yeats, authoritative) texts, and consciously attempted to establish his position as the latest link in an imperishable chain of poets who were at once literary spokespersons, prophets, and *interpreters* of "some great memory that renews the world's and men's thoughts age after age."[8]

It is not surprising, then, (as we saw in "The Phases of the Moon"), that Yeats placed the interpretive act—the act of reading—at the center of the creative experience. In writing his poems, the poet is always in the pose of "reading still": surrounded by ghosts of the great artists of the past, he "seeks in book or manuscript / What he shall never find." My purpose in this essay is to examine the textual implications of Yeats's focus on the act of seeking the answers to his own creative questions in "book or manuscript." In other words, I intend to look at the ways in which Yeats's poems embody Iser's idea that "the need to decipher gives us a chance to formulate our own deciphering capacity."[9] When considered in this light, Yeats's poems reveal a fascinating dialectic between the rhetorical authority granted by the external texts that poets themselves decipher in writing their own texts, and an "opening" of interpretive possibility to the reader, often through a crafted indeterminacy in the language.

Yeats's view of poetry as both a reading of other texts and as a subsequent communication of a new text is repeatedly found in poems based on the image of sexual intercourse. For Yeats, the paradigm of the poet's contact with "the great" is more "Leda and the Swan" (211) than Jacob and the angel. The poet's—and, subsequently, the reader's—meeting with fiction or myth is nothing less than "a sudden blow"—an experience of overwhelming force. But the issue in "Leda" is not, as it is in Bloom's version of the Jacob tale, how the artist can "win" or extricate himself from such a struggle in order to establish his "priority"—his new name—but rather how artists can achieve knowledge while assimilating power.

The viewpoint in "Leda" is uniquely multidimensional: the poet is at once the visionary swan giving form to experience, the swan engaged in a brutal rape, and the helpless Leda overwhelmed by its force. The experience in "Leda" is one in which the mythic and the mortal "know" each other sexually; the question is whether or not carnal knowledge bestows creative knowledge. Rather than "displace the subject of authority," as Geoffrey Hartman has suggested, the subject of "Leda" focuses and reinforces the issue: in terms of the allegory I am suggesting, what can the poet "know" after his union with myth, history, and literature—the various and multiform contexts that frame and shape art? Does the power received at the orgasmic moment, the "shudder in the loins," the "broken wall, the burning roof and tower" inevitably "engender" a new cycle of creativity?[10]

The significance of Yeats's sexual imagery, found throughout his poetry, in fact seems to echo the language of some of our contemporary critics, who characterize the components of the reading process as the "seduction of the text" (Geoffrey Hartman), the tamer and more euphemistic "entanglement" of the reader (Wolfgang Iser), the text that "must prove to me *that it desires me*" (Roland Barthes), the critic who "adores" interpretive closure and who "indulges" in it (Stanley Fish), or the delivering of one's self "bound hand and foot, to the omnipotence of fiction" (Georges Poulet).[11] According to many of these readers, what excites our "entanglement" in the poem is, in fact, its invitation, or "seduction" to unite with it in creating meaning—its temptation to the reader to attempt to formulate his or her own "deciphering capacity."

In "Leda," the reader's involvement in the text is generated by an attempt to sustain the balance between the authoritative and rhetorical power of the received context (the Leda myth) and the structured indeterminacy of the text itself, which both elicits and frustrates repeated attempts to "know." The poet-reader's "moment of knowledge" may be (in the language of Yeats's *A Vision*) his own "fifteenth phase," the point where "all thought becomes an image," a perception or seeing, an imaging of the figures of the poem or, rather, a reperception, and a reimaging. Yeats's vision in the poem is thus not a stasis, but an invitation to necessary revision on the part of the reader.

In the poem, Leda is the artist-as-reader overcome by the force of myth and fiction—that being so different from herself. Simultaneously, she is the reader-as-artist, or the bearer of new myths and fictions. Her vision—and Yeats's re-vision of her vision—engenders subsequent re-visions, her perception, subsequent apperceptions.

The question that concludes "Leda": "Did she put on his knowledge with his power / Before the indifferent beak could let her
drop?" reverberates behind the poem, behind the best of Yeats,
and, perhaps, behind poetry as a whole. Can poets balance the
power and domination of prior language and prior fictive structures
with a *knowledge*—the present moment of the poem? Can he both
seek the answers "in book or manuscript" and at the same time
engender new fictions? Yeats suggests in "Phases" that the poet "is
reading still"; he or she can only continue the attempt, and perhaps
momentarily sustain a precarious balancing, like a juggler in a
circus. I would suggest that the form of "Leda" answers the concluding question by presenting Yeats's re-vision of prior texts, and
at the same time by inviting the reader to continue the process, to
study, like Yeats, "book or manuscript"—in this case, the manuscript of Yeats's "Leda and the Swan."

The rhetoric of the poem turns on three powerful loci. First, the
title of the poem, like the beginning strains of a familiar song,
establishes the context for continued participation—the myth of
Leda.[12] The second locus of the rhetoric develops the first: "a
sudden blow"—the overwhelming force of the encounter described
in strong, convincing language and rhyme:

> . . . the great wings beating still
> Above the staggering girl, her thighs caressed
> By the dark webs, her nape caught in his bill,
> He holds her helpless breast upon his breast (211).

In this poem the rhetorical force of the known—the reader's
recognition of the Leda myth (and, perhaps, a knowledge of Yeats's
discourse on its poetic and typological significance in *A Vision* and
elsewhere)—is brilliantly combined with the more frightening force
of the unknown—the almost surreal "great wings."

The third locus of the rhetoric is found in the lines:

> A shudder in the loins engenders there
> The broken wall, the burning roof and tower
> And Agamemnon dead.

The fact of death, the sudden break in the penultimate line, the hard
"d" in the middle of the sestet, forcing the reader to prolong the
caesura, are all elements contributing to the poem's power—the
power that both poet and reader inevitably encounter when they
seek in "book and manuscript" for those images to enrich their
own. In the face of such power, how can the poet-as-reader and the

reader-as-reader creatively know? In his union with fiction, in which he is overwhelmed by the fictive image, can he yet experience his own vision? If all art is inevitably an "aftering," in Bloom's word,[13] how can the poet and the reader achieve a creative knowledge, however transitory it may be?

We may discover the answer by noting that the very power of the poem's rhetoricity is tempered by an indeterminacy in the language, forcing the reader to try various strategies by which to perceive the poem. The details of the poem, like the pieces of a great puzzle, are presented to the reader, who can use them to compose the image— of Leda and the Swan.[14] The swan itself is not imagined as a whole but as a series of parts, starting from the "great wings," to the "dark webs," the "bill," the "breast." The metonymic nature of the descriptive language creates an effect of indefinite terror: "webs," not not feet; "feathered glory" and "white rush," rather than swan. The overwhelming strangeness of the experience is stressed in "And how can body, laid in that white rush, / But feel the strange heart beating where it lies?" On the mimetic level, Yeats may have emphasized this "otherness" to intensify the element of inscrutability mixed with terror, the inability of the mortal victim to clearly perceive the immortal rapist. This inability to totally "see" may be due to the mythical (and therefore unfamiliar) origins of the swan, but in the context of the allegory I have been suggesting, this obscurity may be a characteristic of the interpretive process itself. In recovering the received text, and in transforming it into the context for a new text, vision becomes re-vision, but only in partial form. Yeats seems to suggest that the whole can never be totally transferred: if you "seek in book or manuscript" for the complete image, you seek what "you shall never find." Something remains forever outside the confines of the new text. The vagueness and disembodiment of the swan—and of Leda herself (thighs, nape, "helpless breast," terrified vague fingers")—is both the response of the poet as reader of prior texts, and an opening of a new "book or manuscript" to the reader of the poem, an invitation to the reader to use his or her own deciphering ability and to be a participant in what Hartman calls "rewriting the figure."[15]

The climactic moment of the poem: the "shudder in the loins," the "broken wall, the burning roof and tower" engenders a rhetorical finality—"and Agamemnon dead." Ironically, however, this rhetorical finality becomes a textual setting-in-motion, as the poem receives its new life, now dependent on the constitutive act of the reader.

The troubling final question artfully balances the feeling of over-

whelming and inevitable conquest generated by the two previous
questions. It is troubling because it suggests the frightening possibility that the artist's or reader's encounters with the authoritative
power of prior fictions may overcome and quash his new perception
into nothingness—"drop" it into a void of insignificance. Yet,
through language that both conveys the power of the past context
with the generative quality of the present, Yeats suggests another
possibility: the translation of the poet-reader's precarious and ten-
uous knowledge into a text as act. Both poet and reader seek vision
not as a static goal, or final knowledge—this (as Michael Robartes
astutely notes) "he shall never find"—but as a vision of recurrence,
a sensitivity to the deciphering activity as the essence of creative
experience. Both poet and reader are "reading still."

It is not surprising, therefore, that "Leda" has been called "a
fable for the hermeneutic situation," one of many to be found in
Yeats's poetry.[16] Although it lacks the sophisticated development of
the more mature poetry, "Solomon and the Witch" (174) is a fine
early illustration of the way in which Yeats balances the power of
received contexts with such a "fable for the hermeneutic situation." The poem has been called "a charming fantasy on the doctrine of the timeless moment in which Yeats at least half believed,"
and, more derogatorily, as "too slight to bear its difficult dialectic."[17] The lightness of the poem's tone, however, and the wit and
economy of its language are neither meager nor merely charming;
such techniques provide an effective balance to the recondite
nature of some of the poem's contexts, and, moreover, underline
Yeats's belief that "vision" (including poetic vision) is neither a
tangible solid nor a palpable finality, but an experience to be
"passed through" again and again. In "Solomon and the Witch,"
Yeats's "timeless moment" becomes not only a metaphysical but
an aesthetic vision—a fable, like "Leda and the Swan," for the
"hermeneutic situation."

"Solomon and the Witch" is informed by a multifaceted context,
one enriched by the authority of sources as various as the Old and
New Testaments; theosophy; the Cabala; Jewish, Christian, and
Arab legend; Christian iconography; and the writings of Flaubert
and Arthur Symons. Because they are less familiar than the Leda
myth, I would like to discuss these contexts briefly, if only to
provide a basis for our understanding of the text as an allegory or
fable of the interpretive process.

Yeats became interested in Solomonic legend through his involvement in the Theosophical Society and the Golden Dawn (two
of the many occult organizations of the 1890s). As has been exten-

sively documented, he was particularly influenced by one of the most powerful figures in these occult circles, S. L. MacGregor Mathers, who, far from being merely a colorful eccentric, was also an accomplished magician and a serious scholar of occult writings. Yeats was familiar with Mathers's version of the *Kaballah Unveiled* and began a personal acquaintance with him after meeting him in the British Museum, where Mathers was engaged in editing and translating the *Clavicula Solomonis* or *Key of Solomon,* a handbook of sorts for kabalistic magical rites.[18]

The prominent position given to Solomon in the works of people like MacGregor Mathers and Madame Blavatsky is firmly based on biblical and Jewish legend, according to which Solomon had dominion over the entire creation—men, animals, demons, and angels—and possessed magical powers in vanquishing demons and in building the Holy Temple.[20]

Like Solomon, Sheba is traditionally associated with occult wisdom and sorcery. In both Arab and Jewish legend, in the *Zohar* (the main text of Cabala), and even in Josephus, Sheba is consistently mentioned in connection with genii, demons, magic, and witchcraft.[21] Because Yeats casts Sheba in the role of "witch," it is more than likely that he was familiar with at least some of these legends (probably, again, through Mathers). We do know that Yeats had read Flaubert's *Temptation of St. Anthony* and Arthur Symons' play, "The Lover of the Queen of Sheba," both of which similarly see Sheba as the possessor of secret wisdom.[22]

The motif of a mystical nuptial love may also derive from a still different kind of "text"—Christian typology and iconography. The sacred "grove" of the poem may be a typological emblem of the Garden of Eden and Paradise Regained; the woman of *caritas* and salvation (in this case, a kind of poetic or anesthetic "salvation"). In Christian iconography, Solomon is the type of Jesus (heavenly wisdom), and Sheba is the gentile Church.[22]

In short, both poet-as-reader and reader-as-reader are asked to contemplate a multitude of varied contexts, reinforcing the immediacy of our original question: how can the poet-reader balance the formidable rhetorical *power* of such a plethora of contexts with the *knowledge* of the present moment of the poem? Moreover, what keeps the poem from being merely a novel and witty play on esoteric sources, or from being inundated by its veritable flood of external references?[23]

As in "Leda," the "hermeneutic situation" is described, but in this case, an exhaustive anatomy is presented. As in "Leda," the image is a nexus, or meeting point between the act of reading and

the act of writing. Although in "Leda" we are invited to picture, to
see, to create the central image by collecting the disjointed details
into a realization of the whole, in this poem, we are asked to follow
the interpretive and imaging process step by step.

The allegory or fable of "Solomon and the Witch" turns on a dual
metaphysical-aesthetic theme. On the metaphysical plane, Yeats
sees Solomon and Sheba as male and female principles of creation,
and their union as bearing cosmic consequences. Solomon says that
the cockerel that crowed to announce the Fall has crowed once
again:

> And would not now but that he thought
> Chance being at once with Choice at last,
> All that the brigand apple brought
> And this foul world were dead at last.

In other words, in the aftermath of their union, the cock that
crowed out eternity is once again active, this time, says Solomon, to
crow "it in again." It may be that the cock crows again because he
thought that Solomon and Sheba had "so nearly transfigured themselves into the divine images."[24] On the aesthetic plane, however,
the cock crows to announce the eternity of the poetic moment
embodied in the dynamic image. Like "Leda and the Swan," (another poem that relates the bird image with male procreative
power), "Solomon and the Witch" is a myth of annunciation—here,
as in "Leda"—the annunciation of the initiating moment of poetic
genesis.

The structure of the poem suggests that the deciphering process
can go on ad infinitum. Like a stone dropped in a pool, "Solomon
and the Witch" reverberates beyond itself—simultaneously back to
the contexts I have mentioned and forward toward the reader in
concentric circles of deciphering. Sheba's "strange tongue" is her
"text" of the cock's crow; Solomon interprets Sheba's version of
the crowing, the reader interprets Yeats's interpretation of Solomon's interpretation of Sheba's cry, the reader of this essay interprets my interpretation of Yeats's interpretation of Solomon's
interpretation of Sheba, and so forth. The first word (and, as we
shall see, the last) in the dialogue between Solomon and Sheba
belongs to Sheba:

> 'Last night, where under the wild moon
> On grassy mattress I had laid me,
> Within my arms great Solomon,

I suddenly cried out in a strange tongue
Not his, not mine'.

Like Yeats's wife George, who began her famous automatic writing
shortly before "Solomon and the Witch" was written, the "Arab
lady" of our poem cries out in a "strange tongue," which demands
interpretation. Like Yeats himself, the "great Solomon" sets about
deciphering the strange sounds spoken by the woman at his side.
Solomon's interpretation, it seems to me, is more than a commentary on an arcane legend; it is a complex allegory on the dynamics
of the image:

'For though love has a spider's eye
To find out some appropriate pain—
Aye, though all passion's in the glance—
For every nerve, and tests a lover
With cruelties of Choice and Chance;
And when at last that murder's over
Maybe the bride-bed brings despair,
For each an imagined image brings
And finds a real image there;
Yet the world ends when these two things,
Though several, are a single light,
When oil and wick are burned in one;
Therefore a blessed moon last night
Gave Sheba to her Solomon'.

On one level, Solomon describes the relationship between two
lovers, particularly noting the cruelties of passion. The "spider's
eye," which revolves, refracts, and sees all, is subtly rhymed and
echoed by the interjected phrase: "Aye, though all passion's in the
glance." The glance is the mask of pure passion, which often
disguises the intensely painful trials and cruelties that the lover may
devise for the loved one.[25]
    The possible result of such a "murder," says Solomon, is de-
spair—"For each an imagined image brings / And finds a real image
there"; in love, Choice never perfectly coincides with Chance, and,
moreover, the inevitable gap between the two may lead to irrevocable despair. What you will never perfectly coincides with what
you get. As the last five lines of the last verse show, the world of
time ends, and eternity is ushered in if the real image of the beloved
and the imagined image become one.
    By now, the reader, like Solomon, is deeply involved in the act of
deciphering texts—not only that of Sheba's strange tongue, but the

text of Solomon's interpretation as well. The emphasis on the word "image" suggests that Yeats uses the sexual union of Solomon and Sheba as an allegory for the kind of fusion that must occur before poetry can be created. The poet, like the lover, goes through trials and agonies, struggling with "cruelties of Choice and Chance" as he attempts to discover the perfect verbal embodiment for his creative perceptions. Like the lover, the artist in the grip of his creative passion may be carried on what Maud Bodkin called a "tidal ebb toward death followed by life renewal," a kind of "murder" followed by "increased awareness . . . of our own lives in their secret and momentous obedience to universal rhythms."[26] Moreover, like the lover, the poet is inevitably disappointed; he discovers that Choice cannot always be imposed on Chance, and that the "imagined image" does not always coincide with the "real image." Yet, if such a synchronization should occur, it would be both the epitome of the poetic act ("a single light, / When oil and wick are burned in one"), and the end of the world.

Interestingly, it is Sheba, the witch, the speaker of the "strange tongue," whose words bring Solomon back to reality: " 'Yet the world stays,' " she says simply. Solomon's response to Sheba's obviously accurate observation is not only a witty continuation of the "plot" of this poem but a further commentary on the writing of poetry:

> 'If that be so,
> Your cockerel found us in the wrong
> Although he thought it worth a crow.
> Maybe an image is too strong
> Or maybe it is not strong enough'.

On the one hand, as Yeats was well aware, (and as readers of some of his poems would agree), an image may be too strong, obscuring perception and overwhelming meaning. On the other hand, the image may not be strong enough, thus failing to evoke perception and significance. In either case, poet as reader, and reader as poet, go through what Iser has called an "oscillation," a process of trial and error whereby "we organize and reorganize the various data offered us by the text."[27]

Like the Fall, however, the failure on both the metaphysical and the aesthetic levels of "Solomon and the Witch" is felicitous. Sheba's " 'O Solomon! Let us try again!' " is spoken with great enthusiasm, and the same verve applies to the never-ending attempts of the poet to find the locus between the act of reading "strange tongues" and the act of writing—the setting-in-motion of other texts that ultimately becomes the realization of a new text. Like Nietzsche's Dionysian artist, Yeats's artist is he who says "yes" to life, who rejoices "over . . . life's own inexhaustibility,"[28] because (as Yeats saw it) it gives him renewed opportunities to realize the perfect image. The activity is necessarily incomplete; we can only "rewrite the figure" imperfectly, but the glory is in the attempt.

As we see in poems like "Byzantium," the state of imagistic perfection is a goal both longed for and dreaded; poets strive continually to unite Choice and Chance, though they know that such perfection means the obliteration of the very time-bound world that nourishes the creation of such images. The position that Yeats takes in such a powerful paradox is thus that of Sheba, not Solomon: the moon is "wilder every minute," ecstasy is within reach—"let us try again." We can only repeat, says Yeats, but it is a glorious repetition; the very failure of the act becomes the victory of the imagination.

The power-knowledge question of "Leda" is thus "answered" by the poetry itself, but, paradoxically, only by reinforcing the question. The authoritative "power" of received contexts (mythic, historical, literary, and linguistic) is necessarily balanced by a creative "knowledge" of the perfect, yet transitory, poetic moment. It has been said that every creator achieves the "uniqueness of his own consciousness through a kind of fall";[29] for Yeats, such a fall "condemns" him, like Solomon and Sheba, repeatedly to "try again" to reach the unity of Choice and Chance. For the readers of these poems—those of us who are "reading still"—such a fall can only be called fortunate.

Notes

1. W. B. Yeats, *Collected Poems,* definitive ed. (New York: Macmillan, 1956), 160–61. All references to Yeats's poems are from this edition; subsequent citations from this work are noted parenthetically in text. For an explanation of the references in this poem, see A. Norman Jeffares, *A Commentary on the Collected Poems of W. B. Yeats* (Stanford: Stanford University Press, 1968), 204–11.

2. W. B. Yeats, "A General Introduction for My Work," *Essays and Introductions* (New York: Collier Books), 1968, 522.

3. Cf. Richard Wilbur, "A World Without Objects is a Sensible Emptiness," in *Poems* (1956; reprint, San Diego: Harcourt Brace Jovanovich, 1963), 117.

4. See Edward Said, *The World, The Text, and the Critic* (Cambridge: Harvard University Press, 1983), 135, and Wolfgang Iser, "Interaction between Text and Reader," in *The Reader in the Text: Essays on Audience and Interpretation,* ed.

Susan R. Suleiman and Inge Crosman (Princeton: Princeton University Press, 1980), 106.

5. Peter Rabinowitz, " 'What's Hecuba to Us?': The Audience's Experience of Literary Borrowing," in Suleiman and Crosman, *Reader in Text,* 241. Peter de Vries, *The Prick of Noon* (Boston: Little, Brown and Company, 1985), 69. "Anteriority," (or "priority"), one of the central terms in Harold Bloom's criticism, refers to the urge of every great poet to be the one who "named something first." See *The Anxiety of Influence: A Theory of Poetry* (New York: Oxford University Press, 1978), 13–15 and 78–83. "Hermeneutic perplexity" is used by Geoffrey Hartman, *Criticism in the Wilderness: A Study of Literature Today* (New Haven: Yale University Press, 1980), 24.

6. Harold Bloom, *Poetry and Repression: Revisionism from Blake to Stevens* (New Haven: Yale University Press, 1976), 3, 5; and Bloom, *Anxiety of Influence,* 26, 96. See also Harold Bloom, *The Breaking of the Vessels* (Chicago: University of Chicago Press, 1982), 45–54. Bloom's emphasis is thoroughly masculine. His conception of the "strong poet" seems to apply to male poets only.

7. In *Anxiety of Influence,* 80–83, and *Poetry and Repression,* 5, Bloom discusses the problems of the "latecomer" poet.

8. Yeats, *Essays and Introductions,* 79.

9. Wolfgang Iser, *The Implied Reader: Patterns of Communication in Prose Fiction from Bunyan to Beckett* (Baltimore: Johns Hopkins University Press, 1974), 294.

10. See Hartman, *Criticism,* 21–27, 34–35. Hartman views Yeats's "Leda and the Swan" in a similar vein, seeing Leda as the imposed upon reader.

11. Ibid., 22–23; Iser, *Implied Reader,* 290; Roland Barthes, *The Pleasure of the Text,* trans. Richard Miller (London: Jonathan Cape, 1975), 6; Georges Poulet, "Criticism and the Experience of Interiority," in *The Structuralist Controversy,* ed. Richard Macksey and Eugenio Donato (1970; reprint, Baltimore: Johns Hopkins University Press, 1972), 58. The remark on closure was made by Stanley Fish at a conference on "The Literary Text and its Audience," Bar-Ilan University, 1985.

12. I thus disagree with Hartman's view that "until we come to the proper name, 'Agamemnon,' we are kept in the aura of an action whose referent is not fixed" (Hartman, *Criticism,* 24).

13. Bloom, *Poetry and Repression,* 4.

14. Giorgio Melchiori, *The Whole Mystery of Art: Pattern into Poetry in the Work of W. B. Yeats* (London: Routledge and Kegan Paul, 1960; Westport, Conn.: Greenwood Press, 1979), 73–163, 276. It is interesting to note that although larger sections of Melchiori's book are devoted to examining the figurative sources in painting and in sculpture for "Leda and the Swan," the text itself almost consistently undermines and even blocks such an investigation, as it presents the "picture" of Leda in strangely disjointed form.

15. Hartman, *Criticism,* 27. Hartman notes that the "ultimate indeterminacy" in the poem, the one that the reader must attempt to resolve, is the "face of Leda that cannot be imagined," the possible look on Leda's face after she has been imbued with both the power and the knowledge of the swan. (25).

16. Hartman, *Criticism,* 35. Obvious examples include the two "Byzantium" poems, "Among School Children," "The Statues," and "Long-Legged Fly."

17. F. A. C. Wilson, *Yeats's Iconography* (London: Methuen, 1970), 280; and Harold Bloom, *Yeats* (New York: Oxford University Press, 1970), 313–14.

18. The essay by Lawrence W. Fennelly, "W. B. Yeats and MacGregor Mathers," in *Yeats and the Occult,* ed. George Mills Harper (London: Macmillan, 1975),

285–307, is a good account of the relationship between Yeats and Mathers. See also Ellic Howe, *The Magicians of the Golden Dawn: A Documentary History of a Magical Order 1887–1923* (London: Routledge and Kegan Paul, 1972); S. L. MacGregor Mathers, *The Kabbalah Unveiled* (1887; reprint, London: Routledge and Kegan Paul, 1962) (translated into English from the Latin version of Knorr von Rosenroth and collated with the original Chaldee and Hebrew text); and Mathers, *The Key of Solomon the King (Clavicula Solomonis)* (London: Kegan Paul, French, Trubner, 1909) (translated and edited from the ancient manuscript in the British Museum). When he first met Mathers, Yeats was working on his edition of Blake, which may have made his mind particularly receptive to new myths and mystical configurations.

19. See *1 Kings* 5:29–34, and Louis Ginzberg, *The Legends of the Jews*, (Philadelphia: Jewish Publication Society, 1936), 4:150, 288–89; 5:302 (translated from the German by Henrietta Szold). Individuals active in occult circles, such as Madame Blavatsky and MacGregor Mathers—Yeats's direct contacts for these myths—expanded these legends for their own purposes. Madame Blavatsky suggests that Solomon "got his secret learning from India through Hiram, the King of Ophir, and through Sheba," and notes that the very Seal of Solomon—conspicuously gyre-like in its form—is of Hindu origin. Solomon was regarded in the Theosophical Society as the original Mason, and the building of the Temple as "an allegory for the gradual acquirement of *secret* wisdom, or magic." See H. P. Blavatsky, *Isis Unveiled: A Master-Key to the Mysteries of Ancient and Modern Science and Technology* (London: Theosophical Publishing Society, 1910), 135–36, 291. In *The Kabbalah Unveiled*, Mathers cites Solomon and David as the figures "most deeply initiated into Kabbalah" (6), and in the introduction to *Key of Solomon*, he prays to God to attain the understanding of "Solomon the son of David the King" (3–4).

20. See, e.g., Ginzberg, *Legends*, 4:152; 5:289–92, 389. See also Raphael Patai, *The Hebrew Goddess* (New York: Ktav, 1967), 207, 233.

21. Gustave Flaubert, *The Temptation of St. Anthony*, trans. Lafcadio Hearn (New York: Boni and Liveright, 1911), 27–70, and Arthur Symons, "The Lover of the Queen of Sheba," in *The Collected Works of Arthur Symons* (London: Martin Secher, 1924), 2:26–36.

22. See D. W. Robertson, Jr., "The Doctrine of Charity in Medieval Literary Gardens: A Topical Approach through Symbolism and Allegory," *Speculum* 26 (1951): 24–49; and Gertrud Schiller, *Iconography of Christian Art*, trans. Janet Seligman (London: Lund, Humphries, 1966), 1:23–26. Sculptures and paintings of Solomon and Sheba can be found in many churches and cathedrals; the best known, perhaps, is the bronze bas-relief by Ghiberti on the doors of the Florence Baptistry.

23. Bloom, *Anxiety of Influence*, 57, defines the concept in his book's title as that tension the poet experiences "in expectation of being flooded" by his precursors.

24. Wilson, *Yeats's Iconography*, 281.

25. T. B. Henn, *The Lonely Tower* (London: Methuen, 1966), 57, notes an allusion here to the "spider love" of Donne's" "Twick'nam Garden." Yeats believed that courtship was a kind of ritual murder. See "Crazy Jane Grown Old Looks at the Dancers," in *Collected Poems*, 255, and a late play, "A Full Moon in March" (1935), in Yeats, *Collected Plays* (1934; reprint, New York: Macmillan, 1952), 380–97.

26. Maud Bodkin, *Archetypal Patterns in Poetry: Psychological Studies of Imagination* (1934; reprint, London: Oxford University Press, 1963), 8–9.

27. Iser, *Implied Reader*, 288.
28. Friedrich Nietzsche, "Twilight of the Idols," *The Portable Nietzsche*, trans. Walter Kaufmann (New York: Viking, 1954), 562.
29. Bloom, *Poetry and Repression*, 13.

References

Barthes, Roland. *The Pleasure of the Text*. Translated by Richard Miller. London: Jonathan Cape, 1975.

Blavatsky, H. P. *Isis Unveiled: A Master-Key to the Mysteries of Ancient and Modern Science and Technology*. London: Theosophical Publishing Society, 1910.

Bloom, Harold. *Yeats*. New York: Oxford University Press, 1970.

———. *The Anxiety of Influence*. New York: Oxford University Press, 1973.

———. *Poetry and Repression: Revisionism from Blake to Stevens*. New Haven and London: Yale University Press, 1976.

———. *The Breaking of the Vessels*. Chicago: University of Chicago Press, 1982.

Bodkin, Maud. *Archetypal Patterns in Poetry: Psychological Studies of Imagination*. 1934. Reprint. London: Oxford University Press, 1963.

Fennelly, Lawrence W. "W. B. Yeats and MacGregor Mathers." In *Yeats and the Occult*, edited by George Mills Harper, 285–307. London: Macmillan, 1975.

Flaubert, Gustave. *The Temptation of St. Anthony*. Translated by Lafcadio Hearn. New York: Boni and Liveright, 1911.

Ginzberg, Louis. *The Legends of the Jews*. Translated from the German by Henrietta Szold. Philadelphia: Jewish Publication Society, 1936.

Henn, T. B. *The Lonely Tower*. London: Methuen, 1966.

Hartman, Geoffrey. *Criticism in the Wilderness: A Study of Literature Today*. New Haven and London: Yale University Press, 1980.

Howe, Ellic. *The Magicians of the Golden Dawn: A Documentary History of a Magical Order 1887–1923*. London: Routledge and Kegan Paul, 1972.

Iser, Wolfgang. *The Implied Reader: Patterns of Communication in Prose Fiction from Bunyan to Beckett*. Baltimore: Johns Hopkins University Press, 1974.

Iser, Wolfgang. "Interaction between Text and Reader." In *The Reader in the Text*, edited by Susan R. Suleiman and Inge Crossman, 106–20. Princeton: Princeton University Press, 1980.

Jeffares, Norman, A. *A Commentary on the Collected Poems of W. B. Yeats*. Stanford, Calif.: Stanford University Press, 1968.

Mathers, MacGregor S. L. *The Key of Solomon the King (Clavicula Solomonis)*. Translated and edited from ancient manuscripts in the British Museum. London: Kegan Paul, French, Trubner, 1909.

———. *The Kabbalah Unveiled*. 1887. Translated into English from the Latin version of Knorr von Rosenroth, and collated with the original Chaldee and Hebrew text. Reprint. London: Routledge and Kegan Paul, 1962.

Melchiori, Giorgio. *The Whole Mystery of Art: Pattern into Poetry in the Work of W. B. Yeats*. London: Routledge and Kegan Paul, 1960. Reprint. Westport, Conn.: Greenwood Press, 1979.

Nietzsche, Friedrich. "Twilight of the Idols." In *The Portable Nietzsche,* translated by Walter Kaufmann, 562. New York: Viking, 1954.

Patai, Raphael. *The Hebrew Goddess.* New York: Ktav, 1967.

Poulet, Georges. "Criticism and the Experience of Interiority." In *The Structuralist Controversy.* 1970. Edited by Richard Macksey and Eugenio Donato, 56–71. Reprint. Baltimore: Johns Hopkins University Press, 1972.

Robertson, D. W., Jr. "The Doctrine of Charity in Medieval Literary Gardens: A Topical Approach through Symbolism and Allegory," *Speculum,* 26 (1951): 24–49.

Said, Edward. *The World, The Text, and the Critic.* Cambridge: Harvard University Press, 1983.

Schiller, Gertrud. *Iconography of Christian Art.* Translated by Janet Seligman. London: Lund, Humphries, 1966.

Symons, Arthur. "The Lover of the Queen of Sheba." In *The Collected Works of Arthur Symons,* 2:26–36. London: Martin Secher, 1924.

Wilbur, Richard. *Poems.* 1956. Reprint. San Diego, New York, London: Harcourt Brace Jovanovich, 1963.

Wilson, F. A. C. *Yeats's Iconography.* London: Methuen, 1970.

Yeats, W. B. *Collected Plays.* 1934. Reprint. New York: Macmillan, 1952.

———. *Collected Poems.* Definitive Edition. New York: Macmillan, 1956.

———. "A General Introduction for My Work." In *Essays and Introductions.* New York: Collier Books, 1968.

11

"All Alone, Little Lady?"

Jane Tompkins

"All alone, little lady?" asks the renegade Yankee soldier of Scarlett O'Hara. He has wandered into Tara shortly after she herself has arrived there, in the final days of the war. The Yankee, thinking that Scarlett is alone in the house, sheathes his pistol. In the next second, Scarlett shoots him in the face, and a few minutes later she and Melanie rifle the corpse and decide to bury it in the grape arbor. Melanie takes off the ragged slip she has been using as a nightgown and wraps it around the soldier's head to stanch the blood that would otherwise give the murder away; as Scarlett drags the body out feet first, Melanie sits naked in the great hall of Tara listening to the soldier's head bump down the back stairs.

This scene contradicts the image that academic criticism has traditionally had of Margaret Mitchell's *Gone With the Wind* as "an escape to ardent romance for those wishing to forget the arduous moment," "prudish, melodramatic, and sentimental," "false to human nature," and written in "women's mag prose."[1] I quote the scene because I want to argue that *Gone With the Wind*[2] is not an escapist fantasy but a novel whose central preoccupations have spoken directly to the experience of millions of men and women, especially during the 1930s when it first appeared. In its presentation of women as the survivors of social cataclysm, *Gone With the Wind* is central to a tradition of American literature in which women are crucially responsible for the spiritual and material survival of the nation. The tradition I refer to is that of popular women's fiction, a tradition that has no authority in twentieth-century literary culture.

The absence of *Gone With the Wind* from the canon of American literature is the most flagrant example of the systematic and complete exclusion of popular women's fiction from our literary tradition. Although Mitchell's novel is the most widely known of all American fictions, enormously popular not just in the United

States but all over the world, although its characters have become bywords in our daily conversations, and its closing line—"Tomorrow is another day"—a piece of folk wisdom, the name of Margaret Mitchell is absent from our literary histories; it does not appear in anthologies of American literature; it hardly ever shows up on course reading lists, and certainly not on the list of books that doctoral candidates study for their Ph.D. examinations. College students who major in English never hear or read Mitchell's name in the course of their formal education, because, as far as the literary establishment is concerned, she does not exist.

Ironically, but not coincidentally, a link exists between the failure of *Gone With the Wind* to command the attention and respect of literary academicians, and the fatal mistake the soldier makes when he sees Scarlett O'Hara appear at the head of the stairs. The resemblance has to do with the relationship in our culture between women and power. The soldier, acting on assumptions about the nature of "little ladies"—that they are weak, that they are physically helpless, that they have no power—fails to take Scarlett seriously because she is a woman. If the person who appeared at the head of the stairs had been a man, the soldier would have kept his pistol out—and lived. The critics, conversely, fail to take *Gone With the Wind* seriously, not because they believe the novel lacks power but for exactly the opposite reason. This novel, and others like it, has *too much* power, power of a kind to make a lot of money and to command the attention of a large popular audience. The critics' move, therefore, is to strip that power of its authority by denigrating its object—the popular audience; its rewards—hard cash; and its source—a woman writer. Here, for example, is Bernard De Voto, representing the Eastern liberal establishment in 1937:

> the slick writers of the highest bracket—they are practically all women—believe firmly in the moral overtones of their stuff, which are what give it cash value. . . . In all ages these simplicities are what the popular audience has most wanted from literature and what it has most rewarded. The women's magazines, and the slicks in general, merely canalize the popular taste.[3]

In another article, De Voto explains his views further:

> GWTW is important as a phenomenon but hardly as a novel. . . . Its author has no eye and no feeling of human character, and its page by page reliance on all the formulas of sentimental romance and all the effect of melodrama is offensive.[4]

It is instructive to note the contradiction implicit in De Voto's trashing of Mitchell's achievement. Although on the one hand he parades his contempt for her ability to earn hard cash and command a vast, popular audience, he nevertheless, in using terms like "sensational romance" and "melodrama" to characterize her work, criticizes it for failing to come to terms with the hard cash and power plays of the real world. What critics blame women's novels for being at one level—commercially successful dominators of the marketplace—is the same thing they blame them for having no grasp of at the level of representation. Popular women's novels are perpetually chastised for being out of touch with reality. So that finally the assumptions the critics bring to the fiction are not unlike those the Yankee soldier makes about Scarlett, in that they posit an inability on the part of women to deal with the real world. If the soldier believes that little ladies cannot hurt him because they are all moonlight and magnolias, the critic believes, or wants to believe, the same about popular women's writing. Here is Malcolm Cowley's famous attack, written in 1936:

> *Gone With the Wind* is an encyclopedia of the plantation legend. . . .
> The big white-columned house sleeping under its trees and the cotton
> fields; the band of faithful retainers, including two that faintly resemble
> Aunt Jemima and Old Black Joe; the white-haired massa bathing in
> mint juleps; the heroine with her seventeen-inch waist and the high-
> spirited twins who came courting her in the magnolia-colored moon-
> light. . . ; it is all here, every last bale of cotton and bushel of moon-
> light. . . ; every last full measure of Southern female devotion working
> its lilywhite fingers uncomplaining to the lilywhite bone.[5]

To see if this estimate of the novel is correct, let us return to the scene on the staircase at Tara. The scene that ends with the murder of the Yankee soldier begins with Scarlett soaking an infected toe in a bucket of water. The festering toe, a result of Scarlett's desperate journey from Atlanta two weeks before, is only one of the innumerable painful and insulting features of her situation: her father is crazy; her sisters and Melanie are sick; no food is at Tara; no crops are in the ground; she has no money that is worth anything; she has no means of transportation and, even if there were, nowhere to go for help. "There was," wrote Mitchell, "no security or haven to which she could turn now" (412). A few days later, Scarlett reaches rock bottom when, scavenging for food in the slave garden at Twelve Oaks, she finds some radishes in the ground:

Hardly waiting to rub the dirt off on her skirt, she bit off half and swallowed it hastily. It was old and coarse and so peppery that tears started in her eyes. No sooner had the lump gone down than her empty outraged stomach revolted and she lay in the soft dirt and vomited tiredly.

. . . As she lay prostrate, too weak to fight off memories and worries, they rushed at her like buzzards, waiting for death. No longer had she the strength to say: "I'll think of Mother and Pa and Ashley and all this ruin later—Yes, later when I can stand it." She could not stand it now, but she was thinking of them whether she willed it or not. The thoughts circled and swooped above her, dived down and drove tearing claws and sharp beaks into her mind. For a timeless time, she lay still, her face in the dirt, the sun bearing hotly upon her, remembering things and people who were dead, remembering a way of living that was gone forever— and looking upon the harsh vista of the dark future. (420–21)

As she lies there, Scarlett realizes that there is no going back; she takes one last look at the ruin of Twelve Oaks, and

then she started down the road to Tara, the heavy basket cutting into her flesh.

Hunger gnawed at her empty stomach again and she said aloud: "As God is my witness, as God is my witness, the Yankees aren't going to lick me. I'm going to live through this, and when it's over, I'm never going to be hungry again. No, not any of my folks. If I have to steal or kill—as God is my witness, I'm never going to be hungry again." (421)

This last quotation may seem to strike exactly the melodramatic note that De Voto and Watkins, among others, found so offensive in Mitchell's novel. But words from a nonliterary source contemporary with *Gone With the Wind* may help us to see this passage as powerfully in touch with the real world.

The quotations that follow come from three of the hundreds of thousands of letters written to President and Mrs. Roosevelt and to various officials during the Depression. The date of this letter is 29 October 1935.

Dear Ladie I read your letter telling me to write to the relif office for help I did they wrote me that they was puting people off the relif now instead of takin them on and I don't want on the relif if I can help it I want to work for my livin but the last thing we have is gone my cow that I ask you to send me some money to save her for my little children to have milk has bin taken and we only get $17.50 on our debt for her we picked cotton at 40 cents per 100 lbs till it was all gone now there isnt one thing her that we can do to get bread to eat my sick child is still livin and takin medicin but the Dr says he cannot keep lettin us have medicine unless we pay him some for he is in debt for it and the man that has let us have a house and land to work wont let us stay in the house if we cant get a mill [to] plow the land with and we cannot get a mill and cant get a house and don't you know its aful to have to get out and no place to have a roof over you sick child and nothing to eat I cant tell all my troubles there isn't any use we only have a few days to stay here in the house now wont you please send me some money. . . . Mrs. C. D. C. Winnsburo. La.

The date of this letter is 6 August 1934. It is written to a Mr. J. Will Taylor, a U.S. congressman from Tennessee.

I am enclosing a few lines for instruction if you pleas I am here with 5 children and a wife and under the new act of law I cant get a days work at eny thing at all I havnt had a days of work for over 2 years I am a disable body man and cant get a days work at all. I am a ruptured man my family is barfooted and naked and suferns and we all are a going to purish if I cannot get some help some way I cant get eny ade at all and if I could not get it in Scot County were it is from me I could not go and get it for it is about 20 miles to the clostly rail rode station from where I live in the county. I have got no horse no autmobel and no nothing to ride can you pleas if possible fix for me some way so my family will not purish.

So hoping to hear from you soon. . . . N. P., New combe, Tennessee.

And, finally, an excerpt from a letter sent to the secretary of the Civil Works Administration by a man in Latrobe, Pennsylvania, in 1934.

[I am] on the mercy of relief with 6 children and a wife to support. Now I am forced with proposition of being set out of my home because I cannot pay my rent. I have 10 days to get another house, no job, no means of paying rent. Can you be so kind as to advise me as to which would be the most human way to dispose of my self and family, as this is about the only thing that I see left to do. No home, no work, no money. We cannot get along this way.[6]

These letters dramatize more forcefully than my own words could the parallels that existed between Mitchell's novel, published in 1936, and the circumstances that Americans in the 1930s were living through. But more important even than the similarity of circumstances is the psychological parallel between the South after the war and America during the depression. I mean the sense that problems can get no worse; that one's back is to the wall; that one will do *anything* in order to survive—even write to the president for money. My contention is that *Gone With the Wind* is a novel about what people will do in order to survive, and that millions of readers in this country responded to it, not because it was "false to human nature," but because it was true to what so many were thinking and feeling at the time. Scarlett's hunger, her vomiting, her infected toe, her murder of the Yankee soldier, his blood, and Melanie's nakedness are not "prudish" or "sentimental"; given the conditions in north Georgia during Sherman's march—and in America during the Depression—they are not even "melodramatic."

Cowley's claim that *Gone With the Wind* replicates the plantation legend does not hold up—and not surprisingly. Academic critics did not grasp the emotional and material realities Mitchell's novel appealed to because their vision of the novel had been shaped by professional and ideological interests that were unrelated to those of the author and her readers. Because *Gone With the Wind* flouted the aesthetic doctrines of literary modernism, it was hardly noticed by the critics centered at Vanderbilt and the University of the South. Because of its commercial success and its female authorship, it was anathema to genteel academic critics like De Voto; its lack of the proper social consciousness offended the political sensibilities of critics like Cowley.

In denying cultural authority to *Gone With the Wind*, however, the critics were doing nothing new. They were carrying on a tradition of rejection, by the elite literary establishment, of popular women's novels like *Charlotte Temple, Uncle Tom's Cabin, The Wide, Wide World*, and *The Gates Ajar*, which were hailed by reviewers and read by millions but denied entry into America's literary hall of fame. In denying the value of *Gone With the Wind* and its predecessors, the critics were only protecting their own interests as arbiters of the national taste. This point, however, should alert us to the fact that the reasons they give for condemning this fiction—that it is "prudish," "sentimental," "false to human nature"—bear about as much relation to the work itself as the Yankee soldier's notions about "little ladies" did to the person who shot him dead.

Notes

1. Floyd Watkins, "GWTW as Vulgar Literature," *Southern Literary Journal* 2 (1970): 86–103.
2. Margaret Mitchell, *Gone With the Wind*, Avon ed. (Macmillan: New York), 1973. Subsequent citations from this edition are noted parenthetically in the text.

3. Bernard De Voto, "Writing for Money," *Saturday Review,* 9 October 1937.

4. Bernard De Voto, "Fiction Fights the Civil War," *Saturday Review,* 18 December 1937.

5. Malcolm Cowley, "Going with the Wind," *New Republic,* 16 September 1936, 161–62.

6. This letter and the preceding ones are from *Down and Out in the Great Depression: Letters from the "Forgotten Man,"* ed. Robert S. McElvaine (Chapel Hill: University of North Carolina Press), 1983. The punctuation and spelling in these letters are reproduced to follow the originals identically.

References

Cowley, Malcolm. "Going with the Wind." *New Republic* (16 September 1936):

Cowley, Malcolm. *Down and Out in the Great Depression, Letters from the "Forgotten Man."* Edited by Robert McElvaine. Chapel Hill, N.C.: The University of North Carolina Press, 1983.

De Voto, Bernard. "Writing for Money." *Saturday Review* (9 October 1937):

———. "Fiction Fights the Civil War." *Saturday Review* (18 December 1937):

Floyd, Watkins. "GWTW as Vulgar Literature." *Southern Literary Journal* 2 (1970):

Mitchell, Margaret. *Gone With the Wind*. Avon Edition. Macmillan: New York, 1973.

12

The Impossible Conclusion: Irony in Gustave Flaubert's *Bouvard and Pécuchet*

Roselyne Koren and Judith Kauffmann

This essay constitutes the first stage of a more ambitious undertaking, whose aim is to make a contribution toward the description and definition of those mutations of irony that dominate the writing of a whole text. Contemporary theories are, essentially, the product of the examination of single statements or the evocation of isolated events. The extended syntagmatic of irony still has to be elaborated. It should be defined in relation to the notions of parody, satire, and comic writing. This point implies that irony should no longer be considered only as a trope but also as a "figure de pensée"[1] (figure of thought) impregnating the whole work, because it is a product of the speaker's ethics and aesthetics.

The task that we are undertaking here is perilous. Can one surrender with impunity to the desire to circumscribe and define the numerous and constantly changing manifestations of a speech-act that wishes to remain ambiguous? We are convinced that it is possible to readapt current techniques of interpretation and create new ones. We owe that conviction to a close reading of a famous ironic text, Gustave Flaubert's *Bouvard and Pécuchet*.[2] We assume that our respective linguistic and literary backgrounds will increase the possibility of achieving fruitful results. As Nietzsche says, "the individual is always wrong," and "truth starts at two."[3]

The ironic enunciation presents the problem of interpretation and textual multivocality in a particularly acute manner. The meaning cannot be found in the text itself, but is a consequence of the interaction of the text and context. Irony, writes Vladimir Jankélévitch, "is not intended to be believed, but to be understood" (i.e., interpreted).[4] Irony is a transitive notion. The impossibility of relying on the literal meaning forces the reader into deducing the author's intentions through hypotheses and interpretative calculations. Alerted through the linguistic or extralinguistic context, decoders realize that they must apply semantic inversion and hope that it will guide them to the intended meaning. Decoders find themselves in a stimulating (albeit perilous) situation, and as much as the situation absorbs them, decoders will have to answer the fundamental question: why does the speaker prefer the ambiguous meandering of the ironic statement to the lineal transparency of conventional discourse?

These difficulties have not discouraged the "ironologists."[5] Definitions of irony abound. Each definition claims to reveal if not the essence (irony only exists in absentia) at least the essential manifestations and intentions of irony. Can any systematic position, however, measure up to an ambiguous discourse? We decided to put some of these theoretical interpretations of irony to the test by applying them to Flauberts's text. His text is made up of two distinct works: a novel, *Bouvard and Pécuchet,* and a dictionary, *The Dictionary of Accepted Ideas,* which is the continuation of the novel. The two texts are usually treated separately. We, on the contrary, intend to examine the connection between the two texts and to show that they are necessarily complementary, and were written for the same reasons. These different approaches must be synthesized in a way that will emphasize the compatibility of the different theories and point out their respective failings. As a discontinous and open speech-act, irony would seem to evade all categorical conclusions.

Contemporary theory recognizes three types of irony: verbal or rhetorical, situational, and citational irony. The first category is the most classic, and we will examine it first. The ironic trope is the result of the convergence of two different but complementary semiotic orientations, the one semantic and the other pragmatic. The first may be recognized by the use of semiotic inversion; the second relates to the interpretative calculations of the reader who strives to deduce the author's intention through the textual signals. Let us take an example used by Henri Morier[6] taken from one of Hermione's speeches in Racine's *Andromaque.*

After having described Pyrrhus's cruelty, the heroine concludes, "What could one refuse such generous blows!"[7] The literal sense awakens the reader's suspicions, through the incoherent assimilation of cruelty and generosity. The uncertainty of such a situation cannot be maintained. The rule of discursive coherence has been transgressed;[8] readers continue their quest for the intentional meaning, using antonymic inversion. "Generous" in this context means "cruel." "The accepted hierarchy of semantic levels has been reversed: the derived value has been promoted to the rank of denotative value, whereas the literal sense has been demoted to a connotative clue."[9] The real sense is that sense in which all the enunciated terms are compatible with each other and with the situation described. The process initiated by the antiphrase represents the *semantic* aspect of the trope. The *pragmatic* aspect is represented by the speaker, whose intention is to accuse his target through his bantering speech. This second component is more typical of irony than the first, and it distinguishes the ironic trope from metaphor or oxymoron. These two figures of speech also draw the reader's attention to the incompatibility of two signifieds. Paul Ricoeur regards these figures of speech as tactics belonging to the same "general strategy," which he defines as "implying something different from that which it affirms" and providing "indices which orient towards a second level of meaning."[10] In the case of the metaphor in absentia two signifieds correspond to a unique signifier, whereas in the case of irony, two signifiers exist—one literal and the other to be deduced. The oxymoron is identified by the "decoder" through the juxtaposition of two terms that are logically contradictory (e.g., black sun or clear darkness).

We would like to express a number of reservations with regard to the arguments in favor of the resemblance between these figures. The metaphor can be lexicalized as a part of everyday speech; irony remains, however, a novelty. According to C. Kerbrat-Orrechioni, "lexical codes cannot accept the existence of terms which designate a notion and its opposite at the same time."[11] Conversely, irony can only exist in absentia. The implied intentional sense justifies its existence. The adjectival or verbal metaphor in *absentia* is opposed to the substantive metaphor in praesentia. This trope is, in fact, a figure of analogic denomination that is used to resolve a problem of representation. The metaphor is not designed to express a value judgment, or "compel agreement with any conclusion."[12] As for the oxymoron, one cannot attempt to assimilate it either to irony or to metaphor or any length of time: it is not a trope. "Semantic telescoping" certainly occurs, but this does not imply the disqualification of the literal signifieds. The general meaning of the syntactic group can be found by readjusting the literal sense of each of the components.[13] Furthermore, it has no argumentative value.

Moreover, is the antiphrase really the quintessential form of irony? Does it enable us to interpret each speech-act in which irony is revealed through textual indicators? Hyperbole constitutes a classic counterexample. The speaker who comments on his own failure by saying "I am a genius" does not necessarily wish to say that he considers himself an imbecile.[13] The scale is thus not qualitative (antonymic) but is quantitative: we are dealing with an exaggerated conclusion and overgeneralization.[14]

Our second example that undermines the antiphrase law in an even more spectacular manner is also borrowed by Henri Morier: "Mr. Johnson, what do you think of our candidate and of his literary essay? He has an excellent memory."[15] The answer is unexpected. It refers to the candidate's memory, where one would expect a value judgment about his reasoning or about how he expresses his ideas. The irony is not revealed through semantic incompatibility but through an argumentative malformation. "He has an excellent memory" does not mean that he has a very bad memory, but it means that your candidate is merely capable of plagiarism or of mechanically repeating arguments about a subject that has already been researched.[16]

These counterexamples show that the speaker's intention of accusing and of calling the target of his speech to account, plays an essential role. The pragmatic orientation of irony is more specific than the semantic. This constitutes the basic difference that enables us to distinguish the ironic trope from both the metaphor and oxymoron.

A metaphor may be used ironically if one employs it to laugh at a target. Henri Morier defines it by means of the qualifiers, "descending" or "burlesque." The subject of the comparison is ridiculed by comparison with someone or something that shows their lowest common denominator. This extract from *Du Côté de chez Swann,* in which asparaguses are compared to comestible young nymphs illustrates his point. "It seemed that these celestial nuances (the colors of the asparagus betray the wonderful creatures who had amused themselves by transmuting themselves into vegetables."[17]

The oxymoron can also become a figure when used to ridicule a victim. The syntactic group, "heroic butchery," which is Voltaire's definition of war, reveals an argumentative and not an informative intention. The speaker presents an argument and its counter-argument simultaneously to condemn the combat so denoted.[18] It is not so much a contradiction "with regard to the referential truth as much as with regard to the argumentative value."

The rhetorical interpretation of irony is stimulated by the perception of an unexpected textual signal. In the case of an untruth spoken on a stormy day—"What wonderful weather!"—the anomaly cannot be interpreted by reference to the linguistic context; it requires an examination of the locutionary situation. The untruth can only be recognized if one possesses extralinguistic data. This type of irony is defined as situational—the figure can be perceived with reference to the common environment of the sender and receiver. The notion of situation is not restricted to the evocation of the material condition in which the speech-act occurs. It also includes "that collection of knowledge, of beliefs, of representational and of evaluative systems of the referential universe which are possessed by the sender and by the receiver at the time of the speech-act."[19] If we say, for example, that a literary work is, "as roguish as a novel by Bernanos," we are trying to discredit it by playing on the fact that this author is thought of as being particularly austere. This "cultural evidence," affirms Berrendonner, is the implied information that reverses the predication of the adjective "roguish" and makes it ironic. The situational irony retains the antonymic inversion that substitutes an extralinguistic reference for the linguistic context.[20]

Two contemporary theoreticians Dan Sperber and Diedre Wilson approach the interpretation of irony from a completely different viewpoint. They see the notion of "implicit intentional sense," and "antiphrase" as inappropriate for the description of the specificity of the ironic speech-act. The key concept in their theory is that of a "mention" or of "citation." If one says "it was unnecessary to be bothered with an umbrella" on a very rainy day, one does not wish to affirm that an umbrella would have been useful but to deride a statement made by someone other than the present speaker. One could even envisage a situation in which the speaker is scoffing at an imprudent statement that he himself had made previously. The speaker wishes to say "something about the statement."[21] The target of the raillery is explicit; it is not an act (going out without an umbrella) but a quoted statement. Sperber and Wilson are using a distinction that is made in logic between use and mention. To say "it is a pity" is to use a formula that expresses regret, but to say "don't say it's a pity, do something!" is to mention an expression that one wants to condemn. Citational irony is a particular case of the discursive strategy of the mention. The mentioned statement is ironic only if the speaker makes it in order to scoff more effectively.

At the risk of upsetting the "ironologists," we would like to point out certain fundamental resemblances. We do not intend to replace three different theories with one uniform theory that would necessarily be reductive but to demonstrate their compatibility. Let us consider the situation in which the receiver notices a semantic incompatibility. Whatever the case is, his or her attention is drawn to a contradiction in the text-context interaction.[22] The antiphrase becomes suspect through its incoherent relationship with its extra-linguistic framework. The statement quoted is identified as such because it contradicts what we know of the speaker's identity or about the situation in which the statement is made. These incompatibilities reveal the fundamentally pragmatic orientation that is common to the three types of irony, that is, the intention of scoffing at a target. With regard to the "antiphrase," Sperber and Wilson certainly do not accord it the status of a distinctive marker of irony, but they do not exclude it from their interpretative calculations. Take for example the following dialogue:

> Arsène Lupin: "I am happy that destiny has chosen you to do justice to the honest man that I am!"
>
> M. Formerie: "Sir, the honest man that you are, has to justify, at this moment, some 344 cases of theft."

Sperber and Wilson give the following explanation: in this example, Arsène Lupin is a dishonest man.[23] The strategy of the quoted statement does not abolish the need for antonymic inversion.

The application of these theories reveals the existence of a difficulty common to both verbal and citational irony. The examples that they have considered have been restricted to a syntactic group or to several consecutive statements. The examination of a restricted linguistic corpus certainly guarantees the scientific nature of the definition of the concepts; but how can they be applied to whole texts impregnated with irony? Only those theoreticians who deal with situational irony can consider manifestations of generalized irony, which are revealed through the internal arrangement of the literary work. Irony as a trope is replaced by an ironic verbalization of a situation engendered by destiny.[24] As Muecke says "It is the irony of the biter bit, of Oedipus in search of himself."[25] This type of verbalization does not necessarily require the use of the "antiphrase," its domain is especially that of the techniques of representing action. The sender and receiver are aware of the implicit signified, whereas the protagonists remain prisoners of the literal signified, which seems to them enigmatic.[26] The citational theory shows the closeness of irony to parody. According to Sperber and Wilson, however, this proximity concerns neither the text seen as a whole nor the statements. Its influence is felt in the "expressions."[27] This position is in accordance with Roland Barthes's definition in S/Z; "Parody is to an extent applied irony"; the extension of this concept of parody to text analysis is excluded, however. We believe that there now seems to be no objection to the compatibility of the notions of ironic citation and of parody: ironic citation is found in single statements, and parody can be aimed at a whole text. Linda Hutcheon defines the phenomenon of parody: "Parody effects a superimposition of texts. At the level of formal structure, a parodic text is the articulation . . . of a parodied text . . . through a parodying text . . . but this parodic duality only aims to mark a difference; parody represents both a deviation from a literary norm and the inclusion of that same norm as interiorized material."[28]

Citational irony plays the same dangerous and subtle game as ironic parody, which consists in taking up the discourse that one condemns in order to reject it from inside more violently and to affirm that the truth should break forth more strongly.

Let us now submit the theories of irony to the test of a reading of Flaubert's text. What will become of rhetorical irony? If one applies the definition of the trope pedantically, then one is reduced to making an inventory of the "antiphrases." Now these are very rare in *Bouvard and Pécuchet*, although there are some. Here is a description of the two heroes' garden: "In the middle of the lawn loomed a rock which resembled a gigantic potato. Something was lacking to complete the harmony" (102). We would like to pause to discuss a very famous passage from the novel, the passage that is probably cited most frequently. It is that moment when "they developed a pitiable faculty within them, that of seeing stupidity and being unable to tolerate it any longer" (319). That aptitude is cruel—unpitying—in all respects because Bouvard and Pécuchet can no longer endure their surroundings: "Small things depressed them; advertisements in the newspapers, the profile of a middle-class man, a stupid remark heard by chance" (319). The two colleagues also become unbearable to others. The critics are unanimous in pointing out a turning point in the novel: "Something irrevocable had happened" (321). Borges, to quote a random example, notes: "The fact is that five years of coexistence have transformed Flaubert into Pécuchet and Bouvard or (to be more precise) Pécuchet and Bouvard into Flaubert."[29] Flaubert has of course made his contribution to the critics' common reading by all sorts of confidences. One can read in the scenario: "They can . . . after each period of study formulate their (i.e. my) opinion through desiderata in the form of axia."[30] All of which causes us to believe that a definite change has occurred, a change that has been prepared by a long and difficult process of preparation.

In fact this new lucidity cannot prevent the two woodlice[31] from speedily reverting into their former idiocy, a process that is already apparent in the suicide scene, or a little later in Bouvard's religious experiences: "He had been taught that the sacrament would transform him: for a number of days he watched for a flowering of his conscience. He remained the same and was seized by a sad wonder" (343).

If the emergence of "the pitiable faculty" marks a turning point in the narration, it is not, as one usually assumes, because the heroes have advanced from stupidity to lucidity. Moreover, Flaubert continues in the asides, which accompany the writing of the book, to complain that he is eaten up with anger because of the stupidity of his heroes. Emphasis is placed, in an intense manner, on the coexistence of the contradictory judgments: Bouvard and Pécuchet are stupid versus Bouvard and Pécuchet are intelligent.

The confrontation between the counterterms is presented in different ways in the text. As the episode of the "pitiable faculty" has shown us, it is revealed in a "diffused" manner by the juxtaposition of different stages in Bouvard and Pécuchet's conquest of knowledge.

They employ methods without bothering to test their practical applicability, condemning themselves to disastrous reverses. From these reverses and from the contradictions that set the scholars consulted, irrevocably, one against the other, they do not draw the conclusion that it is necessary to readjust their instruments or to choose those arguments that can be made credible or comprehensible through experience. They ruin all that passes through their hands. Their superficial, passive and mechanical knowledge shows up their stupidity. Simultaneously, however, they express the exalted desire for self-instruction; their "need for the truth for its own sake" (188); their unbounded curiosity; their suffering because of the feeling of ignorance; and their formulation of pertinent criticism that casts doubts on the examined philosophical, scientific, political, and religious systems. Bouvard declares: "Science is made up of data furnished by one corner of space. Maybe it is not compatible with the unknown remainder which is very much bigger and cannot be perceived" (138). Our two friends criticize didactic bombastic speech several times. Listen to them: "One takes ideas about things for the things themselves. One explains something that one hardly understands by means of words that one doesn't understand at all, e.g. substance, extension, matter and soul. So many abstractions, so many imaginings" (316).

The problematic juxtaposition of opposites is sometimes reduced to a lapidary formula. For example in the entry "battle" in *The Dictionary of Accepted Ideas,* battle always means "blood," and two victors always exist: the winner and loser (492). The neologic use of the word "battant" for winner is in the pair "battant/battu" instead of the usual synonyms "vainqueur/vancu" accentuating the logically impossible association.

The coexistence of the contradictory judgments can effect the interpretation of the whole novel: the circular structure of the novel that returns the comrades to their initial copying work would convince us of their stupidity were it not that the composition of the dictionary presented "the savage and retrograde stupidity" of the others with a virtuosity and Machiavellianism reminiscent of Flaubert's ferocity.[32]

In his work, *Eléments de pragmatique linguistique*, A. Berrendonner analyzes this phenomenon of coexistence in a particularly interesting manner. The ironic speech-act is, in his opinion, a paradoxical argumentative act demonstrating a refusal to submit to the norms of coherence in discourse. An argument employed in language ought to be compatible with a certain type of conclusion, which he calls "r" for the purpose of his demonstration. If he directs the discourse towards r, he cannot simultaneously direct it toward "not-r" (i.e., the opposite conclusion (which belongs to another class of arguments). The act of argumentation imposes on the speaker the need to choose between these two types of subgroups. The ironic speaker rejects this yoke. He practices a type of nonconformist discursive strategy that accumulates argumentative values. No conclusion is excluded: irony is, "the last refuge of the liberty of the individual." A person who practices irony is immune from "any possible sanction"; he has "all coherence" for himself and in case of attack he can take cover behind[33] one or other of the two interpretations in order to evade the offensive.

Thus, for Flaubert, it is not sufficient to suggest a second antonymic signified: he formulates it explicitly in his text. Faced with a discourse that orients him toward two opposite directions simultaneously, the reader-interpreter cannot determine which of the two meanings is valid. Flaubert wrote: "Stupidity is not restricted to one side and spirit to the other; it is like vice and virtue; you have to be artful to distinguish between them."[34] He defines syntheticism from the same viewpoint: "equality of everything, of good and of evil, of beauty and of ugliness, of the insignificant and of the essential," and calls it "a great law of Ontology."[35] The target of the irony is no longer the enunciation of incompatible speech-acts, but the interpreter who believed in the possibility of reaching definite conclusions. "Stupidity consists in wanting to reach a conclusion."[36]

The situational theory allows us the possibility of evaluating the importance of the role that irony plays in destiny. Heroes are naïve, as is demonstrated by a very simple mechanism: they believe what they see—they confuse words with things, the signifier with the signified. Here are a few short examples.

Incapable of distinguishing between the abstract and the concrete, heroes take idioms literally: "The aim of psychology is to study what happens 'within me.' One discovers through observation. 'Let us observe!' For the next two weeks, they sat down after lunch to examine their conscience arbitrarily expecting to make great discoveries and, to their great astonishment, finding nothing" (304).[37] A beautiful name to them is an external sign of intrinsic quality that influences their choice in buying fruit trees: "Having chosen those names which enchanted them, they address themselves to a nursery gardener in Falaise, who promised to supply them three hundred stems which he had not succeeded in selling" (95). The imitation of an attitude passes for a sign of real competence, or, if one prefers, "The appearance is as good as the thing itself." "At times Pécuchet would extract the manual (of digging) from his pocket and would study a paragraph, upright, with his spade by his side, in the pose of the gardener, which ornaments the frontispiece of the book. The resemblance flattered him very much. He conceived even more esteem for the author" (97).

The blindness of the characters causes them to see themselves as martyrs to science. This naïvete is to be contrasted with the clearsightedness of the readers who are guided by the furtive interventions of the narrator who introduces dry mischievous humor in an apparently neutral tone, for example, "They had been delirious about manure" (89).

The appearance-reality duality is a quintessentially comic situation. We, the readers, who have been forewarned, share the knowledge with the narrator to the detriment of the character in the grip of his illusions. This comic device, whose essential aim is to devalue the target and that practices inversion of positive appearance versus negative reality (they seem intelligent versus they are really stupid) satisfies the definition of situational irony.

The characters' repeated setbacks, in confronting us with a sense of our own superiority, have created a framework suitable for their ongoing experiences and for the development of our reasoning. The model thus created is simple. They fail in everything that they undertake—but only apparently because "in spite of the pernicious liming, niggardly hoeing and the untimely weeding, the following year Bouvard had a good wheat harvest" (91). That result, which mystifies the characters, or seems like the irony of destiny, destroys those certitudes that have been progressively acquired by the readers. The violation of the setback rule puts an end to the author-narrator/reader complicity. The target of the situational irony is not exclusively the character. The fooler-fooled can also be the reader.

As for the citational theory, it shows itself to be an excellent tool, but only at the price of a readjustment involving the extension of ironic citation and parody. Sperber and Wilson only see them in the context of the speech-act: reading the novel and the *Dictionary* reveals that they form the major part of the texts. Citational irony is the omnipresent tactic of that narrator, whose target is the erudite or the literary discourse. Flaubert appoints himself a reporter of scientific researches in order to compromise their authority and credibility more successfully; he parodies the romanesque and lexicographic genres to pervert their laws.

In the report of the philosophic adventure related in chapter 8, we find the following text (emphasis added):

They continued with chapter II: the faculties of the soul.
There are *three, no more,* feeling, knowing and wishing.
In the faculty of feeling, *one distinguishes* between physical and moral sensibility.
The physical feelings *can be classed* naturally into five kinds which are brought by the sense organs . . . the moral feeling has *four classes* and its *second class* "moral desires" can be divided into *five kinds. . . .*
In the faculty of knowing, one finds rational perception, which includes *two principal movements* and *four degrees.*

Who is "one" in the preceding text? Is it Bouvard and Pécuchet resuming their reading, is it the author of the philosophical manual, or is it Flaubert, who, prior to writing the book, had devoted himself to innumerable encyclopedia lectures? This polyphonic phenomenon makes it impossible for the reader to identify the target of the irony in a categorical way. It can equally be, perhaps, the artificial method that the two heroes use to master science and the fallibility of science itself. Not only are we in ignorance as to the identity of the enunciator, but we are also faced with the anomaly of a superficial systemization of knowledge.

The care for classification outweighs the spirit of analysis. We know how many units make up the "faculties of the soul," but these subdivisions are neither defined nor even named in most cases. The

arrangement of the abstract makes the definite tone of the enunciator ridiculous, and suggests that the formulation hides a vain and
arbitrary knowledge.

Let us examine two entries from the *Dictionary:*

ACADEMIE FRANCAISE: Decry it but try to become a member if
one can. (486)

AIR: One should always be careful of air currents. The lowest air is
invariably opposed to the temperature: the air is cold if the weather
is hot and vice versa. (487)

It is evident, here, that the reader ought not to be associated with an
enunciator, whose identity is moreover perfectly dissimulated by
the use of infinitives and the impersonal pronoun, "one." It would
be impossible to attribute to Flaubert (for we know how much he
hated moralistic preachings) these definitions from which hypoc-
risy bursts forth and in which he affirms absurd, contradictory, and
gratuitous truth with pedantic authority.

Let us now examine the case of parody. It is essentially concerned with two targets: literary and didactic discourses. We will
consider the following typical examples, perversion of the conventions of a love story, the landscape description, and the lineal
development of action.

The novel opens with a description of the meeting of the two
heroes, who are provided with predestinating patronyms. The con-
sonant *b* of Bouvard and the *p* of Pécuchet are complementary
plosive phonemes in French: *b* is soronous, and *p* is dull. The future
friends sit down, "at the same moment on the same bench" (51).
Their tastes, temperaments, and facial characteristics are shown to
be opposite in a rigorous and mechanical way. They illustrate the
rule that opposites attract. Their meeting is a real "coup de foudre"
(59)—love at first sight—which is underlined by this emphatic
declaration: "Really if we had not gone out for a stroll just now, we
could have died without getting to know each other" (58).

The description of the countryside, which the two friends discover after the first night in their new domain, ironically perverts
the genre's conventions. It consists of a list of details that make up
the garden: "on the right," "on the left," "two alleys . . . in the
form of a cross," "here and there," "on one side," and "on the
other side" (74). The text defies interpretation, it speaks of neither
beauty nor ugliness. We do not know what the two friends feel. The
description is irrelevant to both the progression and the interpretation of the action.[38]

Neither is the global plan of the work immune from the process of undermining. First, through the circularity that we have already mentioned, the desire for knowledge uproots the copyists from their craft and involves them in an infernal quest. The quest reaches its conclusion by their taking up their former activity again, each adventure concluding with the rejection of the science studied. This quest as a whole, however, finishes by developing their intelligence. This progress is still new when they meet a stinging setback at the end of the novel: they pass from the status of students to that of teacher (they throw themselves into the education of two delinquent children).

The *Dictionary* takes up the themes and particularly the stereotyped plot of the novel.[39] Let us restrict ourselves to a brief example, that of the entry "SCIENCE: with regard to religion: a little science moves one away from religion, a lot returns one to it" (551). This theme already figured in the novel, in the form of a declaration by the Count of Faverges: " 'Take care,' said the Count, 'You know the proverb my dear sir, a little science moves one away from religion, a lot leads one back' " (156).

Flaubert undertakes here a trial of his own discourse.[40] He purposely perverts the romanesque, unifying continuous prose that has been designed for lineal and reassuring progress and writes a book against books. The lexicological discourse could have been a subterfuge.[41] Its organization is fragmentary, subordinated to the arbitrary bondage of alphabetic order. Nothing favors the cult of systematic unity and closure. This type of discontinuous prose is the solution chosen by Nietzsche or René Char,[42] at a certain moment of their career, to evade the dangers of the closed text. Because Flaubert suffers from a congenital hate for the Serious, the *Dictionary* is as vulnerable as the novel to the ravages of ferocious parody. The accepted opinions that make up the entries ridicule both the lay Bible as represented by the dictionary and the self-satisfaction of middle-class science.

Each of the three theories of irony, then, tested through a reading of the novel and the *Dictionary* constitutes an effective and enriching instrument for research; none of them, however, succeeds in exhausting the totality of forms in which the Flaubertian irony is clothed. For the moment, we restrict ourselves to an examination of the case of the coexistence of incompatible arguments and our two heroes' excesses of behavior. The necessary distance for the perception of semantic incompatibility cannot be resolved by recourse to the antiphrase alone. Let us take the following passage as a typical example: "The cabbages consoled him. One, especially, gave him hope. It flourished and grew and finished by being prodigious and absolutely inedible. Never mind; Pécuchet was happy to own a monster" (86). The coordination of the adjectives "prodigious" and "inedible" and the subordination of "own a monster" to the adjective "happy" constitute intentional argumentative distortions. The associated vocables are mutually exclusive but not antonyms. They denounce the protagonists' folly.

Let us now examine the narration of the excesses to which the two "wood-lice" give themselves up. It stimulates us to approach the problem of the relationship between comic writing and irony. Here the ironic intention is revealed by the unlikely amplification of the two heroes' "manias."[43] The grotesque portraits that are simultaneously both comic and sinister constitute that "violent" and "exaggerated"[44] magnification of error,[45] which is such a necessary precondition for derision. Here the ironic distance is quantitative and not qualitative as in the case of hyperbole. Hostile to preaching and solemn speech, Flaubert has recourse to comic and grotesque writing to ridicule his victims. We refer, for example, to those pages that denounce our heroes' madness in giving themselves up to "the delirium of manure" (89), in cutting spherical yews in the form of a peacock, or in requiring the exploitation of the benefits of magnetism in the following manner: "Pécuchet . . . put the noses of all the sick people into his mouth and inhaled their breath to take their electricity for himself and at the same time Bouvard clasped the tree in order to increase the fluid" (286).

How can one draw conclusions about the impossibility of concluding, if not by two questions: why does Flaubert prefer the ambiguities of ironic discourse to the univocality of conventional discourse? What has the reading of the two texts taught us about the difficulties of interpretation?

Writers, who are convinced of the omnipresence of the comic at the heart of the serious and the serious at the heart of the comic, can neither argue against the ideas they reject nor defend their conception of justice and morality in didactic language. The aim of Flaubertian irony is serious, but instead of recruiting abstract and systematic arguments to help him, the artist prefers concrete and virulent arguments expressed through events in a story; he prefers the grotesque exaggeration of caricatures incarnating ideas and the inventory of ridiculous speech-acts manipulated with virtuosity. Irony is a defensive position chosen by idealists who feel that they themselves are in danger of becoming ridiculous when they write a book against books. It is also, even more so, the discursive strategy of a "kill-joys" who, throughout their career have suffered harmful attacks and incomprehension from many contemporaries and who wishes to avoid social sanctions. Irony is at least a discursive strategy arguing for an open text. The impossibility of concluding is not necessarily a tragedy. It makes for an excellent antidote to the world of the systematic mind and its intolerances.

If we may then, at least close, if not conclude, we propose that the linguistics of enunciation and text analysis need to integrate amendments regarding the interaction of the two fields into their semantic descriptions. Ambiguity and polysemy in a text do not annul the concept of encoding and do not release readers from their obligations toward the discourse to be analyzed. The interpretation of an ironic text can only approach clarity when the results of researches that have followed the following paths converge: a close and primordial study of the language of the text; key theories of irony; the correspondence, aesthetic, and ethics of the author; and a study of the historical context of the work (in this case of nineteenth-century notions of progress and of romantic irony).

The reading of *Bouvard and Pécuchet* and of the *Dictionary* has been a salutary experience confirming the crucial role of doubt in hermeneutics. The contradictions in scientific systems, the abyss between words and the signified, and the lack of meaning of languages[46] are unsupportable evils for Flaubert. Irony alone can offer a hazardous remedy for these evils, but they no longer destroy the contemporary researcher who considers them as necessary trials in the quest for knowledge.

Notes

1. Cf. Olivier Reboul, "Les figures de pensée," in *La Rhétorique* (Paris: Presses Universitaires de France, 1984), 59: "According to Quintilian, it is necessary to distinguish the ironic trope which applies to several words . . . from the ironic figure of thought, which constitutes a complete discourse or even a complete work."

2. Gustave Flaubert, *Bouvard et Pécuchet,* Claudine Gothot-Mersch's ed. (Gallimard: Folio, 1979). The translations of Flaubert and of all the French texts are our own. Subsequent citations from this work are noted parenthetically in the text.

3. Quoted by Maurice Blanchot in *L'Entretien Infini* (Paris: Gallimard, 1969), 232.

4. Vladimir Jankélévitch, *L'Ironie* (Paris: Flammarion, Champs, 1979), 60.

5. Cf. D. C. Muecke, "Analyses de l'ironie," *Poétique* 36 (1978): 478, fn. 1: "This term [is] utilized for the first time in an ironic fashion by W. C. Booth in *The Carleton Miscellany* (1961)."

6. Henri Morier, *Dictionnaire de Poétique et de Rhétorique* (Paris: Presses Universitaires de France, 1975), 558.

7. For this rule see L. Olbrechts-Tyteca, *Le Comique du discours* (Bruxelles, Editions de l'Université, 1974), 415; and Alain Berrendonner, *Eléments de Pragmatique Linguistique* (Paris: Editions de Minuit, 1982), 230.

8. C. Kerbrat-Orrechioni, "L'ironie comme trope." *Poétique* 41 (1980): 111.

9. *La Métaphore vive* (Paris: Editions de Seuil, 1975), 122.

10. Ibid., 109.

11. Berrendonner, *Pragmatique Linguistique,* 186.

12. Kerbrat-Orrechioni, "L'ironie," 111.

13. Ibid., 119.

14. Berrendonner, *Pragmatique Linguistique,* 187.

15. Ibid., 562.

16. See also F. Recanati, *Les Enoncés Performatifs* (Paris: Editions de Minuit, 1981), 214–15, with regard to the philosophy teacher, "who instead of assessing the student simply says that he is punctual and knows spelling."

17. Berrendonner, *Pragmatique Linguistique.* 685–86.

18. Ibid., 185–87. Cf. also Kerbrat-Orrechioni, "L'ironie," 111: "your clarity is rather obscure." Only the adjective is appropriate. It serves to denounce the impropriety of the substantive whose "literal content is discredited."

19. Kerbrat-Orrechioni, "L'ironie," 116, as well as her *La Connotation* (Lyon: Presses Universitaires de Lyon, 1977). See also Berrendonner, *Pragmatique Linguistique,* 176; L. Hutcheon, Poétique 46 (1981): 150–51; D. C. Muecke, "Analyses," 492; and J. Culler, *Flaubert: The Uses of Uncertainty* (Ithaca: Cornell University Press, 1974), 189.

20. Berrendonner, *Pragmatique Linguistique,* 176.

21. Dan Sperber and Diedre Wilson, "Les ironies comme mentions," *Poétique* 36 (1978): 404.

22. The reference to the linguistic or extralinguistic context is the initial proceeding that permits us to interpret the discourse as ironic. A serious assertive speech-act is self-sufficient. Its meaning is easily accessible. That of the ironic speech-art requires complex interpretative calculations. The ironic assertion does not exist in an intrinsic fashion. Cf. F. Recanati, *Enoncés Performatifs,* 222 and Ch. Perelman and L. Olbrechts Tyteca, *Traité de l'Argumentation: La Nouvelle Rhétorique,* 4th ed., (Bruxelles: Editions de l'Université, 1970), 280.

23. Sperber and Wilson, "Les ironies," 407–8.

24. Muecke, "Analyses," 481–82.

25. Ibid., 480.

26. Cf. Morier, *Poétique et Rhétorique,* 567 (l'ironie "immanente").

27. Sperber and Wilson, "Les ironies," 409.

28. Hutcheon, "Ironie, satire, parodie." 143.

29. J. L. Borgès, "Défense de Bouvard et Pécuchet," in *Discussion* (Paris: Gallimard, 1966), 117.

30. Cited by Maurice Nadeau in *Gustave Flaubert écrivain* (Paris: Denoel, 1969), 298.

31. Cf. Alphonse Jacobs, ed., *Correspondance Flaubert-Sand* (1876; reprint, Paris: Flammarion, 1981), 2:523: "My book about my two wood-lice."

32. Cf. R. Barthes, *S/Z* (Paris: Seuil, 1970), 105; and A. Thibaudet, *Gustave Flaubert* (Paris: Gallimard, 1935), 210: "He had pushed his criticism so far until he produced from his own nature an imbecilic nature by their means. But on the contrary, from their imbecilic nature, he produces a critical nature similar to his own. After he identifies himself with them, he makes them in his own image."

33. Berrendonner, *Pragmatique Linguistique,* 238–39.

34. A letter from Flaubert of 2 August 1855, quoted by M. Crouzet in his study, "Sur le grotesque triste de Bouvard et Pécuchet," in *Flaubert et le comble de l'art* (Paris: S.E.D.E.S.-C.D.U., 1981), 51.

35. The dossier is quoted in Geneviève Bollême, ed., *Le second volume de Bouvard et Pécuchet* (Paris: Denoel, 1966), 29.

36. See the letter to Louise Bouillet of 4 September 1850 in Jacobs, *Correspondance*, 2:239: "Yes, stupidity consists in wanting to conclude. We are one thread and want to know the whole design."

37. Cf. also p. 87: "all the experiments failed. He was very surprised each time"; "Without the least scruple, Bouvard and Pécuchet threw themselves into organic chemistry" (117); "Bouvard retired without the least worry" (91); "All the common premises about age, sex and temperament seemed of the highest importance to them" (122).

38. Cf. Culler, *Flaubert*, 106–9.

39. Cf. C. Gothot-Mersch, "Un roman interminable; un aspect de la structure de *Bouvard et Pécuchet*," in *Flaubert et le Comble de l'Art* (Paris: S.E.D.E.S.-C.D.U., 1981) 18–19.

40. Cf. R. Barthes, "La crise de la verité," in *Magazine Littéraire* 108 (1976): 6–9. "All Flaubert's giddiness is centered in two words ordinarily contradictory but now simultaneous, 'Let us work on finishing the sentence,' on the other hand, 'it is never finished.' Flaubert, from the point of view of style is the last classical writer, but, because his work is excessive, giddy and neurotic, he embarrasses the classical minds from Faguet to Sartre. It is to this that he owes the title of the first modern writer: because he surrenders to folly. The folly is not representative of imitation, of realism, but is a folly of writing, of language" (9).

41. Ibid., 8: "In *Bouvard and Pécuchet* . . . Flaubert appears as a man who stuffs himself with languages. But of all these languages finally, none of them prevails, there is no master-language. . . . Flaubert's favourite book is not the novel but the *Dictionary*. . . . The stupidity theme is to some extent a lure. The great book hidden in Flaubert, is the phraseological dictionary, the dictionary of phrases."

42. Cf. Blanchot, *L'Entretien Infini*, 228–31, 452–53.

43. Cf. e.g., Flaubert, *Bouvard et Pécuchet*, 149: "The flood mania was succeeded by that of erratic blocks." Cf. also Jacobs, *Correspondance*, 1:465. "The comic is the only consolation of virtue. There is, however, another way of looking at it which is lofty. That is what I am going to try and do with my two *good fellows*. Do not fear that it will be too realistic. I am afraid that, on the contrary, it will seem impossible, since I have pushed the idea to such extremes."

44. Crouzet, "Grotesque triste," 49: "The name itself "sad grotesque," which indicates a violent exaggerated and annihilating comedy is corrected by its contrary and returned to the Flaubertian theory of absolute or, of non-relative or of non-arbitrary comic. In contrast to human stupidity which relativizes everything in relation to its own measure, separates the grotesque and the sad . . . the sad grotesque would be just universal, objective, absolute, it is the superior joke."

45. Morier, *Poétique et Rhétorique*, 561: "irony, exaggeration of error, or hyperbole."

46. Cf. Blanchot, *L'Entretien Infini*, 489: "It is the agony of form which is important for Flaubert and not the signification which he lends it here or there, or, to be more precise, this anxiety is infinite, relative to the experience in which he feels himself involved, having nothing but uncertain signposts to define the direction." See also Barthes, "La crise," 6: "One copies because language presents no guarantee, cannot lead to the truth, it is the beginning crisis of modernity. Everything lacks meaning."

References

Barthes, Roland *S/Z*. Paris: Seuil, 1970.

———. "La crise de la verité." *Magazine Littéraire* 108 (1976): 6–7.

Berrendonner. Alain. *Eléments de Pragmatique Linguistique*. Paris: Editions de Minuit. 1982.

Blanchot, Maurice. *L'Entretien Infini*. Paris: Gallimard, 1969.

Bollême, Genviève, ed. *Le second volume de Bouvard et Pécuchet*. Paris: Denoel, 1966.

Borges, J. L. *"Défense de Bouvard et Pécuchet," Discussion*. Paris: Gallimard, 1966.

Crouzet, M. "Sur le grotesque triste de Bouvard et Pécuchet." In *Flaubert et le comble de l'art*. Paris: S.E.D.E.S.-C.D.U., 1981.

Culler, Jonathan. *Flaubert: The Uses of Uncertainty*. Ithaca: Cornell University Press, 1974.

Dictionnaire de Poétique et de Rhétorique. Paris: Presses Universitaires de France, 1975.

Flaubert, Gustave. *Bouvard and Pécuchet*. Paris: Gallimard, 1979.

Gothot-Mersch, C. "Un roman interminable; un aspect de la structure de *Bouvard et Pécuchet*." In *Flaubert et le Comble de l'Art*. Paris: S.E.D.E.S.-C.D.U., 1981.

Hutcheon, L. "Ironie, satire, parodie: Une approche pragmatique de l'ironie." *Poétique* 46 (1981): 140–55.

Jankélévitch, Vladimir. *L'Ironie*. Paris: Flammarion, 1979.

Kerbrat-Orrechioni, C. *La Connotation*. Lyon: Presses Universitaires de Lyon, 1977.

———. "L'ironie comme trope." *Poétique* 41 (1980): 108–27.

Muecke, D. C. "Analyses de l'ironie." *Poétique* 36 (1978): 478–94.

Nadeau, Maurice. *Gustave Flaubert écrivain*. Paris: Denoel, 1969.

Olbrechts-Tyteca, L. *Le Comique du discours*. Bruxelles: Editions de l'Université, 1974.

Perelman, Ch., and L. Olbrechts-Tyteca. *Traité de l'Argumentation: La Nouvelle Rhétorique*. 4th ed. Bruxelles: Editions de l'Université, 1970.

Reboul, Olivier. "Les figures de pensée." In *La Rhétorique*. Paris: Presses Universitaires de France, 1984.

Recanati, F. *Les Enoncés Performatifs*. Paris: Editions de Minuit, 1981.

Ricoeur, Paul. *La métaphore vive*. Paris: Editions de Seuil, 1975.

Sperber, Dan., and Dierdre Wilson. "Les ironies comme mentions." *Poétique* 36 (1978): 399–412.

Thibaudet, A. *Gustave Flaubert*. Paris: Gallimard, 1935.

Contributors

SHARON BARIS, lecturer in the English Department at Bar-Ilan University, has published on Hawthorne, James, and Wallace Stevens. She is currently completing a book on the biblical Daniel in American literature.

TOVA COHEN is a senior lecturer in Hebrew literature at Bar-Ilan University. Her research is on the Hebrew literature of the European Jewish Enlightenment. She has written (in Hebrew) *From Dream to Reality: Descriptions of Eretz Yisrael in Haskalah Literature* and, most recently, a study of Shlomo Levisohn.

HAROLD FISCH, Professor of English at Bar-Ilan University and formerly lecturer at Leeds, has written extensively on Shakespeare, Milton, and on the figure of the Jew in English literature. His most recent books are *A Remembered Future: A Study in Literary Mythology* and *Poetry With a Purpose: Biblical Poetics and Interpretation*.

CLAUDE GANDELMAN is Professor of French literature at Haifa University, author of *Le Regard dans le Texte: Image, Ecriture, du Quattrocento au xxe Siecle* (1986). He is a regular contributor to *Semiotica* and to the American Semiotics Association Journal.

KATHRYN HELLERSTEIN teaches at Haverford College. She is the author of two books of translations of Yiddish poetry by Moyshe-Leyb Halperin and Kadya Molodowsky and is currently writing a book on women Yiddish poets.

E. D. HIRSCH, JR., Professor of English at the University of Virginia, is the author of *Validity in Interpretation* and *The Aims of Interpretation* and, most recently, *Cultural Literacy*. His articles on the theory of interpretation have appeared in *Critical Inquiry, Salmagundi,* and *New Literary History*.

JUDITH KAUFFMANN is a senior lecturer at Bar-Ilan University, where she teaches twentieth-century literature in the French

Culture Department. Her main research interest is indirect speech in humor and irony, and she is also working on the underground poetry of the Second World War.

ROSELYNE KOREN teaches French linguistics at Bar-Ilan University. She is interested in French grammar, poetics, rhetoric, and the theory and practice of argumentation.

KINERETH MEYER teaches English and American literature at Bar-Ilan University, specializing in twentieth-century drama and poetry and generic studies. She has published articles on Yeats, Stevens, and forms of the lyric in journals such as *Genre, Religion and Literature,* and the *Wallace Stevens Journal.*

BETTY ROJTMAN is an associate professor of French at the Hebrew University of Jerusalem. Her special interest is in the conjuction of contemporary literary theory and biblical hermeneutics. Her recent book on the topic is titled *Feu noir sur feu blanc: sur l'herméneutique juive.*

ELLEN SPOLSKY is an associate professor of English and the director of Lechter Institute for Literary Research at Bar-Ilan University. She is the coauthor, with Ellen Schauber, of *The Bounds of Interpretation: Linguistic Theory and Literary Text,* and has just completed *Gaps in Nature: The Possibilities for Change in Literary Systems.*

MEIR STERNBERG, professor in the Department of Poetics and Comparative Literature at Tel Aviv University, is the author of *Expositional Modes and Temporal Ordering in Fiction* and *The Poetics of Biblical Narrative: Ideological Literature and the Drama of Reading.*

JANE TOMPKINS teaches English at Duke University. She is the author of *Sensational Designs: The Cultural Work of American Fiction, 1790–1860.* Her current project, *West of Everything,* is a cultural analysis of Western novels and films of the twentieth century.